Hertfordshire

29 JAN 2007

16|12

Please renew/return this item by the last date shown.

So that your telephone call is charged at local rate, please call the numbers as set out below:

	From Area codes 01923 or 020:	From the rest of Herts:
Renewals:	01923 471373	01438 737373
Enquiries:	01923 471333	01438 737333
Textphone:	01923 471599	01438 737599

L32   www.hertsdirect.org/librarycatalogue

VIRGIN ISLANDS

BOOKS BY GORE VIDAL

NOVELS
Williwaw
In a Yellow Wood
The City and the Pillar
The Season of Comfort
A Search for the King
Dark Green, Bright Red
The Judgment of Paris
Messiah
Julian
Washington, D.C.
Myra Breckinridge
Two Sisters
Burr
Myron
1876
Kalki
Creation
Duluth
Lincoln
Myra Breckinridge and Myron
Empire
Hollywood
Live from Golgotha

SHORT STORIES
A Thirsty Evil

PLAYS
An Evening with Richard Nixon
Weekend
Romulus
The Best Man
Visit a Small Planet

ESSAYS
Rocking the Boat
Reflections upon a Sinking Ship
Homage to Daniel Shays
Matters of Fact and of Fiction
Pink Triangle and Yellow Star
Armageddon?
A View from the Diners Club
United States

MEMOIR
Palimpsest

GORE VIDAL

VIRGIN ISLANDS

•

A dependency of
United States

E S S A Y S
1992 – 1997

ANDRE DEUTSCH

First published in Great Britain in 1997 by
André Deutsch Limited
A subsidiary of VCI plc
106 Great Russell Street
London WC1B 3LJ

A CIP record for this title is available from
the British Library

ISBN 0 233 99136 0

Printed in Great Britain by
Caledonian International Book Manufacturing, Glasgow

Contents

Preface

A few years ago, in a book called *United States*, I collected some of the essays that I had written over forty years. The book weighed three and a half pounds; that's quite enough, I thought, shutting down the old portmanteau. But whatever that is, it is never truly that until Time's Wingéd Wastebasket has collected all. Since then, I have not entirely let slip, as it were, the feather. On the other hand, I've run out of titles. This volume of pieces is, in a sense, a dependency of *United States* as the Virgin Islands are a dependency of the actual United States – hence, the title.

Last time around, an English reviewer took me to task for referring to the USA as an empire when all we had to show in the way of possessions were Guam, the Virgin Islands, Puerto Rico and CNN. I was too tactful to note that our empire is the great globe itself. We still occupy militarily the three nations we defeated in World War Two – Japan, Germany and Italy. Also, rather slyly, we continue to occupy our allies in that adventure through such mystical alliances as NATO which we are now extending ever eastward to the consternation of the Russians and the bemusement of the Chinese. We are, said President Clinton, the one indispensable – or was it indisposable? – nation.*

Whatever. Here are some further reflections on political and literary matters. I've also included a slight piece called 'George' on George Washington. An amiable young man who identified himself as son of an old friend, John F. Kennedy, rang to ask me if I would write a light piece for the first issue of a non-political political magazine that he was starting, to be called *George*. I obliged, but when asked would I add this or subtract that I said, 'Think of this as a birthday present. You can always turn it in for something else.' He did.

GV
15 May 1997

---

* For those interested in the American military occupation of the British Isles, I provide details in the Appendix.

PART I

1
Edmund Wilson: Nineteenth-Century Man

'Old age is a shipwreck.' Like many a ground soldier, General de Gaulle was drawn to maritime metaphors. Of course shipwrecks are not like happy families. There is the *Titanic*-swift departure in the presence of a floating mountain of ice, as the orchestra plays the overture from *Tales of Hoffmann*. There is the slow settling to full fathom five as holds fill up with water, giving the soon-to-be-drowned sufficient time to collect his thoughts about eternity and wetness. It was Edmund Wilson's fate to sink slowly from 1960 to June 12, 1972, when he went full fathom five. The last entry in his journal is a bit of doggerel for his wife Elena: 'Is that a bird or a leaf? / Good grief! / My eyes are old and dim, / And I am getting deaf, my dear, / Your words are no more clear / And I can hardly swim. / I find this rather grim.'

'Rather grim' describes *The Sixties*, Wilson's journals covering his last decade. This volume's editor, Lewis M. Dabney, starts with an epigraph from Yeats's 'Sailing to Byzantium', thus striking the vale-tudinarian note. New Year 1960 finds Wilson at Harvard as Lowell Professor of English. He suffers from angina, arthritis, gout, and hangovers. '*At my age*, I find that I alternate between spells of

3

fatigue and indifference when I am almost ready to give up the struggle, and spells of expanding ambition, when I feel that I can do more than ever before.' He is in his sixty-fifth year, a time more usually deciduous than mellowly fruitful. But then he is distracted by the people that he meets and the conversations that he holds, all the while drinking until the words start to come in sharp not always coherent barks; yet the mind is functioning with all its old energy. He is learning Hungarian, as he earlier learned Hebrew and before that Russian, a language whose finer points and arcane nuances he so generously and memorably shared with Vladimir Nabokov, unhinging their friendship in the process.

During his last decade, Wilson published *Apologies to the Iroquois*, a project that he had set himself as, more and more, he came to live in the stone house of his mother's family at Talcottville in upstate New York. Although brought up in New Jersey, Wilson himself was a classic old New York combination of Ulster and Dutch; and so, in a sense, he had come home to die. Also, to work prodigiously. He made his apologies to the Indian tribes that his family, among others, had displaced. In *O, Canada*, he paid belated attention to the large familiar remoteness to the north which he had visited in youth with his father. He wrote book reviews; spent time at Wellfleet where he had a house; visited New York; went abroad to Israel, Hungary.

The decade was made unpleasant by the fact that he had neglected to file an income tax return between the years 1946 and 1955. The Internal Revenue Service moved in. He was allowed a certain amount to live on. The rest went to the Treasury. He was also under a grotesque sort of surveillance. Agents would ask him why he had spent so much money for a dog's cushion. Wilson's response to this mess was a splendid, much ignored polemical book called *The Cold War and the Income Tax*, which he saw as the two sides to the same imperial coin. The American people were kept frightened and obedient by a fear of the Soviet Union, which their government told them was on the march everywhere, as well as by the punitive income tax, which was needed in order to pay for a military machine that alone stood between the cowed people and slavery. It was better, we were warned, to be dead than red – as opposed to just plain in the red.

Maximum income tax in those days was 90 per cent. Wilson's anarchic response was later, more slyly, matched by the Reagan backlash; instead of raising money to fight the enemy through taxes, the money was raised through borrowing. The result is that, today, even though we have not only sailed to but made landfall in Byzantium, the economy remains militarized, as Wilson had so untactfully noted. At sixty-eight, his present reviewer's green age, he writes, 'I have finally come to feel that this country, whether or not I live in it, is no longer any place for me.' Not that he has any other country in view: 'I find that I more and more feel a boredom with and scorn for the human race. We have such a long way to go. . . .' He, of course, was a professional signpost, a warning light.

Despite boredom and scorn Wilson soldiered on, reading and writing and thinking. He published his most original book, *Patriotic Gore*. He acknowledges a critical biography of him. The book has a preface by a hack of academe who refers to *Patriotic Gore* as a 'shapeless hodgepodge'. Since remedial reading courses do not exist for the tenured, Wilson can only note that his survey of why North and South fought in the Civil War

> is actually very much organized. . . . I don't think that Moore understands that with such books I am always working with a plan and structure in mind. As a journalist, I sell the various sections to magazines as I can. . . . He is also incorrect in implying, as several other people have, that I studied Hebrew for the purpose of writing on the Dead Sea scrolls. It was the other way around: it was from studying Hebrew that I become curious to find out what was going on in connection with the scrolls.

He ends, nicely, with a list of *errata*, even 'though I doubt whether your book will ever get into a second printing'.

5

In the introduction to *Patriotic Gore*, Wilson broods on the self-aggrandizing nature of nation-states, one of which, he is sad to note, is the United States, in all its *un*exceptionalism. A propos the wars,

> Having myself lived through a couple of world wars, and having read a certain amount of history, I am no longer disposed to take very seriously the professions of 'war aims' that nations make. . . .
>
> We Americans have not yet had to suffer from the worst of the calamities that have followed on the dictatorships in Germany and Russia, but we have been going for a long time now quite steadily in the same direction.

Why did North want to fight South? And why was South willing, so extravagantly, to die for what Seward had scornfully called their 'mosquito republics'? Through an analysis of the fiction and rhetoric of the conflict, Wilson presents us with a new view of the matter while dispensing with received opinion. He also places his analysis in the full context of the cold war just as it was about to turn hot in Vietnam. Before anyone knew precisely what our national security state really was, Wilson, thirty years ago, got it right:

> The Russians and we produced nuclear weapons to flourish at one another and played the game of calling bad names when there had been nothing at issue between us that need have prevented our living in the same world and when we were actually, for better or worse, becoming more and more alike – the Russians emulating America in their frantic industrialization and we in imitating them in our persecution of non-conformist political opinion, while both, to achieve their ends, were building up huge governmental bureaucracies in the hands of which the people have seemed helpless.

Predictably, this set off alarm bells. At the Algonquin, May 15, 1962, Wilson meets Alfred Kazin. 'I took Alfred back to a couch and talked to him about his review of *Patriotic Gore*. He showed a certain indignation over my Introduction: I and my people "had it made" and didn't sympathize with the Negroes and people like him, the son of immigrants, who had found in the United States freedom and opportunity. He is still full of romantic faith in American ideals and promises, and it is hard for him to see what we are really doing.'

In *Patriotic Gore*, Wilson questioned the central myth of the American republic, which is also, paradoxically, the cornerstone of our subsequent empire – *e pluribus unum* – the ever tightening control from the centre of the periphery. Wilson is pre-Lincolnian (or a Lincolnian of 1846). He sees virtue, freedom in a *less* perfect union. Today's centrifugal forces in the former Soviet Union and Yugoslavia he anticipated in *Patriotic Gore* where, through his portraits of various leaders in our Civil War, he shows how people, in order to free themselves of an overcentralized state, are more than willing, and most tragically, to shed patriotic gore.

To be fair, Wilson set off alarm bells in less naive quarters. As one reads reviews of the book by such honourable establishment figures as Henry Steele Commager and Robert Penn Warren one is struck by their defensive misunderstanding not only of his text but of our common state. At times, they sound like apologists for an empire that wants to present itself as not only flawless but uniquely Good. Commager zeroes in on the Darwinian introduction. He notes, as other reviewers do, Justice Holmes's *Realpolitik*: 'that it seems to me that every society rests on the death of men.' But Commager is troubled that Wilson 'does not see fit to quote' the peroration of 'The Soldier's Faith', Holmes's memorial address, with its purple 'snowy heights of honor' for the Civil War dead. Yet Wilson quotes the crux of Holmes's speech,

> There is one thing that I do not doubt, no man who lives in
> the world with most of us can doubt, and that is that the faith
> is true and adorable which leads a soldier to throw away his
> life in obedience to a blindly accepted duty, in a cause which

7

he little understands, in a plan of campaign of which he has
no notion, under tactics of which he little understands.

Surely, that is quite enough patriotic tears for spilled gore.

In 1963, as *pontifex maximus* of the old American republic, Wilson
is speaking out with a Roman hardness and clarity, and sadness at
what has been lost since the Union's victory at Appomatox. Our
eighteenth-century *res publicus* had been replaced by a hard-boiled
soft-minded imperium, ever eager to use that terrible swift sword,
presumably for ever, unless, of course, we are struck down by the
current great Satan who threatens our lives and sacred honour in
the high lands of Somalia. Wilson has no great sentimentality about
the Indian-killing, slave-holding founders but he is concerned by
the absolute loss of any moral idea other than Holmes's bleakly
reductive 'every society rests on the death of men'. It is not this sad
truth that Wilson is challenging, thus causing distress to the apologists of empire; rather it is their clumsy ongoing falsifications of
motives, their misleading rhetoric all 'snowy heights of honor' (try
that one on a Vietnam veteran), their deep complicity in an empire
that is now based not only on understandable greed but far worse
on a mindless vanity to seem invincible abroad and in full control
of all the folks at home. Just as the empire was about to play out its
last act in South-east Asia, Wilson's meditation on the Civil War and
war and the nature of our state was published and: 'There is shock
after shock,' as Penn Warren put it, 'to our official versions and
received opinions.' But, surely, shock is what writers are meant to
apply when the patient has lost touch with reality. Unhappily,
many others are in place to act as shock-absorbers. They also
shroud the martyred Lincoln with his disingenuous funeral
address at Gettysburg in order to distract attention from the
uncomfortable paradox that his dictatorship – forbidden word in a
free country – preserved the Union by destroying it.

Commager was also dismayed by Wilson's 'odd interpretation of
World War I – that we were seduced into it by British propaganda,
and the assertion that had we but stayed out we could have "short-
ened the war and left Europe less shattered and more stable." Or

the astonishing statements that we "were gradually and *furtively*" brought into World War II by President Roosevelt who "had been ... *pretending* ... that he had not committed himself" [italics mine].' I happen to agree with Wilson but I acknowledge that others hold defensible contrary views. But, surely, Commager might have refrained from *pretending* (italics mine) to be 'astonished', even in innocent 1962, at hearing Wilson state views that many others have held about our wars; but then we must recall that both historians were writing not so many months after we had all been assured, most attractively, on a snowy day at the Capitol, that we would bear any burden to make sure that something or other would prevail somehow somewhere and in this process each of us might have the opportunity to become truly adorable.

In these last years Wilson returns to Jerusalem for an update on the Dead Sea Scrolls; he leaves the city on the day before the 1967 war starts. Meanwhile, he revises and reissues earlier books, writes regularly for *The New Yorker* and *The New York Review of Books*; he settles with the IRS largely, one suspects, because he was quirkily honoured by President Kennedy at the White House in 1963 with a Freedom Medal. In *Upstate*, Wilson writes that the bureaucracy objected: 'When Kennedy saw the man who remonstrated, he said, "This is not an award for good conduct but for literary merit."' When Kennedy asked Wilson what *Patriotic Gore* was about, Wilson told him to go read it.

> I have sometimes lately had the impression that my appearance and personality have almost entirely disappeared and that there is little but my books marching through me, the Indian book, the Civil War. They live, I am ceasing to live – But this is partly due to too much drinking, reading and thinking at night. . . .

That he could do all three suggests an ox-like physical structure.

*

9

Throughout this period as friends die off and new people tend to blur, certain figures keep recurring. There is quite a lot of Auden in and out. Also, Robert Lowell; also, an unlikely but intense friendship with Mike Nichols and Elaine May, who were then enjoying a success with their comic sketches and improvisations in a series of smoky Manhattan caves. Wilson is plainly smitten by Elaine May: 'It is a good thing I am too old to fall in love with her. I've always been such easy game for beautiful, gifted women and she is the most so since Mary McCarthy in the thirties. I imagine that she, too, would be rough going.'

Anaïs Nin, muse to Henry Miller, Olive Oyl to his Popeye, returns, hustling her jams and jellies. In the forties Wilson had praised her in *The New Yorker*. He had an endearing – to some – habit of falling in love with the work of a woman writer whom he would later want to meet and seduce. Like Montaigne, he thought that a mind and talent of the first order, associated for Montaigne and, perhaps, for Wilson, only with men, should it be combined with a woman's beauty might produce the perfect other half of Plato's whole, to be desired and pursued with ardour. Sometimes this longing had comic results. Wilson once praised a novel by what he took to be a young woman of the highest sensibility, Isabel Bolton. In due course he contrived to meet her. Bolton was indeed intellectually everything that he had ever desired in a woman. She was also a serene dowager of seventy, disinclined to dalliance.

Ms Nin was of sterner stuff. In her diaries she is kittenish about Wilson and herself. In life she told me that they had never had an affair, which – in Nin-speak – meant that they did. But he did not do enough for her work and so she wrote bitterly about him in the diaries that she was now preparing for publication. Since the publishers had insisted that she get a written release from each person mentioned, she writes Wilson, who sees her; finds her enchanting. In the next room, her long-suffering husband, Hugo Guiler, is editing a film. 'What about?' asks Wilson. 'Me,' she replies. Then

she leaned down and put her cheek against mine. She told me that she would send me the first volume of the diary – in which, I believe, I don't appear. . . . I don't know how much her reconciliation and the favorable picture of me may have been due to an eye to publicity on the publication of the diary. . . . She gave me a copy of her last book, *Collages*, and told me it was her first 'funny' book. It is actually not much different from her others: stories about exquisite women told by an exquisite woman.

Later Wilson reads her account of him: 'she found me aggressive, arrogant, authoritative, like a Dutch burgher in a Dutch painting, and with shoes that were too big. She had become frightened of me and had had to escape. . . . I made her correct a few details about Mary [McCarthy] and a few characteristic inaccuracies. She had said that I had given her a set of Emily Brontë – as if there could be such a thing, actually it was Jane Austen – and she had been offended and sent it back – which was not true, she had kept it.'

The relationship between Wilson and Elena, his wife, is occasionally stormy: she prefers her Wellfleet garden and Manhattan to rough Talcottville. Wilson's description of a dinner at the Kennedy White House shows him at his journalistic best and Elena, his handsome German-Russian fourth wife, at her most grand. Wilson's cold eye analyses her, too. 'I had never before been with her anywhere remotely resembling a court, and wasn't prepared for her stiffening attitude. The first sign of this was her "squeamishness", as she calls it – this Russian groping for *brezglivost* . . . in the presence of Tennessee Williams – after all he had been in our house at Wellfleet', but, as they stood in line behind Williams, Elena tells Wilson in Russian that she 'feels such physical repulsion that she . . . cannot stand to be near him.' One would like to think that this was due to his drunkenness.

James Baldwin, as writer and as a black, appeals to both of them. He makes a successful visit to Talcottville. Wilson thought him 'one of the best writers that we have', though 'when Elena left the table to go into the kitchen, he turned on his adjectival "fucking" like the people in his novel. . . . I have been wondering whether ordinary people really talked to one another in that way now. I reflected, after seeing later in New York Albee's play *Who's Afraid of Virginia Woolf?*, whether most of the dirty language in fiction and on stage didn't occur in the work of homosexuals? Albee, Tennessee Williams, Isherwood, Baldwin, Genet, and the beatniks Ginsberg and Burroughs.' Actually, this is off-the-wall. A degree of candour about same-sexuality is the most that these writers have in common. Four-letter words seldom occur in Tennessee's 'poetic' dialogue nor do they in Isherwood or even in Genet except when he is rendering underworld argot where such words are a normal part of speech. Actually 'fuck' entered the general language as ubiquitous epithet thanks to World War II, in which 13 million Americans served. If Wilson had bothered to read *The Naked and the Dead* or *From Here to Eternity* he would have noted the sea-change in language from Hemingway and Dos Passos to our time. But then he liked to say that he himself was a man of the nineteenth century.

Wilson writes a propos Elena's 'theory that Jews are bitterly jealous of the attention that Baldwin and others are directing towards the Negroes':

I did not take this seriously at first, but I now think there's something in it: Podhoretz's article in *Commentary* about his having been persecuted in his childhood by the Negroes, Lillian Hellman's play with its white boy who champions the Negroes, then is robbed by the Negro to whom he has been making an impassioned speech. Elena's conversation . . . with the young Jewish Greek teacher from Brandeis – when Elena asked this young man if he had heard Baldwin's lecture at Brandeis, he had answered certainly not: he had been to school with Baldwin. The Negroes were inferior, they had never produced anything. Why associate with them, or bother about them? They were making capital out of their sufferings, but the Jews had suffered much more. One does get the impression that the Jews regard themselves as having a monopoly on suffering, and do not want the Negroes to muscle in.

Wilson's eye is not only on the great of the world but on those who attract him as well, like Mary Pcolar, who lives in the Talcottville region; she is married with two children and holds various jobs that he describes with Balzacian precision. He is sexually drawn to her but notes his debility in these matters; nothing much happens but then, unlike in the early journals with their sexual graphicness, Wilson seems unable to perform the act to which he had devoted so much time in the past – not to mention so many words; yet, every now and then, oddly there will be a description of a sudden lust for Elena which ends in a successful coupling despite 'half-mast' erections.

I suspect that future literacy chronicles will find it odd that the generation of Wilson and Miller and Williams and McCarthy – names more or less taken at random – should have felt duty-bound to tell us at length exactly what they did or tried to do in bed. The effect is sometimes bracing, like reading a good description of applied physics, say, but it is never erotic. The thought of Wilson in the act is profoundly depressing. D. H. Lawrence – first in this field? – is not much better in his fictive renderings. On the other hand James Boswell delights us with his drunken swoops on complaisant chambermaids, and his poxy member takes on a plangent life of its own: one responds to its rises and falls as one never does to the clinical Wilson's plumbing.

Wilson enjoys Auden's company; Auden's unremitting pedantry matches his own. When they met it was to exchange lectures until, with alcohol, Wilson would start barking and Auden mumbling and wheezing.

> Wystan tends nowadays to plug with me that we both belong to the professional middle class, who are the pillars of civilization. There was, he thought, no distinction [in the United States] between professional people and those in trade . . . I said that when I was in college, there *had* been a marked distinction and this surprised him. He asked me whether it wasn't true that I never felt myself inferior to anybody. I told him that in my youth I had rather resented the millionaires.

I think that he himself had actually resented being looked down upon as a doctor's son.... He said that he *had* regretted not having been sent to Eton.

Auden complains to Wilson that critics never note his mastery of the technicalities of verse.

For example, nobody had mentioned in writing about his last book that it contained a poem in stanzas. I said that I thought William Carlos Williams had ruined American poetry by leading most of the poets to give up verse altogether and lapse into 'shredded prose'. He said he didn't care about the early Williams but that he had learned something from the later Williams. I said I couldn't see any influence. 'It's there.' 'What do you mean?' 'Technically.' 'How?' 'Length of lines.' I still don't know what he meant.

Glumly Wilson notes, 'The last lusts gutter out.' He concludes man-woman sex is nothing to fuss about. 'Yet homosexuals don't seem to have flowered and borne fruit, don't seem to have fully matured. Auden with his appetite for Tolkien.' Surely, Auden's poetry is . . . well, one of the fine mature fruits of this century while a liking for Tolkien can be philological as well as infantile.

What Wilson maintains to the end is a clear eye for what is in front of him, whether a text or a person. Great critics do not complicate a text; they describe it and then report on what they have described, if the description itself is not the criticism. Some of his reports – or even asides – make sense where most readers make none or nonsense. A friend

had just read Tolstoy's *Death of Ivan Ilyich*, which had made a great impression on him. I do not care for this story as much as many people do. I don't believe that a man like Ivan Ilyich could ever look back on his life and find it empty and futile; I don't believe that Tolstoy, in the period when he was writing his great novels, would ever have invented such a character.

This is simply put; it is also, simply, true. Ivan Ilyich would not have regarded his past life as empty and futile any more than Edmund Wilson, despite his aches and pains, could ever have found his life anything but fascinating and full, as through him marched the Iroquois, the protagonists of the Civil War, the Dead Sea Scrolls, recollections of Daisy and Hecate County, *Axel's Castle* and *To the Finland Station*, as well as these journals – first begun at Box Hill in Surrey, close to the small chalet where the great lost poet-novelist George Meredith wrote 'half a dozen great novels'.

The editor, Mr Dabney, notes, I think correctly, that Wilson in his journals, 'was creating an art of portraiture in the tradition of Dr Johnson, Taine and Sainte-Beuve'. He is certainly at his best when he turns the lights on a literary figure whom he knows and then walks, as it were, all around him. He mentions occasionally that he is reading Jules Renard's journals; it is a pity that Wilson has none of that journalist's aphoristic wit. But he might have said, with Renard, 'Be interesting! Be interesting! Art is no excuse for boring people', not to mention 'I was born for successes in journalism, for the daily renown, the literature of abundance; reading great writers changed all that. That was the misfortune of my life.' But their misfortune is our good fortune. They existed to give the dull a glimpse of unsuspected worlds hidden in the one that we daily look at. One admires in Wilson what he admired in Parkman, 'the avoidance of generalization, the description of the events always in concrete detail. The larger tendencies are shown by a chronicle of individualized persons and actions. It is what I try to do myself.' Successfully, one might add. In the four-volume *Literary Criticism, A Short History* (1957), by W. K. Wimsatt, Jr and Cleanth Brooks, the *Almanach da Gotha* of critics, Wilson is cited in *three* footnotes. Three! Fame!

The New York Review of Books
4 November 1993

15

2

Dawn Powell: Queen of the Golden Age

In November 1987, after a year of reading the published works of Dawn Powell (1897–1965), I published my findings in *The New York Review of Books*.* There is now a somewhat blurred perception that she was always very much on the minds of such exciting critics and taste-makers as James Wolcott and John Updike, and that I had simply leapt onto a merrily moving bandwagon. Actually, all her books were out of print and her name was known only to those of us whose careers had overlapped hers. In the twenty-two years that had passed since her death, she had been thoroughly erased, as original writers so often are, in the United States of Amnesia. But then she had never had much success in her lifetime either. She was a wit, a satirist and a woman, a combination that did not enchant the bookchatterers of that era. Worst of all, *she did not affirm warm mature family values*. She herself was the principal third of an interesting *ménage à trois* in Greenwich Village; the other two thirds were her lifelong (*his* lifelong) husband, Joseph Gousha, and Coburn Gilman, a man about town and sometime magazine editor.

* *The New York Review*, November 5, 1987.

16

All three were serious drinkers but then so was everyone else in those days when she could (with no irony) write a book about Manhattan and call it *The Happy Island*.

Since my description of Powell's fifteen novels, she is now almost entirely in print, here and abroad, and some of her work is even, as she would say, compost for movies and television. As I contemplate Dawn's posthumous victory, I feel incredibly smug. With sufficient diligence, bookchat *can* serve a purpose, indeed its only proper purpose: to persuade the few remaining voluntary readers to turn to a writer whom they have never heard of because authority for so long either ignored or disapproved of her. If I sound unduly proprietary, I am. Also, I liked not only the Powell novels but Dawn herself. ('Yes, I know I have the name of an unsuccessful stripper. It is my strong suit.') She was the best company in the world, with a fine savage wit, 'that Irish strain in me'. Now one Tim Page has taken on Powell's case and he is busy editing and republishing her work, most lately the diaries that she kept off and on from 1931 to her death in 1965, aged sixty-eight. He has, he tells us, 'algebraically tightened many of the entries'. Personally, I would have plane geometrically loosened them but then I am old school and would have kept some of the drunken entries. She is, he tells us, 'one hell of a writer', the ultimate canonical praise from the likes of John Crowe Ransom and the New Critics of yesteryear. But so she is, Tim, so she is.

Biographical data: Powell was born at Mt Gilead, Ohio. Shunted about from relative to relative. Obliged to amuse the unamusable. When wicked stepmother destroys her writing, Dawn flees home. Works as a waitress. Eventually graduates from Lake Erie College and heads for New York City where she writes anything to live. But always remains a novelist, writing either of her Ohio home, always further and further away, or tales of Manhattan life.

Now the diaries. For me, it is like having her back to life – very small, very plump – seated at a banquette in the Blue Angel, a long thin shiny black-walled night club, known to our friend John Latouche (of whom more later) as Juliet's Tomb, and presided over by its owner, Herbert Jacoby, a sombre Frenchman who would introduce each comedy act with a melancholy sigh and then turn from Imogene Coca, let us say, with a look of absolute despair. Meanwhile, Dawn would be knocking back fiery waters and the wit would start to rise. It should be noted that she never complained to friends of her ongoing ill health, her retarded son, or chronic poverty. But occasionally in the diary she gives it to Fate for what Fate has done to her; yet at the end, she did have a degree of success with her last (and perhaps best) novels, *The Golden Spur* and *The Wicked Pavilion*. Astonishingly, she was nominated for a literary prize. She notes: 'Will success spoil Dawn Powell? I don't see why not. I'm no better than anybody else, never said so.' She failed to get the award.

Although Dawn was admired as a writer and bright companion by such contemporaries as Hemingway and Dos Passos, it was Edmund Wilson who helped her most, if a bit too late in the game. When finally he praised her in *The New Yorker*, he failed to elevate her to those heights where the important lady writers sunned themselves or, as Dawn characterized one lady writer with inherited money, 'as she doesn't work for her success, therefore has it, along with prestige, handed to her on a silver platter with warning to God, "Right Side Up."' In 1934 she contemplates three fashionables of the day: Nancy Hale, Louise Bogan, Kay Boyle:

I was impressed with how women now made their art serve their female purpose whereas once it warred with their femininity. Each page is squirming with sensitivity, every line – no matter how well disguised the heroine is – coyly reveals her exquisite taste, her delicate charm, her never-at-a-disadvantage body (which of course she cares nothing about and is always faintly amused at men's frenzies over her perfect legs, breasts, etc.). What gallantry, what equalness to any situation in the home, the camp, the yacht, the trenches, the dives – what *aristocrats* these women writers are, whose pen advertises the superiority of their organs. Fit companions and opposites of the he-man writers – Hemingway, Burnett, Cain

– imitation he-manners whose words tersely proclaim their masculinity, every tight-lipped phrase shows the author's guts, his decency, his ability to handle any situation – insurrection (he is an instinctive leader or else too superior to show it), shipwreck, liquor, women. Through the words shot out of the typewriter clip-clip one watches the play of his muscles; one sighs to lay one's head upon that hairy shoulder.

'Started job with Paramount doing over "Quarantine" at $1000 a week.' *Plus ça change*, as they say at the Beaux Arts. Dawn found the girls every bit as hilarious as the boys. This even-handedness is not the surest path to popularity.

'Happiness as a rule brings out the worst in people's characters. No longer afraid, they radiantly flaunt their smugness, small vices and worst sentimentalities. . . . Happiness has given [X] a sword; respectability has given her the right to be stupid.' Although many of Dawn's novels deal with 'career' women in New York who need each other for company between marriages and love affairs, Dawn is constantly suspicious of girlfriends. 'Always be kind to strangers,' she told Elaine Dundy at my house when they first met. 'It's the friends to beware of.' In the diaries she notes: 'I am perpetually surprised at my own stupidity about women and cannot really blame men for the same lack of perception.' But Dawn, though stringent, lacks all malice even when she zeroes in on someone she truly dislikes. She does a splendid send-up of Clare Boothe Luce, in *A Time To Be Born*, which 'I have been denying for years . . . I insist it was a composite (or compost) but then I find a memo from 1939 – "Why not do novel on Clare Luce?" Who can I believe – me or myself?'

There are few intimate revelations in the diaries. There is a hint that she and the Communist playwright John Howard Lawson once had an affair but one doubts that with the other points to her triangle – Joe and Coby – they would have bothered much about sex when wit and work and the company of each other and the passing parade of the Village was more than enough to occupy

19

them. One is astonished at the amount of work that Dawn was obliged to do in order to pay for the institutionalized son, with not much help from Joe, himself feckless in money matters. She even made an obligatory trip or two to Hollywood to write for movies. Of Hollywood: 'The climate picks up up and throws you down in the most amazing way.' That was about it. She endures a production or two in the theatre, dealing, usually unhappily, with the Group Theater and the Theater Guild. Except for Robert Lewis, a director very much on her wavelength, Dawn found the Strasbergs and Clurmans and Crawfords pretty lethal in their egotism and pomposity while actors regard 'the author and his work as nasty stumbling blocks between them and the public.' She was a good comic playwright who had the bad luck to fall into the hands of the Group Theater at its most didactic. After she saw what they had done to one of her plays, she hoped that they would get their heavy hands on Shaw and Pirandello and reduce those masters to agit-prop sermonizers.

Quite by chance, Dawn was at the centre of the American Communist world. Friends of all sorts figure on the left, including a wealthy woman called Margaret de Silver, mistress of the Italian anti-fascist (and later murdered) Carlo Tresca. It was De Silver who came to Dawn's aid when she and Joe had been literally evicted from their apartment and left, along with their furniture, on the sidewalk. De Silver promptly created a trust fund for the retarded son. Dawn herself was apolitical. 'Roosevelt dies', is a single entry in the diary: that was that.

In 1931 Dawn met Edmund Wilson and they remained friends, with the odd up and down, for thirty-four years. Lately, Wilson is being mysteriously attacked by peripheral literary folk as a drunken bully and general lout. It is true that the MLA disliked him as much as he did them, but at least there are good reasons on both sides, which he spelled out in a splendid work on demolition.*

* The Fruits of the MLA: 'I. Their Wedding Journey' (*The New York Review*, September 26, 1968); 'II. Mark Twain' (October 10, 1968).

The current attacks on Wilson may simply be dismissed as 'mere English': unfocused malice, combined with a well-earned sense of inferiority when faced with any powerful wide-ranging mind.

It seems unlikely that Dawn was one of the *femmes fatales des lettres* of the sort that Wilson was often drawn to. Two brilliant, tubby little creatures, deeply involved in literature of every kind, were bound to be companions rather than lovers. She made him laugh. He made her think. Sometimes it was the other way around, which could make him irritable; and make her sharp. Wilson was a man of the previous century and the idea of a brilliant woman as an equal was always intriguing (he married one, after all, Mary McCarthy, and duly suffered) but somehow against nature. On the other hand, he was that unusual phenomenon, the born teacher who never stops learning new things about everything, from the Iroquois Indians to the intricacies of Hungarian grammar. Inevitably their interests often overlapped (though not I suspect on the Iroquois).

March 23, 1943: 'Reading for the first time a fine book (Flaubert's *Sentimental Education*) I am again impressed by the importance of satire as social history and my theory that what reviewers call satire is "whimsy" and what they call realism is romanticism. . . . The only record of a civilization is satire – Petronius, Aristophanes, Flaubert.' April 2: 'Cocktails with Bunny [Edmund Wilson]. . . . I find Bunny a great devotee of [*Sentimental Education*], though he feels it loses in translation, being, like poetry, built on the cadences of its own language. . . .' Wilson then tells her that, from his own journal, he is about to extract ' "the greatest love story ever written" in pornographic detail. . . . It was exhilarating to spend time again with a sharp, creative literary mind, a balance so necessary in the hoodlum world I live in.'

But there are clouds: Wilson wrote her a letter 'depressing in its way. Men really dislike a literary woman (especially if she is good) and prefer not reading works of their women friends, hoping and even saying that they must be bad.' She was distressed at Wilson's dim review of her best Ohio novel *My Home is Far Away*: 'It is very discouraging to have someone (who actually has told me I'm infinitely better than John Marquand and equal to Sinclair Lewis at his best) do me so much genuine damage. I have enough damage done me already, merely by the desire to write. . . .'

By 1945 Dawn is seriously on the warpath: 'All relations with Bunny are dictated by him – he is the one to name the hour, the place, the subject of conversation. . . . He is mystified and annoyed by the simple process of creation; he is furious at the things he does not understand – furious, blind and bored. What he does not understand is all life that is not in print. . . . He wants to see his ladies alone so he can attack them . . . [tell] them that everything they like is impossible. . . . He beams with joy and well-nourished nerves as he leaves, like a vampire returning from a juicy grave.'

But there were autumnal joys between the old friends. Wilson's daughter, Rosalind, has said that of all the guests who stayed at Wilson's family place in upstate New York, only Dawn knew how to sit comfortably on the porch and do nothing but watch people pass. As Dawn remarks, 'Bunny, Dos [Passos], etc., are so completely selfish that they allow it in others.' There is one splendid drunken quarrel in a cab: Dawn blasted Bunny's wife Elena as a social climber, which, as Dawn promptly notes, 'all this wrong, because [the previous wife] Mary McCarthy was the climber. . . . Sudden silence in cab as I raged, then Bunny said "I wish you weren't so jealous of me, Dawn. It makes it very hard for you." This was a wonderful switch, which I snatched at and said, "It's because you keep me on that little back street and never let me meet your set and you're always going back to your wife and I have never seen you except when you're in town selling—" "Yes I know it's been hard on you, dear," he said. So we were saved from a real embarrassment.' (For those who don't recognize the powerful scene they played, it is from the great best-seller of the day *Back Street* by Fannie Hurst.)

Next day I was ashamed but hardly could call and apologize for murder. So I sent wire to him – 'Darling, what happened to us? Was it my money or your music? Was it the Club?

Where did we go wrong, dear? Aurore.' Today a postcard from him says "Dear Aurore. Perhaps it might be as well for us not to see each other for awhile. The strain of our relationship is becoming difficult. I am leaving for Boston tomorrow. *Mille baisers* – Raoul.'

They also conducted a correspondence in which she was the lofty Mrs Humphrey Ward and he a seedy academic called Wigmore.

'There are so many kinds of fame for a writer that it is astonishing the number of us who never achieve one.' A lifetime of near-misses depressed but did not discourage her. Also, the examination of such monsters as her friend Hemingway made her suspect that the first requisite of earthly glory was a total lack of humour or (the same thing?) self-knowledge. 'I tried once again to read *Farewell to Arms* and it seems as clumsily written as ever to me. . . .' Of the protagonist of *For Whom the Bell Tolls*: 'a fictional movie hero in Spain with the language neither Spanish nor English. When someone wishes to write of this age – as I do and have done – critics shy off – the public shies off. "Where's our Story Book?" they cry. . . . This is obviously an age that Can't Take It.' Dawn's conclusion is that 'Success is a knack – like a knack for weaving something out of a few strings – which for the rest of us are nothing but a few strings.' Nor was she about to ingratiate herself with book reviewers like the New York *Herald Tribune*'s Lewis Gannett, as serenely outside literature as his confrère in the daily *New York Times*, Orville Prescott, currently divided into two halves of equally bewildered density.

At Margaret's Lewis Gannett flung an affectionate arm around me and introduced me: 'Dawn's a good girl except she drinks too much and one of these days she's going to do a good novel.' 'If I did, you wouldn't know it,' I said. 'As for drinking too much you've never seen me at these parties in the last five years where you were drinking more than anyone. That's why you can never be a writer or know good writing when you see it – generalizing about a person's habits from public performances instead of private understanding.' He was mad. I lectured him that if ever I wrote something he considered 'good' I would know I was slipping. '*Pas des mouches sur* Dawn,' as Raoul would say.

But then, 'All my life has been spent killing geese that lay golden eggs and it's a fine decent sport – superior to killing small birds, horses or lions.'

It was Dawn Powell's fate to be a dinosaur shortly after the comet, or whatever it was, struck our culture, killing off the literary culture – a process still at work but no less inexorable – and replacing it with the Audiovisual, as they say at Film School. The Hemingway, Faulkner, Fitzgerald, Dreiser, and Powell American generation was the last to be central to the culture of that part of the world where Gutenberg reigned. By the next generation, it was clear to most of us that the novel had been superseded by the film while popular writing of the sort Dawn was reduced to turning out – stories and serials for slick mass magazines – has, in the last four decades, been replaced by television sitcoms and mini-series. Today few magazines publish fiction of any kind. Few people read fiction of any kind other than what those chains of book shops in the bright malls of America feel that the mallsters are capable of grasping, which is not very much beyond thinly disguised stories about showbiz celebrities, competing with tell-all biographies or autobiographies of the few people that television has acquainted our unread public with. For Dawn Powell's generation, there was still the romantic, if somewhat sappy, notion of The Great American Novel that someone was bound to write – and altogether too many people did write. You were, if serious, a writer for life, with an ever-growing public if you were any good.

All that changed in the Fifties. Writers can still be minor celebrities, good to flesh out a talk show if they can be counted on not to say anything of interest. But the writer as definer of the prospect has no role at all in the 'first world'. Our serious writers teach other serious writers who in turn teach *them* in classrooms. But for the bright inventive woman who kept these diaries the scene was no different from what it was for George Sand – a novel one year, a play the next year, and a life in the stream of her time. When she noted that the reader wants his simple-minded Story Book, she had not realized that the story had already started its leap from dull page to bright moving picture, and when she mourned that this is the age that Can't Take It, she is quite right except that she thought the 'it' was realistic observation – satire – that they couldn't take when the 'it' they can't, and won't, take is literature itself.

The New York of the Golden Age (1945–1950 – the only period when we were not kept at war) glitters in her diary, as she reflects on all sorts of wonders and novelties and even genius. Among the wonders was John Latouche, a short chunky Irish wit (with the obligatory Jewish mother). Although himself an outlander from Virginia he was, like Dawn herself, the personification of Manhattan, particularly its nightside, when ten thousand musicians in dives played songs for which he had written the lyrics – 'Taking a Chance on Love', 'Cabin in the Sky', 'Lazy Afternoon' (written at my house on the Hudson one hot summer day). Latouche talked and talked and kept everyone excited and laughing. It was he who first told me of a writer with the unlikely name, Dawn Powell; she had just written a novel called *The Locusts Have No King*. I met Dawn with him. They looked alike except that he had bright blue eyes in his disproportionately large head, while hers were, I think, brown.

> Latouche came out Saturday and Sunday and left me exhausted. He is so multi-gifted that he seems to leave people as worn as if they'd been to a circus, and while he shoots sparks in all directions, in the end it is the others who are depleted and he is renourished. . . . It is unconsciously deliberate on his part. He wants people not-to-do, just as he doesn't-do. He likes their doing well – no envy there – but it's actual *doing* he minds.

25

When, to survive, I wrote a dozen plays for live television in one year, Latouche was deeply saddened. 'Whoever suspected that you would end up as the Lope de Vega of television?'

> March 11, 1954: Latouche's *Golden Apple* opened at Phoenix – thoroughly fresh and delightful. At end, saw him by stairs in middle of cheers. He was weeping. 'They've ruined my second act – they've ruined it – spoiled everything! Come downstairs and have champagne!' Down was a vast Sardi's. Gore Vidal – Luciferian-looking young man who called a couple of times. Very gifted, brilliant, and fixed in facility as I am.

Thus, I first appear in her diaries: and though we saw each other far too seldom, the condition of an active life in the golden age, she – like Touche – made the weather for us all or, as she put it, 'The way Latouche and I always knocked ourselves out to entertain morons. The more useless and blah they were, the harder we worked for their amusement – as if they were such a waste that only by converting these ciphers into something (in fact nothing more than audience) could they be endured.'

Then the memorable August 7, 1956: 'Latouche died! – in Calais, Vermont. Luckily his opera "Baby Doe" had been a great peak last month in Central City, a peak he might not pass. Incredible that this dynamo should unwind and I think I can guess how. Talentless but shrewd users pursued him always . . . trying to get him in a corner room, lock him up and get out the gold when he wanted only to talk all day and all night. . . . I'm sure this was a desperate, hysterical escape from Lillian Hellman and others waiting for his output to finish up *Candide*.' He was thirty-nine.

In later years Dawn reviewed books, shrewdly if somewhat wearily, in *Mademoiselle*. Although like every regular reviewer she was pretty much stuck with the daily output (Capote? 'The Southern white trash and *crème de menthe* school as against the old mint julep school') but her own views on literature, particularly the superiority of Petronian satire to everything else in the prose line, are interesting. ' "Realism" is the only completely vague word. "Satire" is the technical word for writing of people as they are: "romantic" the other extreme of people as they are to themselves – but both of these are the truth. The ability to put in motive is called satire; the ability to put in vision is romanticism.' She duly noted that the rich and the poor could be satirized with impunity (because they were – then – so few and never read books?) but 'The middle class is wit-proofed. . . . If there is to be satire it must not bite at the bread-winner.' And 'the human comedy is always tragic but since its ingredients are always the same – dupe, fox, straight, like burlesque skits – the repetition through the ages is comedy.'

Powell seems to have got the point to Edith Wharton long before others did. In 1951, 'Read Edith Wharton's *The Reef* and strug-gling with *Wings of the Dove* by James simultaneously. Curiously alike, but she is so superior in this. Odd, her reputation for "moral-izing novels" when it was her *age* which read its own moralizing into her. Not one word could be called moralizing – no villains, no heroes in the noble sense. Villainy is done by a group of characters behaving in the only way they, in all honesty, feel they can decently behave. . . . I must write to Sophy Viner, I woke up thinking. I must tell her – tell her what? She never existed. What a precise miracle of illusion Edith Wharton created – never showing Sophy's room, giving her only one dress, one cloak, describing her only as fresh-faced – but she is *real*.'

Dawn is very much on to Mary McCarthy: 'Read Mary McCarthy's piece – another beginning of novel. . . . These last two starts are invigorating – like a brisk whiff of the stable on a clear wintry day. She has her two manners – her lace-curtain Irish, almost unbelievably genteel lady scholar torn between desire to be Blue Stocking without losing her Ladyship; and then her shanty Irish where she relaxes, whamming away at her characters like a Queen of the Roller Derby, groin-kicking, shin-knifing, belly-butting, flailing away with skates and all arms at her characters and jumping on them with a hoarse whoop of glee when they are felled.'

Finally, she comes to James through that curiously enchanting nouvelle, *The Reverberator*, so prescient in its grasp of the general horror of publicity at the dawn of the age of the tabloid newspapers. 'James's work nearly always stirs the writing imagination. Some object to "involuted writing", "obtuseness" – but none of this is irrelevant. He is like a sculptor in wood, chopping his own trees, hacking and sawing to get to the exact core of his design, examining each branch and bit of sap for its effect on the inner meat. He is after his story for truth's sake, not yours. He is not a tailor, whipping up a pretty costume for your delight. Authors have been stealing his plots for years not because they are inventions (which always wear out with me) but because they are imperishable human truths. That is why he is caviar for the wise and old and experienced – nothing false.'

A few months before death, Dawn wrote a definite non-Valentine to the rising generation of American writers.

> Most important thing for novelist is curiosity and how curious that so many of them lack it. They seem self-absorbed, family-absorbed, success-absorbed, but the new social-climbing writer professes indifference to the couple across the aisle, the noise from the next apartment – as if a gentleman does not concern himself with things not his business.
>
> I contend that a writer's business is minding other people's business. . . . The new writers disdain human curiosity; they wish only to explore and describe their own psyches; they are too egotistical and snobbish to interest themselves in neighbors. The urge to write now is no longer the love of story-telling or even the love of applause for a neat turn or dramatic twist. It is the urge to show off, the author as hero is a big sex success and leaves them gasping. The book's drive is only the desire to strip the writer's remembered woes and wrongs and show his superiority to the reader – not to communicate with him or entertain.

Since then, of course, text and context have been replaced by

Theory, and Author – he dead. Dawn, if alive, would have been one of the first to make it to the Internet as rollicking Queen of the Cyber Punks, carefully digging potholes in the Information Highway.

In 1962 Joe Gousha dies, painfully, of cirrhosis. Dawn writes: 'As for his death, this is a curious thing to say but after 42 years of life together – much of it precarious and crushing – we have been through worse disasters together, and I'm sure Joe would feel the same way about me.' The next-to-last entry in the diaries records that 'Bunny came in': Raoul faithful to the end to his Aurore. She died November 14, 1965, at St Luke's Hospital. 'I cannot exist without the oxygen of laughter,' she wrote not long before the end. One might add that those who can (or must) exist without are – what else? – a sad lot.

The New York Review of Books
21 March 1996

3
The Romance of
Sinclair Lewis

1

Elmer Gantry. It Can't Happen Here. Babbit. Main Street. Dodsworth. Arrowsmith. Sinclair Lewis. The first four references are part of the language; the next two are known to many, while the last name has a certain Trivial Pursuit resonance; yet how many know it is the name of the writer who wrote *Elmer Gantry*, played in the movie by Kirk Douglas – or was it Burt Lancaster?

Sinclair Lewis seems to have dropped out of what remains of world literature. The books are little read today, and he's seldom discussed in his native land outside his home town, Sauk Centre, Minnesota. Although Sauk Centre holds an annual Sinclair Lewis Day, the guide to his home recently admitted, I've never read *Main Street*. . . . I've been reading the biographies.' Elsewhere, the Associated Press (July 18) tells us, 'About forty copies of Lewis's books are on the shelves of the town library. For the most part, that's where they stay.'

'I expect to be the most talked-of writer,' Lewis boasted before he was. But the great ironist in the sky had other plans for him. In the end, Lewis was not to be talked of at all, but his characters – as types – would soldier on; in fact, more of his inventions have gone into the language than those of any other writer since Dickens.

People still say, in quotes as it were, 'It can't happen here,' meaning fascism, which probably will; hence, the ironic or minatory spin the phrase now gets. In the half century since Sinclair Lewis (one wants to put quotes about his name, too) what writer has come up with a character or phrase like Babbitt or Elmer Gantry that stands for an easily recognized type? There is 'Walter Mitty' and Heller's 'Catch-22'; and that's that. Of course, much of this has to do with the irrelevance of the novel in an audio-visual age. It is 'Murphy Brown' not 'Herzog' that registers, if only for the span of a network season. Finally, even if the novel was of interest to the many, its nature has certainly changed since the first half of the century when serious novelists, committed to realism/naturalism, wrote about *subjects* like the hotel business, the sort of thing that only pop novelists go in for nowadays.

That said, it would seem impossible that a mere biographer could effectively eliminate a popular and famous novelist; yet that is exactly what Mark Schorer managed to do in his 867-page biography, *Sinclair Lewis*.* Schorer's serene loathing of his subject and all his works is impressive in its purity but, at the end, one is as weary of Schorer himself as of Lewis. I once asked Schorer, an amiable man who liked to drink almost as much as Lewis did, why he had taken on a subject that he so clearly despised. The long answer was money; the short, too. In this Schorer did *not* resemble Lewis who, as much as he liked every sort of success, had a craving for Art in an *echt*-American way, and a passion for his inventions; also, he believed that somewhere over the rainbow there was a great good place that would prove to be home. As it turned out, he was never at home anywhere; and his restless changes of address take up altogether too many pages in Schorer's survey, as they must have used up too much psychic energy in Lewis's life, where the only constant, aside from frantic writing and frantic drinking, was, as his first wife sadly observed, 'romance is never where you are, but where you are going.' Since he never stayed put, he never

* *Sinclair Lewis: An American Life* (McGraw-Hill, 1961).

got there. Wives and women came and went; there were hardly any friends left after the end of the great decade of his life, 1920–1930.

In 1920, the unadmired great man of American letters, William Dean Howells, died, and Lewis published *Main Street*; then *Babbitt* (1922); *Arrowsmith* (1925); *Elmer Gantry* (1927); *Dodsworth* (1929). The Nobel Prize followed in 1930. That was the period when the Swedes singled out worthy if not particularly good writers for celebration, much as they now select worthy if not particularly interesting countries or languages for consolation. Although the next twenty-one years of Lewis's life was decline and fall, he never stopped writing; never stopped, indeed: always in motion.

'He was a queer boy, always an outsider, lonely.' Thus Schorer begins. Harry Sinclair Lewis was born in 1885 in Sauk Centre, Minnesota, population 2,800. At the same time a couple of dozen significant American writers were also being brought up in similar towns in the Middle West and every last one of them was hell-bent to get out. Lewis's father, a doctor, was able to send him to Yale. Harry or Hal or Red was gargoyle ugly: red-haired, physically ill-coordinated, suffered from acne that was made cancerous by primitive X-ray treatments. He was a born mimic. He had a wide repertory of characters – types – and he was constantly shifting in and out of characters. But where Flaubert had only one act, The Idiot, Lewis had an army of idiots, and once started, he could not shut up. He delighted and bored, often at the same time.

Although Lewis had been born with all the gifts that a satirist needs to set up shop he was, by temperament, a romantic. Early writings were full of medieval fair ladies, gallant knights, lands of awful Poesie where James Branch Cabell was to stake out *his* territory, now quite abandoned. Lewis also had, even by American standards, absolutely no sense of humour. In a charming memoir his first wife, Grace Hegger, noted, '*Main Street* was not a satire until the critics began calling him a satirist, and then seeing himself in that role, is it possible that [his next book] *Babbitt* became true satire?' The question is double-edged. Like Columbus, Lewis had no idea where he had gone, but the trip was fun. He loved his high-toned heroine, Carol Kennicott, but if others thought her a joke, he was willing to go along with it.

In youth Lewis wrote yards of romantic verse, much of it jocose; yet he had heard Yeats at Yale and was much impressed by the poetry of the early Yeats. Like most born writers, he read everything: Dickens, Scott, Kipling were his first influences. But it was H. G. Wells's *The History of Mr Polly* that became for him a paradigm for his own first novel. Like most writers, again, he later claimed all sorts of grand literary progenitors, among them Thoreau, but it would appear that he mostly read the popular writers of his time and on the great divide that Philip Rahv was to note – Paleface versus Redskin – Lewis was firmly Redskin; yet, paradoxically, he deeply admired and even tried to imitate those Edith Wharton stories that were being published when he was coming of age, not to mention *The Custom of the Country*, whose Undine Spragg could have easily served time in a Lewis novel.

The literary world before 1914 is now as distant from us as that of Richardson and Fielding. In those days novels and short stories were popular entertainment. They were meant to be read by just about everybody. Numerous magazines published thousands of short stories of every kind, and a busy minor writer could make as good a living as a minor bank president. Writing was simply a trade that, sometimes, mysteriously, proved to be an art. William Dean Howells had balanced commerce and art with such exquisite tact that he was invaluable as editor and friend to both the Paleface Henry James and the Redskin Mark Twain. Howells himself was a very fine novelist. But he lived too long. For the rising generation of the new twentieth century, he was too genteel, too optimistic (they had carelessly misread him); too much Beacon Street not to mention London and Paris and the Russia of Dostoevsky, whose first translations Howells had brought to the attention of those very conventional ladies who were thought to be the principal audience for the novel in America.

While still at Yale, Lewis headed straight to the action. Upton

Sinclair had started a sort of commune, Helicon Hall, at Englewood, New Jersey, and in 1906 Lewis spent two months there, firing furnaces and writing. By 1909 he was at Carmel with his classmate William Rose Benét, another professional bookman. Lewis worked on the San Francisco *Bulletin*, and wrote. When Jack London had come to Yale to speak for socialism, Lewis had met him. Although Lewis was to be, briefly, a card-carrying socialist, he was never much interested in politics, but he very much admired the great Redskin writer, and he got to know him at Carmel.

London wrote short stories for a living. Unfortunately, he had trouble thinking up plots. Although Lewis was not yet making a living from short stories, he had thought up a great many plots. So, in 1910, Lewis sold Jack London fourteen short story plots for $70. Two became published short stories; the third the start of a not-to-be-finished novel. Lewis later described London at that time as someone more interested in playing bridge than sea-wolfing. He also described how 'Jack picked up James's *The Wings of the Dove* . . . and read aloud in a bewildered way. . . . It was the clash between Main Street and Beacon Street that is eternal in American culture.' Well, eternity is a long time in bookchat land.

In 1910 Lewis moved on to Washington, DC, which was to become, more or less, his home base in the United States. Meanwhile he worked for New York publishers as reader, copywriter, salesman. He was also selling fiction to the flagship of commercial publishing, *The Saturday Evening Post*, as well as to other magazines. From 1913–1914 he produced a syndicated book page that was carried in newspapers all around the country. By putting himself at the centre of bookchat, he ensured good reviews for his own books in much the same way that in England now ambitious young writers not only review each other's books but also often act as literary editors in order to promote their future reviewers. Those destined for greatness will eventually review television programmes in a Sunday newspaper, thus getting to know the television and film magnates who will, in due course, promote them personally on television as well as buy their products for dramatization. The English literary scene today is very much like that of the US pre-1914.

*

Lewis's first novel, *Our Mr Wrenn*, is very much school of Wells; it was, of course, well-reviewed by his fellow bookmen. In the next four years Lewis published four more novels. Each had a subject, of which the most interesting was early aviation, *The Trail of the Hawk* (1915). Lewis had got to know Paul Beck, one of the first army flyers, and the novel presages, rather eerily, Lindbergh's career. In my memory these books are rather like those of Horatio Alger that I was reading at the same time, something of an agreeable blur. Since the Subject comes before the Characters and since Lewis was a thorough researcher, there are many little facts of the sort that pop writers today provide as they take us on tours of the cosmetics or munitions businesses, subjects they usually know very little about beyond idle, as opposed to dogged, research. Only James Michener, through hard work, has mastered the fictional narrative as a means of instruction in a subject of interest to him, like Hawaii; and then to millions of others.

The first five novels established Sinclair Lewis as a serious if not particularly brilliant novelist; but one with, as they say at *Billboard*, a bullet. As a careerist, Lewis was an Attila. In his pursuit of blurbs, he took no prisoners. He cultivated famous writers. *Main Street* is dedicated to James Branch Cabell *and* Joseph Hergesheimer, the two classiest novelists of the day. *Babbitt* is dedicated to Edith Wharton, who took it all in her magnificent ruthless stride.

In 1915 his old mentor Upton Sinclair was invited to assess the product. He did:

You seem to me one of the most curiously uneven writers I have ever known. You will write pages and pages of interesting stuff, and then you will write a lot of conversation which is just absolute waste, without any point or worthwhileness at all; and you don't seem to know the difference. Everything of yours that I have read is about half and half . . . wherever you are writing about the underworld, you are at your best, and when you come up to your own social level or higher, you are no good.

35

Nicely, Upton Sinclair adds a postscript: 'Don't be cross.' Writers usually get other writers' numbers rather more quickly than critics ever do. After all, as contemporaries, they have been dealt much the same cards to play with.

By 1929, the apprenticeship of Sinclair Lewis was over. He had married and become the father of a son, Wells, named for H. G., whom he had yet to meet (Lewis was deeply irritated when people thought that *he* had been named for Upton Sinclair when his father had named him after one Harry Sinclair, a dentist of the first rank).

The genesis of Lewis's ascent can be located in the year 1916 when he and his wife, Grace, came to stay in Sauk Centre with Dr Lewis and his wife, Sinclair's stepmother. In her memoir, Grace Hegger Lewis is very funny about what must have been a fairly uncomfortable visit. 'One morning when "the curse" was upon me', Grace asked for breakfast on a tray. The Lewises said no, while Hal, Grace's name for her husband, was 'furious. He had always taken for granted his affection for his parents and their behavior he had never questioned. But seeing his family through the eyes of New York and of marriage he was appalled by his father's overbearing rudeness.' Grace suggests that this visit forced Lewis to see his home town in an entirely new way and shift the point of view from that of a lonely off-beat lawyer in what was to be called *The Village Virus*, to that of Carol, a girl from outside the village who marries the local doctor, Will Kennicott, and so observes the scene with big city (in her case Minneapolis) eyes.

Grace reports that Dr Lewis did apologize; the young couple stayed on; and the town magnates were brought to their knees when they learned just how much Lewis had been paid for a two-part serial in the *Woman's Home Companion* ($1,500). 'When he told them that it had taken him two weeks to write the serial, the banker, dividing so much per diem, was visibly awed. . . . The young Lewises were to find that this measuring of talent by dollars was fairly universal, and Hal was hurt at first by the lack of interest in the writing itself.'

Their later life in Washington sounds agreeable. She tells us how they would walk to the Chevy Chase Club with the young Dean Achesons and how Lewis also frequented the Cosmos Club and got to know General Billy Mitchell, Clarence Darrow, and the scarlet lady of our town, Elinor Wylie – murmur her name, as indeed people were still doing a few years later when I was growing up. The Lewises seem not to have known the Achesons' friend, Grace Zaring Stone, author of *The Bitter Tea of General Yen*, who, when told by a lady novelist that she was writing a novel about Evil, sighed, 'If only I had thought of that!'

Lewis maintained that the idea for a novel whose subject would be a small Midwestern market town came to him in 1905. I should suspect that it was always there. Village life was the first thing that he had known and, sooner or later, writers usually deal with their origins. The real-life lawyer Charles T. Dorion was to be the main character, an idealistic soul, able to see through the pretences, the hypocrisies, the . . . the . . . the absolute boredom of Sauk Centre (renamed by Lewis Gopher Prairie). But the 1916 homecoming gave Lewis a new point of view, that of his elegant New York wife, to be called Carol. Dorion was demoted to supporting cast, as Guy Pollock.

In July 1920, in a Washington heat wave, Sinclair Lewis finished *Main Street*. He gave the book to his friend Alfred Harcourt, who had started a new publishing house to be known, in time, as Harcourt, Brace, in which Lewis had invested some of his own money. In the business of authorship he seldom put a foot wrong.

October 23, 1920, *Main Street* was published and, as one critic put it, 'if *Main Street* lives, it will probably be not as a novel but as an incident in American life.' Even Schorer, not yet halfway through Lewis's career, concedes, a bit sadly, that the book was 'the most sensational event in twentieth-century American publishing history.' As of 1922 an estimated two million Americans had read the book; and they went right on reading it for years. With Howells gone, Lewis took his place as numero uno and reigned both at home and abroad until 1930, after which, according to Schorer, 'with the increasing conformity at the surface of American life and the increasing fragmentation at its base, there have been no contenders at all.' I'm not sure that Bill or Ernest or Scott or Saul or Norman or . . . would agree. The contenders are all in place. The problem is that fiction – stories intended to be read by almost everyone – ceased to be of much interest to a public 'with no time to read' and movies to go to and, later, television to watch. *The Saturday Evening Post* serial, often well-written by a good writer, would now be done, first, as a miniseries on television or as a theatrical film. Today nonfiction (that is, fictions about actual people) stuffs our magazines and dominates best-seller lists.

In any case, *pace* Schorer, conformity in American life, whatever that means, would certainly be a spur to any writer. As for fragmentation, it is no worse now as the countryside fills up with Hispanics and Asians as it was when Lewis was describing the American hinterland full of Socialist Swedes and comic-dialect Germans. Actually, to read about the career of Sinclair Lewis is to read about what was a golden age for writing and reading; now gone for good.

Lewis's energetic self-promotion among the masters of the day paid off. His dedicatees Cabell and Hergesheimer wrote glowing testimonials. Predictably, the novel appealed to the English realists if not to Bloomsbury. The former wrote him fan letters – John Galsworthy, H. G. Wells, Rebecca West; presently he would be taken up by the monarch of bookchat and the master of the fact-filled realistic novel, Arnold Bennett. At home a fellow Minnesotan wrote him 'with the utmost admiration', F. Scott Fitzgerald. But five years later Fitzgerald is wondering if *Arrowsmith* is really any good. 'I imagine that mine [*Gatsby*] is infinitely better.' Sherwood Anderson leapt on and off the bandwagon. Dreiser ignored the phenomenon but his friend H. L. Mencken was delighted with Lewis, and praised him in *Smart Set*. When Lewis's sometime model Edith Wharton won the Pulitzer Prize for *The Age of Innocence*, Lewis wrote to congratulate her. As for this uncharacteristic lapse on the part of a committee designed to execute, with stern impartiality, Gresham's Law, Mrs Wharton responded with her usual finely wrought irony: 'When I discovered that I was being rewarded by one of our leading Universities – for uplifting American morals, I confess I *did* despair.' She praises Lewis vaguely; later, she is to prove to be his shrewdest critic.

While Mr and Mrs Sinclair Lewis toured restlessly about Europe, trying to enjoy his success, he was already at work on *Babbitt*.

2

The Library of America has now brought out both *Main Street* and *Babbitt* in a single volume, and it was with some unease that I stepped into the time-warp that is created when one returns after a half century not only to books that one had once lived in but almost to that place in time and space where one had read the old book – once upon a time in every sense. It was said of Lewis that, as a pre-1914 writer, he had little in common with the rising gener- ation of post-World War writers like Hemingway, Dos Passos, Faulkner. It might equally be said that those of us who grew up in the Thirties and in the Second War made as great a break with what had gone before as today's theoreticians made with us. Literary history is hardly an ascending spiral, one masterpiece giving birth to an even greater one, and so on. Rather there are occasional clusters that occur at odd intervals each isolated from the others by, no doubt, protocreative dust. Lewis was pretty much his own small star set to one side of Twain, Crane, James, and Wharton, and the small but intense postwar galaxy which still gives forth radio signals from that black hole where all things end. In the Twenties, only Dreiser was plainly Lewis's superior but Dreiser's reputation was always in or under some shadow and even now his greatness is not properly grasped by the few who care about such things.

*

What strikes one first about *Main Street* is the energy of the writing. There is a Balzacian force to the descriptions of people and places, firmly set in the everyday. The story – well, for a man who supported himself by writing stories for popular magazines and selling plots to Albert Payson Terhune as well as Jack London, there is no plot at all to *Main Street*. Things just happen as they appear to do in life. In Minneapolis, Carol Milford meets Will Kennicott, a doctor from the small town of Gopher Prairie. There are events, some more dramatic than others, but the main character is Main Street and the intense descriptions of the place are most effective, while the people themselves tend to be so many competing arias, rendered by a superb mimic usually under control. Later, Lewis would succumb to his voices and become tedious, but in *Main Street* he is master of what Bakhtin (apropos Dostoevsky) called 'the polyphonic novel. . . . There is a plurality of voices inner and outer, and they retain "their unmergedness".' Lewis is splendid on the outer voices but he lacks an idiosyncratic inner voice – he is simply a straightforward narrator without much irony – while his attempts to replicate the inner voices of the characters are no different, no more revelatory, than what they themselves say aloud.

'On a hill by the Mississippi where Chippewas camped two generations ago, a girl stood in relief against the cornflower blue of Northern sky.' The first sentence is brisk; it places us in time – reminds us that this was Indian territory a half century ago, and so the white man is new to the scene, and his towns are still raw. 'Cornflower' is *Saturday Evening Post*. 'Corn' itself is a bit dangerous, as in corny. 'Blue' isn't all that good either. Yet, paradoxically, Lewis had a lifelong hatred of the cliché in prose as well as a passion for sending up clichés in dialogue: this can cause confusion.

Anyway, he has now begun the story of Carol Milford, enrolled at Blodgett College, a girl full of dreams even more vivid that those of Emma Bovary – dreams rather closer to those of Walter Mitty than to Flaubert's Emma, though, in practice, as it later proves, Carol has more than a touch of Bouvard and Pécuchet in her when she takes to the field with one of her projects to bring beauty to a drab world. Lewis maintained that, as of 1920, he had read neither *Madame Bovary* nor Edgar Lee Masters's *Spoon River Anthology*, whose set of arias from the simple dead folk of a small-town cemetery inspired a generation of writers, achieving a peak, as it were, in Thornton Wilder's *Our Town*.

Carol is involved in the 'tense stalking of a thing called General Culture'. Ostensibly on her behalf, Lewis drops Culture names all over the place. First, Robert G. Ingersoll, the nineteenth-century agnostic, and then Darwin, Voltaire. One can't really imagine her liking any of them – she is too romantic; she dreams of truth and beauty. Ingersoll is a hardbitten, dour free-thinker. The other two are outside her interest. Later he tells us that she has read Balzac and Rabelais. Since she becomes a librarian, the Balzac would be inevitable but neither Carol nor Sinclair Lewis ever read Rabelais. There are some things that an experienced dispenser of bookchat knows without *any* evidence.

At a Minneapolis party, Carol meets Dr Will Kennicott, a doctor in the small town of Gopher Prairie. He is agreeable, and manly, and adores her. In a short time: 'He had grown from a sketched-in stranger to a friend.' Will is 'sincere' (a favourite word of Carol's is 'insincere'). Carol meanwhile (as a result of Mrs Wharton on interior decoration and *Italian Gardens?*) has dreamed that 'what I'll do after college [is] get my hands on one of those prairie towns and make it beautiful. Be an inspiration. I suppose I'd better become a teacher then. . . . I'll make 'em put in a village green, and darling cottages, and a quaint Main Street!' Hubris is back in town. One doubts if the worldly Grace Hegger Lewis ever thought along those lines in Sauk Centre in 1916. But Lewis has got himself a nice premise, with vast comic potentialities. But instead of playing it for laughs and making satire, he plays it absolutely straight and so achieved total popularity. Irony.

In 1912 Carol and Will get married. They take the train to Gopher Prairie. It is all very much worse than she expected. But Will exults in town and people. Although Lewis is noted for his voices, the best of the novel is the description of things and the author's observations of the people who dwell among the things.

> The train was entering town. The houses on the outskirts were dusky old red mansions with wooden frills, or gaunt frame shelters like grocery boxes, or new bungalows with concrete foundations, imitating stone. Now the train was passing the elevator, the grim storage-tanks for oil, a creamery, a lumber-yard, a stock-yard muddy and trampled and stinking.

They are met by Will's friends, the elite of the village. There is a lot of kidding. Mock insults. Ho-ho-ho.

> Main Street with its two-story brick shops, its story-and-a-half wooden residences, its muddy expanse from concrete walk to walk, its huddle of Fords and lumberwagons, was too small to absorb her. The broad, straight, unenticing gashes of the streets let in the grasping prairie on every side. She realized the vastness and emptiness of the land.

This is 'home'. She is in a panic. She notes 'a shop-window delicately rich in error' (this is worthy of Wharton), 'vases starting out to imitate tree-trunks but running off into blobs of gilt – an aluminum ash-tray labeled "Greetings from Gopher Prairie."' And so she makes her way down Main Street, all eyes, later ears.

Carol entertains the village magnates, only to discover 'that conversation did not exist in Gopher Prairie . . . they sat up with gaiety as with a corpse.' Nothing stirs them until one says, '"Let's have some stunts, folks."' The first to be called on is Dave, who gives a 'stunt about the Norwegian catching a hen'. Meanwhile, 'All the guests moved their lips in anticipation of being called on for their own stunts.' A stunt was usually an imitation or ethnic joke. One can imagine Lewis's own lips moving as he would prepare to hold captive some party with a monologue in a character not his own. As it turns out, there *is* conversation in Gopher Prairie – about 'personalities', often in the form of lurid gossip, usually sexual. Carol is not happy.

*

Lewis is good at tracing Carol's ups and mostly downs. She puts on a play. Everything goes wrong. She joins the Library Board to encourage reading, only to find that the librarian believes that their function is not to lend but to preserve books. This, of course, was the ancestor of today's Sauk Centre Library where Lewis's books are preserved but not read. Carol joins the Jolly Seventeen, the fashionable young matrons of the village in whose circle bridge is played and personalities dissected. Carol is thought a bit too citified and definitely stuck-up when she tries to talk of General Culture and town improvements. She does her best to fit in but she 'had never been able to play the game of friendly rudeness.'

In time, Carol flirts with the lawyer, Guy Pollock. He loves literature and disdains the town and one can see that Lewis had it in mind to bring them together but Guy is too damp a character. She drops him; then she goes off in two unexpected directions. A beautiful young Swedish tailor has come to town, Erik Valberg. A townswoman soliloquizes: 'They say he tries to make people think he's a poet – carries books around and pretends to read 'em, says he didn't find any intellectual companionship in this town. . . . And him a Swede tailor! My! and they say he's the most awful mollycoddle – looks just like a girl. The boys call him Elizabeth. . . .' Plainly, the influence of Willa Cather's curiously venomous short story 'Paul's Case' of 1905 was still strong enough for Lewis to ring changes on the sissy boy who dreams of art and civilization and beauty.

As it turns out, Erik is not hot for Will but for Carol. They talk about poetry; they lust for each other. They are two against the town. He is randy Marchbanks to her Candida. But nothing happens except that everyone suspects, and talks; and Lewis is at his best when he shows Carol's terror of public opinion in a place where it is not physically possible to escape from eyes at windows. This sense of claustrophobia and of no place to hide is the heart of the book. Even the metaphor of the unending 'grasping' prairie contributes to the stifling of the individual.

Erik is a farm boy turned tailor turned autodidact: he has got the point. 'It's one of our favorite American myths that broad plains necessarily make broad minds, and high mountains make high purpose. They do just the opposite.' Carol's attempts to integrate him in the town fail. Will observes them walking together at night. There is no scene, but it is clear that Erik must leave town, which he does.

The other counterpoint voice to Gopher Prairie is Miles Bjornstam, unfondly known as 'the Red Swede'. He is a self-educated labourer; he cuts wood, does odd jobs, lives in a shack like Thoreau. He reads Veblen. Reading lists of the characters are all-important to Lewis. Carol has not only read but *bought* 'Anatole France, Rolland, Nexe, Wells, Shaw, Edgar Lee Masters, Theodore Dreiser, Sherwood Anderson, Henry Mencken.' Of those on this list, three subsequently gave Lewis blurbs. Ambitious penpersons take note.

Daringly, Carol pays Miles a call; he shocks and delights her by putting into words her own thoughts about the village. Then he goes into business for himself; prospers with a dairy; marries Carol's best friend, her maid-of-all-work, Bea Sorenson, who comes from the hinterland and though she peaks with a comic Scandinavian accent her heart is gold. Earlier, the village was scandalized that Carol had treated her as an equal. Now, although Mr and Mrs Bjornstam are hard-working and prosperous, they are still shunned, partly because of their foreignness and low class but mostly because the agnostic Miles has been 'lippy' about the greatest nation in the country and the most perfect of its Main Streets. With the arrival of the First World War everyone is now a super-American, busy demonizing all things foreign – like Miles and Bea. But Carol continues to see the Bjornstams and their child. She, too, has a son.

It is during these scenes that Lewis must do a fine balancing act between melodrama and poetic realism in the Hardy vein (sometimes Hardy, too, lost his balance). The Bjornstams are the only people Carol – and the reader – likes. But the villagers continue to hate them even though Miles has done his best to conform to village ways.

Bea and her child get typhoid fever, from the bad water that they must drink because the neighbour with the good water won't share. Will Kennicott does his best to save Bea and her child but they die. Carol is shattered. Miles is stoic. When the ladies of the village unexpectedly call with gifts, not knowing that mother and child are dead, Miles says, 'You're too late. You can't do nothing now. Bea's always kind of hoped that you folks would come see her. . . . Oh, you ain't worth a God-damning.' Like Erik, he, too, leaves town.

Set piece follows set piece. There is a trip to California where Will searches for fellow villagers and, unhappily for Carol, finds them. She is now ready to leave Gopher Prairie, 'Oh, is all life always an unresolved but?' She resolves the 'but'. She will get out into the world, *any* world but that of the claustrophobic censorious village folk. Will accepts her decision even though he continues to be In Love With Her. (Rather unlikely this.) Carol and son set out for Washington, DC – the city from which we locals used to set out for New York as soon as we could. On the train east, the boy asks where they are going and Carol says, 'We're going to find elephants with golden howdahs from which peep young mahara-nees with necklaces of rubies, and a dawn sea colored like the breast of a dove . . .' John Cheever would, years later, redo this bit of purple most tastefully.

The elephants turn out to be the Bureau of War Risk Insurance, where she does clerical work, and in mythical, magical Washington 'she felt that she was no longer one-half of a marriage but the whole of a human being.' She moves among army, navy, minor officialdom. She revels in 'the elm valley of Massachusetts Avenue . . . the marble houses on New Hampshire Avenue . . .' and the splendours of the restaurant on the roof of the Powhatan Hotel.

Will pays her a call; she is now a whole woman and so able to return to Gopher Prairie; she is, somehow, mysteriously, at peace with its boredom and mean-spiritedness. But she will not be coopted; she will not be a booster. She has another child. She sees Erik again – at the movies, up there on the silver screen; he had found his way to Hollywood. 'I may not have fought the good fight,' Carol says at the end to Will, 'but I have kept the faith.' On those words of the great Populist William Jennings Bryan, the book ends.

3

Babbitt was intended to be the account of a single day in the life of the eponymous protagonist, a realtor in the great city of Zenith, an extension and enlargement of Gopher Prairie, with elements of sultry Duluth where the Lewises had lived for a season and were – what else? – the cynosure of all eyes. The day that Lewis had picked was one in April 1920, and we follow George F. Babbitt from the moment that he awakens with, significantly, a hangover to the end of the day, but by that time Lewis had decided that one day wasn't going to be enough for him to do his stunts in, so the story continues another year or two, and a Midwestern Bloom was not to be.

Lewis's eye for detail is, as always, precise. We get an inventory of bathroom and house and sleeping porch, a fad of the day that I have just recalled with the sense of having slipped several notches back in time. There is a long-suffering wife, a son, two daughters – one at Bryn Mawr. Babbitt is forty-six years old. Prohibition has been in place for a year, so everyone drinks too much. There is talk of the coming election, and the great shadow of Warren Gamaliel Harding is already darkening the land and his famous injunction, 'Don't knock, boost', is on every Zenith businessman's lip. Babbit himself is vaguely unhappy: 'the Babbitt house', apparently, 'was not a home.' But all the latest gadgets are on display. There is chintz, but no heart. The real estate business is booming.

Even so, he dreams of 'a fairy child', a recurring dream that somehow underscores Lewis's uneasiness with sex, mature or otherwise. Babbitt has been true to his wife, Myra, since he married her, something that is hard for us plague-ridden *fin-de-siècle* types to fathom. As a result, he lusts for other women in his heart and, sooner or later, lust must be served. This gives the story what small impetus it has: how – and for whom – will he fall, and what kind of mess will he make?

As in *Main Street* there is no plot, only set scenes. Lewis notes the class divisions. There is the class above Babbitt that belongs to the Union Club as best emblemized by Charles McKelvey; then there is the Athletic Club where Babbitt and his fellow boosters hang out and denounce socialism and labour unions and anarchists. Meanwhile, at the wheel of his new car, a 'perilous excursion', Babbitt daydreams enroute to his office, the 'pirate ship'. He has had his first conversation of the day with a neighbour, and they have talked of the weather in great detail and though their exchange should be as tedious as the real thing, Lewis is a master of those grace notes of boring speech that put one in mind of Bach. 'There was still snow at Tiflis, Montana, yesterday,' says the neighbouring Bore; then goes for a crescendo: 'Two years ago we had a snow-squall right here in Zenith on the twenty-fifth of April.'

Next, a loving description of Zenith – skyscrapers now – and old houses, movie billboards, drugstores, factory suburbs, a proper city where once the Chippewas roamed. At the office there is a young partner, a secretary – Babbitt's father-in-law is senior partner, and seldom seen. Babbitt is having what now would be called a midlife crisis of a sexual nature: 'In twenty-three years of married life he had peered uneasily at every graceful ankle, every soft shoulder; in thought he had treasured them; but not once had he hazarded respectability by adventuring.' Plainly, Lewis is not drawing on autobiography. Although he preferred drink to sex, he had, at least once, in Italy, cheated on Grace, and one does not suppose him to have been pure premarriage. What is interesting about Lewis's description of Babbitt's sex life is whether he is distorting it deliberately to give American readers, a high-toned, censorious, prudish lot, a picture of an average American businessman, true as steel to the little lady, or whether he has some arcane knowledge of how Zenith males denied themselves. It is hard to know what to think. Even in the Gopher Prairie of Springfield, Illinois, in the 1840s there were girls to be rented by young lawyers like A. Lincoln and J. Speed. Yet in 1920 Babbitt has only masturbatory images, and the recurring mawkish dream of the 'fairy girl'.

Babbitt has only one actual friend, even though he himself is a prototypical gregarious regular fellow and very well liked. But he had been at a school with Paul Riesling, who had wanted to be a musician; instead Paul married a virago (whom he will later shoot but not, alas, kill – he does serve time). Paul and Babbitt revert to adolescence when together. They romanticize their common past. Babbitt was to have been a powerful tribune of the people and Paul a world-class violinist. But since neither is articulate, when they are together they can only tell jokes, as they try, rather wistfully, to go back in time to where they had been, if nothing else, real. They dream now of going off together on a hunting trip.

Babbitt has lunch at the Athletic Club. Lewis delights in repro-ducing the banalities of the Joshers, Good Fellows, Regular Guys. Kidding, chaffing, 'stunts' – all these pass for communication and the fact that Lewis could reproduce this sort of conversational filler delighted those who went in for it, which was most Americans, while British book reviewers acknowledged that Lewis's Joshers confirmed their worst fears about the collective cretinism of the separated cousinage. I cannot think how the French took Lewis's dialogue in translation. Bouvard and Pécuchet are like figures from Racine when compared with the Boosters of the Athletic Club. In any case, Lewis had somehow struck a universal class nerve and, for a time, everyone was delighted by his hyper-realism. Even so, Edith Wharton struck a warning note. She was, she wrote, duly grateful for the dedication to herself of *Babbitt* but she saw fit to make one suggestion: 'In your next book, you should use slang in dialogue more sparingly. I believe the real art in this respect is to use just enough to *colour* your dialogue, not so much that in a few years it will be almost incomprehensible.' She admired his 'irony', wondering how much of it Americans got.

I suspect they got none; the book was taken as just like life and Lewis was hardly more critical of Americans and their values than his readers were. They, too, hankered after fairy girls in dreamland as well as magic casements elsewhere, preferably in Europe, through which they might, like Alice, step into Wonderland. The secret of Lewis and his public was that he was as one with them. Grace thought that the crown of ironist he had been mistakenly awarded by those who read *Main Street* obliged him to go for the real diadem in *Babbitt*. But I think he just kept on recording.

The story proceeds with random events. Babbitt becomes an orator for the realtors; he takes part in the election of a Republican mayor; tries to move up socially and fails; he drinks more and more; the most vivid description in the book is the way booze was sold clandestinely at an ex-saloon, a sordid place, 'giving that impression of forming a large crowd which two men always give in a saloon.'

Lewis makes an odd obeisance to Howells, whom he will dismiss, so foolishly, at the Nobel Prize ceremony of 1930. Lewis calls the state capital Galop de Vache, in memoriam of the hometown of the journalist hero of Howells's Florentine tale *Indian Summer*, who hailed from Des Vaches, Indiana.

Babbitt is essentially a *roman fleuve* despite its snappy scenes and bright 'stunts'. In due course, the river deposits Babbitt on the not-so-wild shore of love. He meets a demi-mondaine lady of a certain age, Mrs Tanis Judique. She is arty; she has a salon of marginal types. Tactfully, Myra Babbitt has retreated, temporarily, to her family and so Babbitt is able to conduct his love affair in relative peace while drinking more and more in the company of the feckless young. Business is affected: deals are lost. He falls in with the town radical, Seneca Doane, another variation on the original Dorion, with a bit of Upton Sinclair thrown in. Doane has been defeated for mayor. He now supports a local strike. Babbit falls under his spell for a time (they had known each other in college). Then the town turns on Babbitt. Adultery does not disturb the boosters so much as Babbitt's timid support of the strikers. In a series of confrontations almost as terrible as the ones at the end of *The Age of Innocence* Zenith threatens to destroy him; and Babbitt caves in. He has not fought the good fight, and he has not kept much of any faith to anything but, at the end, he will "start something": he vowed, and he tried to make it valiant.' Meanwhile, happy ending. Tanis and Seneca slink away; wife comes home. Valiant.

March 26, 1925, Lewis wrote his publisher, 'Any thoughts on pulling wires for [*Arrowsmith*] for Nobel Prize?' There were such thoughts, there were such wires. By 1930 the Swedes were at last ready to pick an American. Earlier, Henry James had been airily dismissed in favour of Maurice Maeterlinck, the Belgian beemaster. The choice was now between Dreiser and Lewis and, as these things are ordered in the land of the great white night, Lewis was inevitably chosen. Mark Schorer writes of all this with distinct sadness. Even the President of the United States, a New England wit called Calvin Coolidge, broke his usual silence – he was a school of Buster Keaton comic – to declare, 'No necessity exists for becoming excited.'

Lewis lived for twenty-one more years. He produced a great amount of work. He turned to the theatre; even acted on stage. He married the splendid journalist Dorothy Thompson, who never stopped talking either. They opposed America's entry into World War Two, a war in which his son Wells was killed. It is painful to read of Lewis's last days as recorded by Schorer. Drink had estranged him from most people; and so he was obliged to hire young secretaries to play chess with him and keep him company; among those paid companions were the writers-to-be Barnaby Conrad and John Hersey, who has prepared the exemplary Library of America *Sinclair Lewis*.

Mr Schorer, enraged to the end, notes, finally, 'He was one of the worst writers in modern American literature, but without his writing one cannot imagine modern American literature. That is because, without his writing, we can hardly imagine ourselves.' This is not a left-handed compliment so much as a rabbit-punch. Whatever Lewis's faults as a writer he never knowingly wrote a bad book or, indeed, one on any subject that he could not at least identify with in imagination. Curiously enough, his ex-wife, Grace Hegger, is more generous (and writes rather better prose) than the biographer:

> Even though Lewis's first successful novels can be recognized as written by him, it is significant that he created no school of writing as have Hemingway and Faulkner, Henry James and Flaubert. He influenced public thinking rather than public writing.

Surely, that is something. As for the man, after his ashes were returned to Sauk Centre, she writes, 'Dear, dear Minnesota Tumbleweed, driven by the winds of your own blowing, rootless to the day when your ashes were returned to the soil which had never received your living roots, I offer you these memories. With love from Gracie.'

The New York Review of Books
8 October 1992

4

Twain on the Grand Tour

1

Both Mark Twain and his inventor, Samuel Clemens, continue to give trouble to those guardians of the national mythology to which Twain added so much in his day, often deliberately. The Freudians are still on his case even though Dr Freud and his followers are themselves somewhat occluded these days. Yet as recently as 1991, an academic critic* tells us that Clemens was sexually infantile, burnt-out at fifty (if not before), and given to pederastic reveries about little girls, all the while exhibiting an unnatural interest in outhouse humour and other excremental vilenesses. It is hard to believe that at century's end, academics of this degraded sort are still doing business, as Twain would put it, at the same old stand.

As is so often the case, this particular critic is a professor emeritus and emerituses often grow reckless once free of the daily grind of dispensing received opinion. Mr Guy Cardwell, for reasons never quite clear, wants to convince us that Twain (we'll drop the Clemens because he's very much dead while Twain will be with us as long as there are English-speakers in the United States)

---

* Guy Cardwell, *The Man Who Was Mark Twain* (Yale University Press, 1991). This oddly repellent work might have been more accurately – and more modestly – called *The Mark Twain Nobody Else Knows*.

'suffered from erectile dysfunction at about the age of fifty. . . .
Evidence that he became impotent ranges from the filmy to the
relatively firm.' This is a fair example of the good professor's style.
'Filmy' evidence suggests a slightly blurred photograph of an
erection gone south, while 'relatively firm' is a condition experienced by many men over fifty who drink as much Scotch whisky as
Twain did. But filmy – or flimsy? – as the evidence is, the professor
wants to demolish its owner, who, sickeningly, *married above his
station* in order to advance himself socially as well as to acquire a
surrogate mother; as his own mother was – yes! – a strong figure
while his father was – what else? – cold and uncaring.

No Freudian cliché is left unstroked. To what end? To establish
that Twain hated women as well as blacks, Jews, foreigners,
American imperialists, Christian missionaries, and Mary Baker
Eddy. Since I join him in detesting the last three, I see no need to
find a Freudian root to our shared loathing of, say, that imperialist
jingo Theodore Roosevelt. Actually, Twain was no more neurotic or
dysfunctional than most people and, on evidence, rather less out of
psychic kilter than most other figures in the American literary
canon.

Twain was born November 30, 1835, in Missouri. He spent his boyhood, famously, in the Mississippi River town of Hannibal. When
he was twelve, his father died, becoming *truly* absent as Dr Freud
might sagely have observed, and Twain went to work as a printer's
apprentice. Inevitably, he started writing the copy that was to be
printed and, in essence, he was a journalist to the end of his days.
Literature as such did not really engage him. *Don Quixote* was his
favourite novel (as it was Flaubert's). He could not read Henry
James, who returned the compliment by referring to him only
once in his own voluminous bookchat, recently collected and published by the Library of America.

Exactly where and how the 'Western Storyteller', as such, was
born is unknown. He could have evolved from Homer or, later,
from the Greek Milesian tales of run-on anecdote. In any case, an
American master of the often scabrous tall story, Twain himself was

predated by, among others, Abraham Lincoln, many of whose stories were particularly noisome as well as worse – worse! – *politically incorrect*. Our stern Freudian critic finds Twain's smutty stories full of 'slurs' on blacks and women and so on. But so are those of Rabelais and Ariosto and Swift, Rochester and Pope and . . . Whatever the 'true' motivation for telling such stories, Twain was a master in this line both in print and on the lecture circuit.

Primarily, of course, he was a popular journalist, and with the best-seller *Innocents Abroad* (1869) he made the hicks back home laugh and Henry James, quite rightly, shudder. Yet when the heavy-handed joky letters, written from the first cruise liner, *Quaker City*, became a text, it turned out to be an unusually fine-meshed net in which Twain caught up old Europe and an even older Holy Land and then, as he arranged his catch on the – well – deck of his art, he Americanized it in the most satisfactory way ('Lump the whole thing! Say that the Creator made Italy from designs by Michael Angelo!'), and made it possible for an American idea to flourish someday.

Twain was far too ambitious to be just a professional hick, as opposed to occasional hack. He had social ambitions; he also lusted for money (in a banal anal way, according to the Freudian emeritus – as opposed to floral oral?).

In the great tradition of men on the make, Twain married above his station to one Olivia Langdon of the first family of Elmira, New York. He got her to polish him socially. He also became a friend of William Dean Howells, a lad from the Western Reserve who had superbly made it in Boston as editor of the *Atlantic Monthly*. Howells encouraged Twain to celebrate the American 'West' as the sort of romanticized Arcadia that Rousseau might have wanted his chainless noble savage to roam.

While knocking about the West and Southwest, Twain worked as pilot on Mississippi steamboats from 1857 to 1861; he joined the Civil War, briefly, on the Confederate side. When he saw how dangerous war might be, he moved on to the Nevada Territory, where his brother had been made secretary to the governor. He wrote for newspapers. In 1863, he started to use the pseudonym 'Mark Twain', a river pilot's measurement of depth, called out on approaching landfall – some twelve feet, a bit on the shallow side for a proper ship.

After the war, Twain began to use life on the river and the river's bank as a background for stories that were to place him permanently at the centre of American literature: *The Adventures of Tom Sawyer* (1876); *Life on the Mississippi* (1883); *The Adventures of Huckleberry Finn* (1884). He liked fame and money, the last perhaps too much since he was forever going broke speculating on experimental printing presses and under-financed publishing houses. He lived in considerable bourgeois splendour at Hartford, Connecticut; oddly for someone who had made his fortune out of being *the* American writer, as he once described himself, Twain lived seventeen years in Europe. One reason, other than *douceur de la vie*, was that he was admired on the Continent in a way that he never was, or so he felt, by the eastern seaboard gentry, who were offended by his jokes, his profanity, his irreligion, and all those Scotch sours he drank. Fortunately, no one then suspected his erectile dysfunction.

Whenever cash was needed and a new book not ready to be sold to the public, Twain took to the lecture circuit. An interesting, if unanswerable question: Was Mark Twain a great actor who wrote, or a great writer who could act? Or was he an even balance like Charles Dickens or George Bernard Shaw? Much of what Twain writes is conversation – dialogue – with different voices thrown in to delight the ear of an audience. But, whichever he was, he was always, literally, a journalist, constantly describing daily things while recollecting old things. In the process, he made, from time to time, essential literature, including the darkest of American novels, *Pudd'nhead Wilson* (1894).

Mark Twain's view of the human race was not sanguine, and much has been made of the Calvinism out of which he came. Also, his great river, for all its fine amplitude, kept rolling along, passing villages filled with fierce monotheistic folk in thrall to slavery, while at river's end there were the slave markets of New Orleans.

Calvinist could easily become Manichean if he brooded too much on the river world of the mid-1800s. In *Pudd'nhead Wilson*, Twain's as yet unarticulated notion that if there is a God (*What is Man?*, 1906) he is, if not evil in the Manichean sense, irrelevant, since man, finally, is simply a machine acted upon by a universe 'frankly and hysterically insane' (*No. 44, The Mysterious Stranger*): 'Nothing exists but You. And You are but a *thought*.'

The agony of the twin boys in *Pudd'nhead Wilson*, one brought up white, the other black, becomes exquisite for the 'white' one, who is found to be black and gets shipped down river, his question to an empty Heaven unanswered: 'What crime did the uncreated first nigger commit that the curse of birth was decreed for him?' All this, then, is what is going on in Mark Twain's mind as he gets ready for a second luxury tour, this time around the world.

2

When one contemplates the anti-imperialism of Mark Twain, it is hard to tell just where it came from. During his lifetime the whole country was – like himself – on the make, in every sense. But Mark Twain was a flawed materialist. As a Southerner he should have had some liking for the peculiar institution of slavery; yet when he came to write of antebellum days, it is Miss Watson's 'nigger', Jim, who represents what little good Twain ever found in man. Lynchings shocked him. But then, *pace* Hemingway, so did Spanish bullfights. Despite the various neuroses ascribed to him by our current political correctionalists, he never seemed in any doubt that he was a man and therefore never felt, like so many sissies of the Hemingway sort, a need to swagger about, bullying those not able to bully him.

In 1898, the United States provoked a war with Spain (a war with England over Venezuela was contemplated but abandoned since there was a good chance that we would have lost). The Spanish empire collapsed more from dry rot than from our military skills. Cuba was made 'free', and Puerto Rico was attached to us while the Spanish Philippines became our first Asian real estate and the inspiration for close to a century now of disastrous American adventures in that part of the world.

Mark Twain would have had a good time with the current demise of that empire, which he greeted, with some horror, in the first of his meditations on imperialism. The pamphet 'To the Person Sitting In Darkness' was published in 1901, a year in which we were busy telling the Filipinos that although we had, at considerable selfless expense, freed them from Spain they were not yet ready for the higher democracy, as exemplified by Tammany Hall, to use Henry James's bitter analogy. Strictly for their own good, we would have to kill one or two hundred thousand men, women, and children in order to make their country into an American-style democracy. Most Americans were happy to follow the exuberant lead of the prime architect of empire, Theodore Roosevelt – known to the sour Henry Adams as 'our Dutch-American Napoleon'. But then, suddenly, Mark Twain quite forgot that he was *the* American writer and erupted, all fire and lava.

The people who sit in darkness are Kipling's 'lesser breeds', waiting for the white man to take up his burden and 'civilize' them. Ironically, Twain compares our bloody imperialism favourably with that of the white European powers then abroad in the 'unlit' world, busy assembling those colonial empires that now comprise today's desperate third world. Twain, succinctly for him, lists who was stealing what from whom and when, and all in the name of the 'Blessings-of-Civilization Trust'. But now the American writer is so shocked at what his countrymen are capable of doing in the imperial line that he proposes a suitable flag for the 'Philippine Province': 'We can have just our usual flag, with the white stripes painted black and the stars replaced by the skull and cross-bones.'

In 1905, Twain published a second pamphlet (for the Congo Defense Association), 'King Leopold's Soliloquy', subtitled 'A Defence of His Congo Rule'. On the cover there is a crucifix crossed by a machete and the cheery inscription 'By this sign we prosper.'

The soliloquy is just that. The King of the Belgians is distressed by reports of his bloody rule over a large section of black Africa. Leopold, an absolute ruler in Africa if not in Belgium, is there to 'root out slavery and stop the slave-raids, and lift up those twenty-five millions of gentle and harmless blacks out of darkness into light. . . .' He is in rather the same business as Presidents McKinley and Roosevelt of the earlier pamphlet.

Leopold free-associates, noting happily that Americans were the first to recognize his rule. As he defends himself, his night-mind (as the Surrealists used to say) gets the better of him and he keeps listing his crimes as he defends them. He notes that his enemies 'concede – reluctantly – that I have *one* match in history, but only one – the *Flood*. This is intemperate.' He blames his current 'crash' on 'the incorruptible *kodak* . . . the only witness I have encountered in my long experience that I couldn't bribe.' Twain provides us with a page of nine snapshots of men and women each lacking a hand, the King's usual punishment. Twain's intervention was not unlike those of Voltaire and Zola or, closer to home, Howells's denunciation of the American legal system – and press – that had found guilty the non-perpetrators of the Haymarket riots. Imperialism and tyranny for Twain were great evils but the more he understood – or thought he under-stood – the human race, the darker his view of the whole lot became, as he would demonstrate in the epigraphs from *Pudd'nhead Wilson's New Calendar* at the head of each chapter of his travel book *Following the Equator* (1897).

3

In Paris, 1895, Twain, his wife, Olivia, and their daughter Clara started on a round the world lecture tour. They crossed the Atlantic; then the United States; then, on August 23, they set sail from Vancouver bound for Sydney, Australia. For several years Twain had suffered a series of financial setbacks. Now the lecture tour would make him some money, while a look at the whole world would provide him with a great deal of copy, most of which he was to use in *Following the Equator*.

At the start of the tour, Twain seems not have been his usual resilient self. 'Mr Clemens,' wrote Olivia to a friend, 'has not as much courage as I wish he had, but, poor old darling, he has been pursued with colds and inabilities of various sorts. Then he is so impressed with the fact that he is sixty years old.' Definitely a filmy time for someone Olivia referred to as 'Youth'.

The pleasures of travel have not been known for two generations now; even so, it is comforting to read again about the soothing boredom of life at sea and the people that one meets aboard ship as well as on shore in exotic lands. One also notes that it was Twain in Australia, and not an English official recently testifying in an Australian court, who first noted that someone 'was economical of the truth'.

In Twain's journal, he muses about the past; contemplates General Grant, whose memoirs he had published and, presumably, edited a decade earlier. One would like to know more about that relationship since Gertrude Stein, among others, thought Grant our finest prose writer. When the ship stops in Honolulu, Twain notes that the bicycle is now in vogue, and 'the riding horse is retiring from business everywhere in the world.' Twain is not pleased by the combined influences of Christian missionaries and American soldiers upon what had once been a happy and independent Pacific kingdom.

They pass the Fiji Islands, ceded to England in 1858. Twain tells the story that when the English commissioner remarked to the Fiji king that it was merely 'a sort of hermit-crab formality', the king pointed out that 'the crab moves into an unoccupied shell, but mine isn't.'

A great comfort to Twain aboard ship is *The Sentimental Song Book* of the Sweet Singer of Michigan, one Mrs Julia A. Moore, who has, for every human occasion, numerous sublimely inapt verses that never, even by accident, scan.

> *Frank Dutton was as fine a lad*
> *As ever you wish to see,*
> *And he was drowned in Pine Island Lake*
> *On earth no more will he be,*
> *His age was near fifteen years,*
> *And he was a motherless boy,*
> *He was living with his grandmother*
> *When he was drowned, poor boy.*

As one reads Twain's own prose, written in his own character, one is constantly reminded that he is very much a stand-up comedian whose laugh lines are carefully deployed at the end of every observation, thus reducing possible tension with laughter. Of the colonists sent out to Australia by England, Twain observes that they came from the jails and from the army. 'The colonists trembled. It was feared that next there would be an importation of the nobility.'

In general, Australia gets high marks. Twain and family travel widely; he lectures to large crowds: 'The welcome which an American lecturer gets from a British colonial audience is a thing which will move him to his deepest deeps, and veil his sight and break his voice.' He is treated as what he was, a Great Celebrity, and 'I was conscious of a pervading atmosphere of envy which gave me deep satisfaction.'

Twain continually adverts to the white man's crimes against the original inhabitants of the Pacific islands, noting that 'there are many humorous things in the world; among them the white man's notion that he is less savage than the other savages.' The Freudian critic cannot quite fathom how the Twain who in his youth made jokes about 'Negroes' now, in his filmy years, has turned anti-white and speaks for the enslaved and the dispossessed. Dr Freud apparently had no formula to explain this sort of sea change.

New Zealand appeals to Twain; at least they did not slaughter the native population though they did something almost as bad: 'The Whites always mean well when they take human fish out of the ocean and try to make them dry and warm and happy and comfortable in a chicken coop', which is how, through civilization, they did away with many of the original inhabitants. Lack of empathy is a principal theme in Twain's meditations on race and empire. Twain notes with approval that New Zealand's women have been able to vote since 1893. At sixty, he seems to have overcome his misogyny; our Freudian critic passes over this breakthrough in dark silence.

Ceylon delights. 'Utterly Oriental', though plagued by missionaries who dress the young in Western style, rendering them as hideous on the outside as they are making them cruelly superstitious on the inside. Twain broods on slavery as he remembered it a half-century before in Missouri. He observes its equivalent in Ceylon and India. He meets a Mohammedan 'deity', who discusses Huck Finn in perfect English. Twain now prefers brown or black skin to 'white', which betrays the inner state rather too accurately, making 'no concealments'. Although he prefers dogs to cats, he does meet a dog that he cannot identify, which is odd since it is plainly a dachshund. He tries to get used to pyjamas but goes back to the old-fashioned nightshirt. Idly, he wonders why Western men's clothes are so ugly and uncomfortable. He imagines himself in flowing robes of every possible colour. Heaven knows what this means. Heaven and a certain critic. . . .

Benares has its usual grim effect. Here, beside the Ganges, bodies are burned; and people bathe to become pure while drinking the polluted waters of the holiest of holy rivers. It is interesting that Twain never mentions the Buddha, who became enlightened at Benares, but he does go into some detail when he describes the Hindu religion. In fact, he finds the city of Benares 'just a big church' to that religion in all its aspects. In Calcutta, he broods on the Black Hole, already filled in. The Taj Mahal induces an interesting reverie. Twain notes that when one has read so many descriptions of a famous place, one can never actually see it

because of all the descriptions that crowd one's mind. In this perception, Twain anticipates the latest – if not the last – theory of how
memory works. He also broods on the phenomenon of Helen
Keller, born deaf, dumb, and blind; yet able to learn to speak and
think. How *does* the mind work?

From India, Twain and company cross the Indian Ocean to
Mauritius. Although he often alludes to his lecturing, he never tells
us what he talks about. He does note, 'I never could tell a lie that
anybody would doubt, nor a truth that anybody would believe.' We
learn that he dislikes Oliver Goldsmith and Jane Austen. As a prose
writer, the imperialist Kipling beguiles him even though Twain
likens empires to thieves who take clothes off other people's
clotheslines. 'In 800 years an obscure tribe of Muscovite savages
has risen to the dazzling position of Land-Robber-in-Chief.' He is
more tolerant of the English. But then he is a confessed
Anglophile.

Meanwhile, the ship is taking Twain and family down the east
coast of Africa. South Africa is in ferment – Boers against English
settlers, white against black. Cecil Rhodes is revealed as a
scoundrel. But Twain is now writing as of May 1897, one year after
his visit to South Africa, and so the outcome of all this is still
unclear to him. He sides with the English, despite reservations
about Rhodes and company. 'I have always been especially fond of
war. No, I mean fond of discussing war; and fond of giving military
advice.' As for that new territorial entity, Rhodesia, Twain remarks
that it is 'a happy name for that land of piracy and pillage, and puts
the right stain upon it'; and he also has Puddn'head Wilson
observe: 'The very ink with which all history is written is merely
fluid prejudice.'

Finally, 'Our trip around the earth ended at Southampton pier,
where we embarked thirteen months before. . . . I seemed to have
been lecturing a thousand years. . . .' But he had now seen the
whole world, more or less at the equator, and, perhaps more to the
point, quite a few people got to see Mark Twain in action, in itself
something of a phenomenon, never to be repeated on earth unless,

of course, his nemesis, Mary Baker Eddy, were to allow him to exchange her scientific deathless darkness for his limelight, our light.

The New York Review of Books
23 May 1996

5
Reply to a Critic

While writing about Mark Twain's views on imperialism, I checked some recent 'scholarly' works to see how his reputation is bearing up under the great fiery cross of political correctness. We were all astonished, some years ago, when a squad of sharp-eyed textual investigators discovered, to their manifest surprise and horror, that the noblest character in Twain's fiction was called 'Nigger' Jim. There was an understandable outcry from some blacks; there was also a totally incomprehensible howl from a number of fevered white males, many of them professors emeritus and so, to strike the tautological note, career-minded conservatives unused to manning barricades.

In an apparently vain effort at comprehension, I quoted a number of malicious and, worse, foolish things that these silly-billies are writing about Twain. Thanks to an editorial quirk, one hot-head was mentioned by *name*, for which I apologize. I always try to shield the infamous from their folly in the hope that they may, one day, straighten up and fly right. But a single name *was* mentioned and now we have its owner's letter at hand. For serene duplicity and snappy illogic it compares favourably to some of the screeds, I believe they are called, from my pen pals in the Lincoln priesthood.

Although my new pen pal does acknowledge that I am reporting the views of other critics on Twain's impotence, sexual infantilism, fondness for small girls, he declares mysteriously that this is 'not what I say'. But it is what he says and presumably means. The Jesuits like to say: 'The wise man never lies.' But in the army of my day, any soldier (or indeed discomfited general) who spent too much time twisting about the language of regulations in his own favour was called a guardhouse lawyer. I now put the case on the evidence at hand, that we have here a compulsive guardhouse lawyer or quibbler. Straight sentences must be bent like pretzels to change meanings to score points. But then much of what passes for literary discourse in these states is simply hustling words to get them to mean what they don't. 'That Clemens dreamed of little girls is well known.' Thus Quibbler wrote but now he has – tangential? – second thoughts. Actually who knows what Twain's dreams were. But let us agree that he doted on the company of Dodsonesque girls and so may well have dreamed . . . fantasized about them in a sexual way. Why not? But Quibbler is getting a bit edgy. He thinks, too, that I have given him a splendid chance to open the guardhouse door. Now we improvise: 'that his dreams and reveries were pederastic is not said in my book by me or by anyone else.' But, of course, that's what the professor (and presumably, those whom he adverts to) means in the course of a chapter entitled 'Impotence and Pedophilia'.

But Quibbler has leapt at the adjective 'pederastic'. Like so many Greekless Americans with pretensions, he thinks that the word means a liking for boys by men with buggery on their mind. But I had gone back to the original root noun, *paedo*, from which comes pederasty, paedophilia, etc.; and *paedo* means not boy but child. A quibble can be made that, as vulgar usage associates the word with boys, that's what I mean but, as context makes clear, it is Lolita-*paedo* – not Ganymede-*paedo* – that Twain *may* be dreaming of. So this quibble is meaningless.

'The idea of impotence excited Clemens's anxious interest: apparently he suffered from erectile dysfunction at about the age of fifty.' I noted in my review that 'so do many men over fifty who drink as much Scotch whisky as Twain did.' Next: 'Psychoanalysts have noted many cases in which diminished sexual capacity . . . has been related to a constellation of psychic problems like those which affected Clemens.' All right. Which psychoanalysts? Did any know him? As for his psychic problems, did he really have a 'constellation's' worth? 'Evidence that he became impotent ranges from the filmy to the relatively firm' – I had some fun with those two loony adjectives. 'Likelihood is high that diminished capacity may be inferred . . .' All these 'apparentlys', 'likelihoods', 'inferreds' as well as filmy to firm 'evidence' appear in one short paragraph.

What we have here is not a serious literary – or even, God help us, psychoanalytic – view of Twain's sex life as imagined by a politically correct school teacher but what I take to be outright character assassination of a great man who happens to be one of the handful – small hand, too – of good writers our flimsy culture has produced. ('Filmy', of course, may be the *mot juste* if we count the movies.) At one point, in the midst of a prurient flow of nonsense, the professor suddenly concedes, 'We do not know the intimate details of Clemens's life very well. . . .' I'll say we don't, so why go to such imaginative length to turn him into an impotent pederast, or paedophile?

Point two. Here we get the denial-of-meaning quibble based on Absence of Quotation Marks. I remark on Twain's having, sickeningly, in the professor's view, *'married above his station* in order to advance himself socially.' Blandly, the professor quibbles that he never used the italicized words. Yet they are an exact paraphrase of how he interprets Twain's marriage to Olivia Langdon. Quibbler has reinvented his own text. Actually, it is his view that Twain did not marry above his station in any but the economic sense although, 'like the most bourgeois of the bourgeois he delighted in money, and high living, and he fervently wished to become a member of the eastern establishment.' Surely, to get from Hannibal, Missouri, to the Gold Coast of Hartford was going to take a bit of social climbing, which he did by marrying into the Langdon family.

'Clemens was what Freud would call a narcissistic suitor.' Quibbler acts as if he is quoting some sort of authority in these matters. Ward McAllister might have been more to his point on American social climbing. '[Clemens] ardently wished to marry a woman who typified not what he was but what he wished to be – rich and possessed of status, a member of the eastern social order.' So, as I said in a phrase to which Quibbler objects, for no clear reason, 'he married above his station.' (I'm surprised he does not make the point that Grand Central *Station* was not in use that hymenal year.) My use of the adverb 'sickeningly' was meant to be ironic, something to which the teaching of school tends to make impervious even the brightest and the best. Anyway, Twain's hypergamous marriage was a happy one, so what's the big deal?

A lust for money that is banal anal (as opposed to floral oral) is simply a verbally symmetrical way of setting up Freud's notion of money as 'faeces'. How did I happen to get this juxtaposition in my head? At one point, our author suddenly quibbles that Twain didn't marry Olivia for her money, at least 'not in any banal sense of the phrase; but he very much wanted to be rich.' As I read the word 'banal', I knew that Freud's theory of anality was coming up. I turned the page. There it was. 'Freud stresses the anal character of money and equates money and feces: it means power, vitality, potency.' The one good thing about bad writing is that one is never surprised by any turn an argument, much less a cliché, may take.

Let me now indulge in quibbler creativity. Freud would never have characterized Twain as narcissistic – an adjective currently used to describe anyone better-looking than oneself. As performerwriter Twain took by storm Vienna in general and Freud in particular. Freud was also something of a connoisseur of jokes and he enjoyed Mark Twain in person and on the page quite as much as he would have revelled in the letter of Professor Emeritus Guy Cardwell. *Ich kann nicht anders*, I can hear Sigmund chuckle through his cigar smoke. (cf. *The Strange Case of Dr Luther Adler* by an Unknown Actress – op. cit. Just about anywhere.)

The New York Review of Books
19 September 1996

6

Rabbit's Own Burrow

A decade ago, thanks to the success of America's chain book stores with their outlets in a thousand glittering malls, most 'serious' fiction was replaced by mass-baked sugary dough – I mean books – whose huge physical presence in the shops is known, aptly to the trade, as 'dumps': outward and visible sign of Gresham's Law at dogged work. In spite of this, the fact that John Updike's latest novel, *In the Beauty of the Lilies*, briefly made it to the bottom of the *New York Times* bestseller list is remarkable. As it is a rare week when any 'serious' novel is listed, one is usually so grateful that there are still those who want to read an even halfway good novelist, one ought never to discourage those readers whom he attracts. Also, what is the point of attacking writers in a period where – save for prize-mad pockets of old London – they are of so little consequence?

In observance of this law of a dying species, I have hardly mentioned, much less reviewed, Updike in the past, and he has observed the same continence with regard to me. But, lately, as I turn the pages of *The New Yorker*, where his poems, short stories and book reviews have been appearing for so many years, I note an occasional dig at me. Apparently, I do not sufficiently love the good, the nice America, is the burden of his *épingles*. In sere and yellow leaf, Updike is now in super-patriot mood and on the attack. For instance, apropos the movie star Lana Turner (whom, to his credit, he appreciates): 'Fifty years ago we were still a nation of builders and dreamers, now whittlers and belittlers set the cultural tone.' O vile Whittlers! O unGodly Belittlers! Of whom, apparently, I am one.

Although I've never taken Updike seriously as a writer, I now find him the unexpectedly relevant laureate of the way we would like to live now, if we have the money, the credentials and the sort of faith in our country and its big God that passes all understanding. Finally, according to the mainline American press, Updike has now got it all together, and no less an authority than *The New Yorker*'s George Steiner (so different from Europe's one) assures us that Updike now stands alongside Hawthorne and Nabokov, when, surely, he means John P. Marquand and John O'Hara.

Prior to immersion in next year's Pulitzer Prize novel, I read Updike's memoir, *Self-Consciousness* (1989), written in the writer's fifty-seventh year. Self-consciousness is a good theme, if meant ironically. After all, save to self, we are, none of us, worth much fussing about, run-of-the-mill poor, bare forked animals – or was it radishes? – that we are. Anyway, I hoped that he would make some self-mocking play on his own self-consciousness as opposed to Socrates' examined life. Hope quickly extinguished. There is no examination of the self, as opposed to an unremitting self-consciousness that tells us why he was – is – different – but not too much different – from others and what made him the way he is – always *is*, as he doesn't much change in his own story, a small-town Philoctetes whose wound turns out to be an unpretty skin-condition called psoriasis. 'Yet what was my creativity, my relentless need to produce but a parody of my skin's embarrassing over-production?'

John Updike's father was of Dutch-American stock; his mother German. He was born in 1932, in modest circumstances at Shillington, Pennsylvania. The mother was a would-be writer, constantly typing away and sending out stories that returned to her like so many boomerangs. The son would soon outdo the mother, *his* stories returning home in the pages of *The New Yorker*.

The Shillington that he describes is a sunny place, despite the Depression of the 1930s and some labour strikes; more than once, Updike edgily refers to the election by the nearby city of Reading of a *socialist* mayor. Happily, for his school of Biedermeier novels, the world outside himself seems never to have caught his proper interest until the dread 1960s, when 'bright young men who are born with silver spoons in their mouth . . . were selling this nation out'. But that was long after he was a 'plain child, ungainly youth. Lacking brothers and sisters, [he] was shy and clumsy in the give and take . . . of human exchange.' Of contemporaries who did not care for school, 'I could not understand how anybody could rebel against a system so clearly benign.' But then he is always true to his 'docile good child nature'.

Yet under all this blandness and acceptance of authority in any form, there is a growing puzzlement. 'Social position in America is not easy to be precise about', he notes; then, warily, he tries to place his high-school teacher father: 'My family sold asparagus and pansies for odd money, embarrassing me.' But unlike a Fitzgerald or an O'Hara (most Irish Catholic writers in America are born with perfect radar on how to make it all the way to the blue light at landing's end – or pass out at the bar in the attempt), Updike seems to have missed whatever gentry there may have been in the neighbourhood. All he knows is that his mother says that we are much 'nicer' than a lot of other people, which is important if not very useful, as his father is a definite non-success, and so Updike concludes that:

> Life breeds punchers and counterpunchers, venturers like my father and ambushers like me: the venturer risks rebuff and defeat; the ambusher . . . risks fading away to nothing. . . . All those years in Shillington, I had waited to be admired, waited patiently . . . burrowing in New York magazines and English mystery novels for the secret passageway out, the path of avoidance and vindication. I hid a certain

determined defiance . . . I would 'show' them, I would avenge all the slights and abasements visited upon my father – the miserly salary, the subtle tyranny of his overlords at the high school, the disrespect of his students, the laughter in the movie house at the name of Updike.

Not exactly Richard III. Rather the inner rebellion of a shy, ambitious, small creature – a rabbit? – preparing to abandon its nice safe burrow for a world elsewhere, for a place across the water in nearby sinful Manhattan.

Shillington was to remain central to Updike's intense consciousness of self. In footnotes to his memoir, he solemnly quotes from his own work to show just how he has used the 'real' life of his small town in fiction. Over and over again he writes of the Lutheran Grace Church, the elementary school, the post office, of youthful revels at Stephens' Luncheonette. Not since Sinclair Lewis has a naturalistic writer been so merciless to his reader as Updike. Endlessly, he describes shops and their contents, newspaper advertisements, streets that go here, there and everywhere except into the – this – reader's mind. Places and people seem to interest him only when reduced, as cooks say, to receipts not dishes. Certainly all the words he uses are there on the page, but what they stand for is not. Only he himself is recorded with careful attention, as he notes his aim of 'impersonal egoism', and 'always with some natural hesitation and distaste' when it comes to memoir-writing; yet he soldiers on, and we learn that only after the family moved from Shillington does he masturbate – and so a lifelong adhesion to heterosexuality begins, at least in the mind. With *jouissance*, he comes into his kingdom, love in hand.

As a fellow *New Yorker* writer, S. J. Perelman, puts it in a letter to Ogden Nash in 1965, 'J. Updike . . . read extracts from three works of his to the assembled scholars, which I didn't personally hear as I was overtaken by the characteristic nausea that attacks me when this youth performs on the printed pages. But Cheever brought me tidings that all dealt with masturbation, a favourite theme of Updike's.' Of course, Perelman was a bit of a grouch; and who could have foretold that in three years' time this onanistic 'youth' would write *Couples*, a celebration of marriage and its saucy twin, adultery, the only important subjects of middlebrow fiction, saving God Himself and His America? It should be noted that Christianity seems always to have been a fact for Updike, starting with the Grace Lutheran and other churches of Shillington; later, as an outward and visible sign of niceness and of belongingness, he remains a churchgoer when he moves up the social scale to Ipswich, Massachusetts, where he achieves that dream of perfect normality which is not only American and Christian but – when in the company of other upwardly mobile couples – ever so slightly bohemian.

Although Updike seems never to have had any major psychic or physical wound, he has endured all sorts of minor afflictions. In the chapter 'At war with my skin', he tells us in great detail of the skin-condition that sun and later medicine would clear up; for a long time, however, he was martyr to it as well as a slave to his mirror, all the while fretting about what 'normal' people would make of him. As it proved, they don't seem to have paid much attention to an affliction that, finally, 'had to do with self love, with finding myself acceptable . . . the price high but not impossibly so, I must pay for being me.' The price for preserving me certainly proved to be well worth it when, in 1955, he was rejected for military conscription, even though the empire was still bogged down in Korea and our forces were increased that year from 800,000 to 3 million – less Updike, who, although 'it pains me to write these pages', confesses that he was 'far from keen to devote two years to the national defence.' He was later to experience considerable anguish when, almost alone among serious writers, he would support the Vietnam war on the ground that, who am I 'to second-guess a president?' One suspects that he envies the clear-skinned lads who could go fight for the land *he* so deeply loves.

'I had a stammer that came and went.' But he is ever game: 'As with my psoriasis, the affliction is perhaps not entirely unfortunate.' Better than to be born with a silver spoon in one's mouth is to be born at the heart of a grey cloud with a silver lining. The stammer does 'make me think twice about going on stage and appearing in classrooms and at conferences', but 'Being obliging by nature and anxious for approval, I would never say no if I weren't afraid of stuttering. Also, as I judge from my own reactions, people who talk too easily and comfortably . . . arouse distrust in some atavistic, pre-speech part of ourselves; we turn off.' Take that, Chrysostom Chatterbox! Characteristically, he is prompt to place a soothing Band-Aid on his own wound: he quotes Carlyle who observes of Henry James: 'a stammering man is never a worthless man.' Whatever that means. (Also, *pace* Carlyle, the Master did not stammer; he filibustered elaborately, cunningly, with pauses so carefully calculated that if one dared try to fill one, he would launch a boa-constrictor of a sentence at the poor mesmerized, oh, dear, rabbit! of an auditor.) Finally, Updike confesses to unease with certain groups that your average distinguished author must address. He is afraid of New York audiences especially: 'They are too smart and left wing for me. . . .' This seems to mean politically minded Jews, so unlike the *nice* Southern college audiences with whom he is most at home.

Dental problems occupy many fascinating pages. But then I am a sucker for illness and debilities and even the most homely of exurban *memento mori*. Finally, relatively late in life, he develops asthma! This splendid coda (to date) of the Updike physical apparatus is something of a master-stroke, and, as I once coughed along with Hans Castorp and his circle, I now find myself wheezing along with Updike; but then I, too, am mildly asthmatic.

The psychic Updike is dealt with warily. The seemingly effortless transition from the Shillington world to Harvard and then to the *New Yorker* staff is handled with Beylesque brevity. He notes, but does not demonstrate, the influence on him of such Christian conservative writers as G. K. Chesterton and C. S. Lewis and Jacques Maritain, while the names Karl Barth and Kierkegaard are often treated as one word, Barthegaard. He tells us that, as a novelist, 'My models were the styles of Proust and Henry Green – dialogue and meditation as I read them (one in translation).' Which one?

We shall never know. But for those of us who revelled in the French translations of Green, I can see how attractive those long irregular subjunctive-laden 'tender explorations' must have been for Updike, too. Although every other American novelist of the past half-century seems to regard Proust as his 'model', one finds no trace of Proust in Updike's long lists of consumer goods on sale in shops as well as of human characteristics that start with external features, followed by internal 'meditations' on the true character of the Character.

Despite all of Updike's book-reviewing, one gets the sense that books have not meant much to him, young or old; but then he was originally attracted to the graphic arts (he attended the Ruskin School at Oxford), and the minor technical mysteries of lettering nibs and scratchboard. . . . 'And my subsequent career carries coarse traces of its un-ideal origins in popular, mechanically prop-agated culture.' This is endearing; also, interesting – 'I was a cultural bumpkin in love not with writing, but with print.' And, like everyone else of the time, with the movies, as he will demonstrate in his latest novel.

Easily, it would appear, he became an all-round writer for *The New Yorker* 'of the William Shawn era (1951–87) . . . a club of sorts, from within which the large rest of literary America . . . could be politely disdained. . . . While I can now almost glimpse something a bit too trusting in the serene sense of artistic well-being, of virtual invulnerability, that being published in *The New Yorker* gave me for over thirty years. . . .' During much of this time, he seemed unaware that the interesting, indeed major, writers of the period did not belong to his club, either because they were too disturbing for the mild Shawn or because they could not endure the radical editing and rewriting that the quintessential middlebrow magazine imposed on its writers. 'I shook with anger,' Perelman wrote in 1957, 'at their august editorial decisions, their fussy little changes and pipsqueak variations on my copy.' Nabokov, published at Edmund Wilson's insistence, needed all of Wilson's help in fighting off editorial attempts to make his prose conform to the proto-Ralph Lauren house impersonation of those who fit, socially, in the roomy top-drawer-but-one. Unlike that original writer, Nabokov, Updike, ever 'the good child', throve under strict supervision and thought himself on Parnassus, a harmless, even beguiling mis-understanding so long as the real world never confronted him, which, of course, it did.

The Vietnam war jolted Updike into the nearest he has yet come to self-examination as opposed to self-consciousness. 'I was a lib-eral,' he notes at some point. That is, he didn't like Nixon when he was at Harvard, and he voted for Kennedy. But now he strikes the Pecksniffian note as he invokes class distinctions. Of liberals at Harvard, 'they, Unitarian or Episcopalian or Jewish, support Roosevelt and Truman and Stevenson out of enlightenment, *de haut en bas*, whereas in my heart of hearts, I, however, veneered with an education and button-down shirts, was *de bas*. They, secure in the upper-middle class, were Democrats out of human sympa-thy and humanitarian largesse, because this was the party that helped the poor. Our family had simply *been* poor, and voted Democrat out of crude self-interest.' He is now moving into McCarthy, Wallace, Buchanan country. Resentment, for Updike a slow-blooming plant, is starting to put forth lurid flowers, suitable for funeral wreaths to be laid upon his carefully acquired affluent niceness as well as upon the sort of company that it had earned him, which, almost to a man, stood against the war that he accepts and even, for a time, favours. Suddenly he starts scrabbling in search of peasant roots to show that he is really *dans le vrai* – unlike those supercilious silver-spoon-choked snobs who dare 'second-guess' presidents.

'Was I conservative? I hadn't thought so, but I did come from what I could begin to see' (after a third of a century?) 'was a con-servative part of the country. . . . The Germans of Berks County didn't move on, like the typical Scots-Irish frontier-seeking Americans. They stayed put, farming the same valleys and being buried in the same graveyards. . . .' Presumably, this stay-put mindset ought to have made him isolationist and anti-war when it came to military adventures in far-off places where other

Americans, whom he knew little of, fought Asians, whom he knew nothing of. But, startlingly, he chooses to interpret the passivity of his ancestral tribes as the reason for his own unquestioning acceptance of authority: if the president wants you to go fight the Viet Cong in order to contain the Viet Cong's mortal enemy, China, you must not question, much less second-guess him. You will go fight when and where he tells you to, unless you are lucky enough to be kept safe at home by psoriasis. For the first time, the apolitical, ahistorical Updike was faced with what pop-writers call an Identity Crisis.

'By my mid-thirties, through diligence and daring' (if one did not know better, one might think the second adjective ironic), 'I had arrived at a lifestyle we might call genteel bohemian – nice big house (broad floor-boards, big fireplaces). . . . We smoked pot, wore dashikis and love beads, and frugged ourselves into a lather while the Beatles and Janis Joplin sang away on the hi-fi set. I was happy enough to lick the sugar of the counter-culture; it was the pill of anti-war, anti-administration, anti-'imperialist' protest that I found oddly bitter.' He notes that the frugging technocrats *et al* of his acquaintance simply sloughed off the war as an 'administration blunder'. But writers, artists, even the very voices to whose sound Updike frugged, began very early to object to the war, while 'I whose stock in trade as an American author included an intuition into the mass consciousness and an identification with our national fortunes – thought it sad that our patriotic myth of invincible virtue was crashing, and shocking that so many Americans were gleeful at the crash.' This is worthy of Nixon at his unctuous best; yet to give that canny old villain his due, Nixon wouldn't have believed a word he was saying. Incidentally, who was 'gleeful' at so much mindless carnage? And what honest citizen would *not* be grateful that a 'myth' of any kind, no matter how 'patriotic', be dispelled?

When intellectuals, for want of any other word, were asked to contribute their views to a book called *Authors Take Sides on Vietnam*, Updike admitted that he was 'uncomfortable' about our military adventure, but wondered 'how much of the discomfort has to do with its high cost, in lives and money, and how much with its moral legitimacy'. This is wondrously callous. Of course, television had not yet shown us too many lives, much less money, being lost on prime time, but Updike weighs them as nothing in the balance when compared to the moral decision made by our elected leaders, who must know best – otherwise they would not be our elected leaders. Loyal to authority, he favours intervention 'if it does some good', because 'the crying need is for genuine elections whereby the South Vietnamese can express their will. If their will is for Communism, we should pick up our chips and leave.' But the American Government had stopped the Vietnamese from holding such elections a decade earlier, because, as President Eisenhower noted in his memoirs, North and South Vietnam would have voted for the Communist Ho Chi Minh and 'we could not allow that'. Updike's ignorance – innocence, to be kind – is not very reassuring, even when he echoes Auden on how 'it is foolish to canvass writers upon political issues'. Our views, as he says, ' "have no more authority than those of any reasonably well-educated citizen" '. Certainly, the views of a writer who knew nothing of the political situation in Vietnam weren't worth very much, but, as an American writer identified with our national fortunes, Updike does acknowledge that writers are supposed to be attuned to the human as well as to the moral aspects of engaging in war, particularly one so far from our shores, so remote from our interests. As Updike's wife at the time told him, 'It's their place.' But by then it was too late. Mild Rabbit had metamorphosed into March Hare.

Letter to *The New York Times*: 'I discover myself named . . . as the lone American writer "unequivocally for" the United States intervention in Vietnam.' He notes that he is not alone. Apparently James Michener, 'an old Asia hand', and Marianne Moore, an old baseball hand, thought that the Commies should be stopped by us anywhere and everywhere . . . or, in Updike's case, by *them*, the Americans obliged to fight. He finds such opponents as Jules Pfeiffer and Norman Mailer 'frivolous'. Mailer had written, 'The truth is maybe we need a war. It may be the last of the tonics. From Lydia Pinkham to Vietnam in sixty years, or bust.' Mailer was being Swiftian. But Updike is constitutionally unable to respond to satire, irony, wit, rhetorical devices that tend to be offensive to that authority which he himself means to obey.

Updike takes offence at a 'cheerful thought by James Purdy: "Vietnam is atrocious for the dead and maimed innocent, but it's probably sadder to be a live American with only the Madison Avenue Glibbers for a homeland and a God."' Rabbit will go to his final burrow without ever realizing the accuracy of Purdy's take on the society in which Updike was to spend his life trying to find a nice place for himself among his fellow Glibbers.

For a certain kind of quotidian novelist, there is nothing wrong in leaving out history or politics. But there is something creepy about Updike's over-reaction to those of us who tried to stop a war that was destroying (the dead to one side) a political and economic system that had done so well by so many rabbits. Updike is for the president, any president, right or wrong, because at such a time: 'It was a plain citizen's duty to hold his breath and hope for the best.' For thirteen years? Then, with unexpected passion, he sides with what he takes to be the majority of Americans against those members of the upper class whom he once emulated and now turns upon: 'Cambridge professors and Manhattan lawyers and their guitar-strumming children thought they could run the country and the world better than this lugubrious bohunk from Texas (Johnson). These privileged members of a privileged nation . . . full of aesthetic disdain for their own defenders.' At some point, unclear to me, the Viet Cong must have bombed San Diego. 'At a White House dinner in June of 1965, I saw what seemed to me a touching sight: Johnson and Dean Rusk . . . giving each other a brief hug in passing – two broad-backed Southern boys, trying to hold the fort.'

After the thrill of watching those whom Unser Gott had placed over us, Updike turns manic ('My face would become hot, my voice high and tense and wildly stuttery'). He grieves for 'the American soldiers, derided and mocked at home. . . .' This is purest Johnson. Whenever LBJ was attacked for having put the troops in Vietnam for no clear reason, he would charge those who questioned presi-

dential mischief with disloyalty – even treason – against our brave
boys, when, of course, it was he and Eisenhower and Kennedy and
Ford and Nixon who supported the sacrifice of our brave boys in a
war that none of these presidents could ever, with straight face,
explain; a war whose long-time executor, Robert McNamara, now
tells us that he himself never did figure out. But in the presence of
Authority, Updike is like a bobby-soxer at New York's Paramount
Theater when the young Frank Sinatra was on view. Out of control, he writes, 'Under the banner of a peace-movement . . . war
was being waged by a privileged few upon the administration and
the American majority that had elected it.' The reverse was true.
Finally Wall Street marched against the war, and Nixon surrendered, weightier matters, like impeachment, on his mind.

'Reading a little now, I realize how little I knew, for all my
emotional involvement, about the war itself, a war after all like
other wars. . . .' But it was not like other wars. No matter, the
March Hare has turned his attention to other legitimacies, such as
God. 'Western culture from Boethius to Proust had transpired
under the Christian enchantment.' What an odd pairing! Plainly,
Updike doesn't know much about Boethius. It is true that after his
execution by the Emperor Theodoric in AD 525, he was taken over
by the Christian establishment (Latin team) as a patristic authority,
even though, in his last work, *The Consolation of Philosophy* (a
'golden volume', according to Gibbon), he is mostly Platonist
except when he obeys the injunction 'follow God' in imitation not
of the tripartite Christian wonder but of Pythagoras. As for the
half-Jew Proust, so emotionally and artistically involved in the
Dreyfus case, Christianity in action could hardly have been
'enchanting'. But Updike, in theological mood, is serenely
absolutist: 'Among the repulsions of atheism for me has been its
drastic uninterestingness as an intellectual position.' This is very
interesting.

At times, reading Updike's political and cultural musings, one
has the sense that there is no received opinion that our good rabbit
does not hold with passion. 'The fights for women's rights and gay
rights emerged enmeshed with the Vietnam protest and have out-

lived it. Though unconsciously resisting the androgyny, which swiftly became – as all trends in a consumer society become – a mere fashion, I must have felt challenged.' As American women have been trying to achieve political and economic parity with men for two centuries, how can these activities be considered 'mere fashion' or a new consumer trend? For Updike, fags and dikes are comical figures who like their own sex and so cannot be taken seriously when they apply for the same legal rights under the Constitution that fun-loving, wife-swapping exurbanites enjoy. Reality proved too much for him. 'I found the country so distressing in its civil fury' that he, along with current wife and Flopsy, Mopsy and Cottontail, fled to London 'for the school year of 1968–69'. The year, one should note, of the three 'decadent' bestsellers, *Portnoy's Complaint*, *Myra Breckinridge* and his own *Couples*.

Today, Rabbit seems at relative peace. He addresses a letter to his grandchildren full of family lore. Along the way, he has acquired an African son-in-law. He is full of Shillington self-effacing gracefulness on what – if any – race problem there might still be in the grand old United States, converted during the Reagan years – golden years for bunnies – to a City on a Hill where he can now take his ease and enjoy the solace of Religion, pondering 'the self [which] is the focus of anxiety; attention to others, self-forgetfulness and living like [*sic*] the lilies are urged'.

Between *Self-Consciousness* (1989) and the current *In the Beauty of the Lilies*, Updike has published three novels, a book of short stories and one of critical pieces. He is, as Dawn Powell once said of herself, 'fixed in facility', as are most writers-for-life; a dying breed, I suspect, as, maw ajar, universal Internet swallows all. Meanwhile, Updike has written his Big Book, the story of four generations of American life, starting in 1910 and ending more or less today in – and on – television, as practically everything does in what the bemused Marx thought might be our 'exceptional' republic.

Before the outbreak of the Civil War, John Brown, a yeoman from Connecticut, destined to be forever connected with Osawatomie, Kansas, set himself up as a unilateral abolitionist of slavery in a state torn between pro- and anti-slavery factions.

Updike probably first encountered him, as I did, in the film *Santa Fe Trail* (1940), where he was made gloriously incarnate by Raymond Massey. With a band of zealots, Brown occupied the federal arsenal at Harpers Ferry, Virginia. The nation suddenly was afire. Inevitably, Brown was defeated and hanged by the state of Virginia, thus making him a martyr for the North, while a song, 'John Brown's Body', was set to a rousing old English folk tune. The poet, Julia Ward Howe, listening to troops sing the demotic words to 'John Brown's Body', in a Delphic fever of inspiration, wrote her own words for what would later be known as 'The Battle Hymn of the Republic', one of the few stirring pieces of national music to give the 'Marseillaise' a run for its Euro-francs.

Updike has chosen for his title one of the least mawkish, if not entirely coherent, quatrains from Howe's lyrics. 'In the beauty of the lilies Christ was born across the sea / With a glory in his bosom that transfigures you and me / As he died to make men holy, let us die to make men free / While God is marching on.' Precisely why God has chosen this moment to go marching – on to where? – is a secret as one with the source of the sacred river Alph. But, no matter, this is rousing stuff. It is patriotic; it favours the freedom of black slaves at the South; it is botanically incorrect – no lilies at Bethlehem in December, as opposed to all those iconographic lilies during April's immaculate conception. But the text fits Updike's evening mood; it also provides him with an uplifting sonorous title, though a more apt title could have been found in the quatrain that begins, 'I have seen Him in the watch-fires of an hundred circling camps; / They have builded Him an altar in the evening dews and damps.' Updike has well and truly builded us a novel that might well and truly be called 'The Evening Dews and Damps'. He has also written easily the most intensely political American novel of the last quarter-century.

The story begins in the grounds of a baronial estate in Paterson, New Jersey. Shillington territory. But this is not your usual Rabbit story. On the lawn, D. W. Griffith is making a film with Mary Pickford. We hear little more about this film, but the modern note has been struck. Now we must defer satisfaction, as Updike gives us a list of things, visible and invisible, in the immediate neighbourhood – like New York City only fifteen miles to the east of Paterson 'lying sullenly snared within the lowland loop of the Passaic River'. One wonders what editor Shawn might have made of that 'sullenly'. Surely, there must have been a house ukase against the pathetic fallacy. But Updike has always liked to signal with his adverbs as he conforms with his adjectives. Besides, he is now off *The New Yorker* page and on to his very own page.

The first section is titled 'Clarence'. The Reverend Clarence Arthur Wilmot of the Fourth Presbyterian church, whose address we are given as well as the church's dimensions, physically and spiritually, along with those of Clarence himself, 'a tall narrow-chested man of forty-three', etc, etc who has, at this moment, suddenly, almost idly, lost his faith. A promising beginning which might have been more effective without the weeds of description that precede it. Even so, there *it* is, on the third page – the Problem. In order to refute a lapsing parishioner, Clarence has been reading the atheist Robert Ingersoll's *Some Mistakes of Moses*, and, in the process, in a flash of utter darkness, he comes to the conclusion that Ingersoll was 'quite right'. Shaken, Clarence makes his way home through a forest of description and into his house with its 'leaded rectangles of stained glass the colour of milky candies and the foot of the dark walnut staircase that, in two turnings punctuated by rectangular newel posts whose point had been truncated. . . .' We are spared nothing, rectangular or otherwise.

Clarence ponders free will versus predestination, the sort of thing that at a church school like St Albans, to the south of Paterson in Washington, DC, most boys had pretty much wrapped up before the onset of puberty – or Grace, whichever took place first. We meet wife and mother, Stella, supervising the cook in the kitchen. Tonight there will be supper for some important Presbyterians. Money for the church will be discussed. Clarence listens to kitchen chatter: 'The eavesdropping clergyman, numbed by his sudden atheism. . . .' Then we're off to a description of lots and lots of things in the house including a Tiffany-glass chandelier, with scalloped edges. Updike never quite knows what to do with his lists of random objects or physical human characteristics. In this, he resembles a more graceful James Michener, whose huge books are simply compendia of thousands of little facts collected by researchers and deposited helter-skelter in his long 'novels'.

Updike also provides us with reading lists of those books that encourage and discourage Christian faith. Clarence is suffering from a mini-vastation, somewhat diluted by Updike's sudden introduction of 'real people' into the book, or at least of real names culled from contemporary newspapers. There is Mary Pickford at the start. Then a son of Theodore Roosevelt gets married. We are given the list of ushers, dazzling society names of the day. Updike will keep on doing this for the entire sixty-year period covered by his narrative. But a technique that worked so well for John Dos Passos in *USA* simply stops dead what story Updike has to tell.

Updike, unlike his alleged literary models, Henry Green and Proust, describes to no purpose. In fact, Green, as I recall, describes hardly anything, relying on a superlative ear for a wide variety of speech patterns, while Updike's characters all speak in the same tone of voice, their dialogue a means to get them from one plot point to the next. As one trudges through these descriptions, one wishes that Updike had learned less from his true models, Marquand and O'Hara, and more from the middle James who, as a lord of the pertinent and the relevant, knew that nothing need be described or, indeed, *told* unless it suggests, while never naming, the presence in the deep of monsters, as the author, off-page, turns ever tighter the screw.

Although in *The Spoils of Poynton* mother and son fight over the contents of a great house, we are never told just *what* is being fought over. James leaves the details to the reader's imagination. But such continence has never been the way of the commercial American writer, no matter how elevated his theme or resourceful his art. For Updike, Poynton is a Sotheby's catalogue.

James only needed to describe – was it one crucifix? – to represent a house full of rare furniture and objects worth killing for. The naturalistic Dos Passos used movie-like cuts and inter-cuts of head-lines to act as useful counterpoint to a narrative that takes place in public, as opposed to strictly private, time. As most people get the news of their day through press and television, why not use or at least mimic these sources? The naturalistic Updike seems to think that just about any item will do in the way of colour, and, in a sense, he is right; one has only to consider the huge popularity of Michener's myriad-fact novels with an unsophisticated reading public that likes to think that valuable time is not being wasted on a made-up story, that the reader is really getting the inside dope on, let's say, Detroit and the auto business or, in Updike's case, on the United States's second most profitable export after aerospace – showbiz and Hollywood. But whereas a few million small facts are the object of the Michenerian enterprise, Updike is more con-ventionally ambitious. He wants to dramatize the forces that have driven the United States ever leftward, even further away from the marching, lily-born God, away from family values and obedience to Authority, away from *The New Yorker*'s benign fact-checkers and sentence-polishers, so sadly absent now when he really needs them.

After James's disasters in the theatre, he famously returned to prose with a new sharp intensity. He had learned that nothing is to be noted unless it is absolutely essential to the dramatic revelation of even the vaguest figure in the carpet. As far as I know, Updike has never submitted himself to the strict discipline of relevance one learns from theatre. And yet, parenthetically, his one attempt at a play, *Buchanan Dying* (1974), though probably unstageable as writ-ten, is a superb work of mimesis, the last thoughts of the enigmatic president from Pennsylvania whose cautious inertness helped bring on the Civil War and imperial Lincoln. The effect is startling and unique, unlike. . . .

'Dialogue and meditation' is how Updike, inaccurately, describes the manner of his early 'model', Henry Green. Updike himself writes long, long descriptions interspersed with brief snatches of dialogue. In theory . . . no, no theory! . . . *ideally*, both description and dialogue should forward narrative, as in most pop writing. Realistic story-tellers in English oscillate between the *démeublement* of Raymond Carver and the richly detailed settings, physical and psychic, of James Purdy. For a true master of effects, either way works. But if, like Updike, one means to go into the wholesale furniture business, one had better be prepared to furnish, in appropriate manner, great Poynton itself. I realize that in a world where democracy is on the rise everywhere except in American politics, one style can never be better than another, 'cause my feelings are just as deep as yours and how can you criticize my voice, my style which is Me? To which some of us old meanies must respond, well, dear, if you choose to send your letter to the world then here's the answer, assuming the letter was not returned to sender for lack of correct address or sufficient postage.

Years ago, in unkind mood, Norman Mailer referred to Updike's writing as the sort of prose that those who know nothing about writing think good. Today, theory, written preferably in near-English academese, absorbs the specialist, and prose style is irrelevant. Even so, what is one to make of this sentence: 'The hoarse receding note drew his consciousness . . . to a fine point, and while that point hung in his skull starlike he fell asleep upon the adamant bosom of the depleted universe'? Might Updike not have allowed one blind noun to slip free of its seeing-eye adjective?

Plot, four generations of the Wilmot family. After Clarence's loss of faith, he sells encyclopaedias, perseveres in his failure, as did Updike's own father, each to be avenged by a descendant; though not by Clarence's son, Teddy, who occupies the next chunk of time – and novel-space. Now we go into the Updike time-machine. 'And then it was a new decade, and drinking was illegal all across the nation, and Attorney General A. Mitchell Palmer accused the IWW of causing the railroad strikes. . . . Mary Pickford and Douglas Fairbanks were married in a Hollywood dream come true, and Europe twisted and turned with coups and riots and little wars' (which ones?), 'and the Democrats at their convention put up James Cox and another Roosevelt, and Bill Tilden . . . and . . . and . . . and. . . .'

Teddy doesn't know what to do with his life. He is passive and not very bright. He works in a bottle-top factory; studies accounting. Meanwhile, he struggles for light beneath his author's thick blankets of research, intended to give us the sense of a world and a time in which Teddy himself has neither place nor perceptible interest: 'And now the sordidness of illusions was leaking out of Hollywood itself. . . . Fatty Arbuckle, unsolved mystery of director William Desmond Taylor. . . .' But there is some point to all this news from outside, because, in the next slice of the Wilmot saga, Teddy's daughter, Esther or Essie, will become a Movie Star and avenge – 'ambush', as Updike did – a world that paid no attention to his father, her grandfather. When Teddy goes to work in Addison's Drug Store (Stephenson's back in Shillington), we are given page after page of what is sold in the store. Then Teddy marries a crippled girl with a strong character. Teddy gives up being a soda jerk and becomes a career postman. He endures a happy marriage, until his wife, as fictional characters tend to do, falls through one of the interstices in Updike's web of Passing Parade notes on world events: 'Jews and Arabs fought in Jerusalem; Chinese and Russians battled along the Manchurian border.' Social notes from all over. Teddy smokes Old Golds.

Part Three. We shift from Teddy to Essie/Alma. I found myself curious that Updike did not choose to shift from third to first person in his studies of four generations. Since all his character writing is in essentially the same tone of voice, he might have dramatized – well, differentiated – his four protagonists by giving each a distinctive voice. But he remains in the lazy third person: Now she thinks this . . . now she does that . . . now Japan invades Manchuria.

In Essie's section, the Shillington/Basingstoke movie house is central, and Essie, now a beauty, is thrilled by what she sees on the screen, ideal life writ large in celluloid. Ambitious, for a dull Wilmot, she enters a beauty contest where she meets a photographer from New York. 'There was something mystical in the way the camera lapped up her inner states through the thin skin of her face. She had known as a child she was the centre of the universe and now proof was accumulating, click by click.' She becomes a model. An actress. A star, as Alma De Mott.

But for Updike, Essie is early blighted. Even before Hollywood and stardom she is taken in by liberals – Commies, too. Plainly, sinister osmosis was taking place at the movie house in her home town. The liberal image of America the Bad was like some insidious virus contained in the celluloid, bacteria which, under the optimum condition of hot light projected through its alien nesting-ground on to the screen, bred discontent in those not sufficiently vaccinated against Doubt by benign school and good church. So ravaged was Essie by Red films like *Now, Voyager* ('Why ask for the moon when we have the stars?') that she actually objected to the loyalty oaths inflicted on so many Americans by President Truman's administration, oaths that the self-conscious Updike cannot, like his father, find objectionable. When Essie's little brother, Danny, says, 'I hate Communists', she says, 'What do you know about anything? Who do you think beat Hitler's armies?' And so the green twig was bent by the product of MGM and the Brothers Warner.

Before Essie leaves New York for Hollywood, Updike helpfully tells us the names 'of the big Hollywood movies at the end of the Forties'. He also lists the foreign films that ravished Essie. Curiously, he forgets to rate the Italian neo-realists for Leftist content. In New York, Essie is taken up by a queer cousin, Patrick. He is worldly, knows his Manhattan: like all homosexuals, he is 'sensitive' but 'frustrating . . . and not just sexually; some inner deflection kept him on the sidelines of life, studying painting but not wanting to paint himself, and even sneering at those that did try'; but then 'the arts, especially minor arts like window dressing, were dominated by them'. Patrick manages her career for a time: 'A comforting accreditation . . . to have a poof bring her in.'

Before Alma makes it to the silver screen, she serves time in live television. Updike tells us all about what it was like; but then there is a firm in New York that will do intensive research on any subject a writer might want – from the Golden Age of Television, say, to the flora and fauna of Brazil. I am certain that Updike, the artist, would never resort to so brazen a crib; even so, many of his small piled-up facts are so rote-like in their detail, and his use of them so completely haywire that – well, *vichyssoise qui mal y pense*.

'Alma would play opposite, within the next few years, both Gary Cooper and . . . Clark Gable.' Boldly, Updike tells us a lot of personal things about Cooper and Gable which he could only have got from fan magazines or showbiz biographies. Updike is now frugging wildly into Collins Sisters territory. But where the Bel-Air Brontës are well advanced in the art and arts of popular fiction and write *romans à clef* with phallic keys, Updike, ever original, disposes with the keys. Confidently, he tells us about 'Coop's' aches and pains, about Clark's career anxieties and sex. Updike has now made it to the heart of the heart of pop fiction: 'there was in Gable a loneliness too big for Alma to fill. Where Cooper was a sublime accident (he reached over, while the wind rushed past and the sun beat sparkling dents in the Pacific below, and cupped his hand around her skull) . . . Gable had never been anything but an aspiring actor. . . . He had been so long a star he had forgotten to find mortal satisfactions.' Why ask for the butterscotch when we can have the fudge?

For a beautiful heroine like Alma, sex is *de rigueur*, but though she fucks like a minx, the sexagenarian Updike has lost some of his old brio. Alma marries a nobody with a body; he never makes it in the business but makes a baby. Meanwhile, she grows more and more unAmerican. Proud to be a Hollywood liberal, she is prone to quarrel with her kid-brother, Danny, now a CIA honcho. 'Well, Danny darling, the movies have never pretended to be anything except entertainment. But what you're doing pretends to be a great deal more.'

'It pretends to be history,' he said quickly. 'It *is* history. Cast of billions. The future of the globe is at stake. I kid you not.' Nice touch, this last. Television slang of the 1950s.

Alma De Mott rises and falls and rises again. She is clearly based – research to one side – on Yvonne de Carlo's performance as an up-down-up movie star of a certain age in Sondheim's musical comedy *Follies*, whose signature song was 'I'm still here'.

Time now to shift to Alma's son, Clark, named for . . . you

guessed it. In the family tradition, he is a born Shillington loser. He is, of course, conscious of being a celebrity as a star's son. But the connection does him no particular good. He also has a stepfather called Rex. When he asks Alma why she married Rex, she 'told him calmly, Because he is all cock.'

Clark is in rebellion against the Communism of his mother and her friends – pinks if not reds – and, worse, unabashed enemies of the United States in the long, long, war against the Satanic Ho Chi Minh. 'Mom, too, wanted North Vietnam to win, which seemed strange to Clark, since America has been pretty good to her.' As irony, this might have been telling, but irony is an arrow that the Good Fiction Fairy withheld from the Updike quiver. Consequently, this *non sequitur* can only make perfect sense to a writer who believes that no matter how misguided, tyrannous and barbarous the rulers of one's own country have become, they *must* be obeyed; and if one has actually made money and achieved a nice place in the country they have hijacked then one must be doubly obedient, grateful, too. Under Hitler, many good Germans, we are told, felt the same way.

There is nothing, sad to say, surprising in Updike's ignorance of history and politics and of people unlike himself; in this, he is a standard American and so a typical citizen of what Vice-President Agnew once called the greatest nation in the country. But Updike has literary ambitions as well as most of the skills of a popular writer, except, finally, the essential one without which nothing can ever come together to any useful end as literature, empathy. He is forever stuck in a psychic Shillington-Ipswich-New York world where everything outside his familiar round is unreal. Because of this lack of imagination, he can't really do much even with the characters that he does have some feeling for because they exist in social, not to mention historic, contexts that he lacks the sympathy – to use the simplest word – to make real.

Many of Updike's descriptions of Hollywood – the place – are nicely observed. Plainly, he himself *looked* at the Three B's – Beverly Hills, Bel Air, Brentwood – 'the palm trees, the pink low houses, the Spanishness, the endlessness . . . the winding palm-lined streets of Beverly Hills, where there was no living person in sight but Japanese and Mexican gardeners wheeling dead palm fronds out from behind hedges of oleander and fuchsias'. 'The wealth here was gentle wealth, humorous wealth even; these fortunes derived from art and illusion and personal beauty and not, as back home, from cruel old riverside mills manufacturing some ugly and stupid necessity like Trojans or bottlecaps.' The 'humorous' is an inspired adjective, proving there is a lot to be said for first-hand observation. But then, alas, he must tell us about *how* films were made in the 1950s and what the makers were like, including Columbia's Harry Cohn, a much-written-about monster. Once inside the celluloid kitchen, Updike falls far, far behind the Bel-Air Brontës at their cuisine-art.

Alma is still here, as the song goes, while the son, Clark, works at a Colorado ski resort, owned by his great-uncle. Clark has gone through the usual schools and done the usual drugs and had the usual run-of-the-mill sex available to a movie star's child. Now he must *find* himself – if there is a self to find – in a partially pristine Colorado rapidly being undone by ski resorts and the greenhouse effect.

Except for Alma, who knew from the beginning that she was unique in her beauty and sweet self-love, none of Updike's protagonists has any idea of what to do with himself during the seventy years or so that he must mark time in this vale of tears before translation to sunbeam-hood in Jesus' sky-condo. Happily, if tragically, true meaning comes to Clark in Colorado.

Updike, nothing if not up-to-date, re-creates the celebrated slaughter at Waco, Texas, where the charismatic David Koresh and many of his worshippers were wiped out in their compound by federal agents. In Updike's fiction, a similar messiah and his worshippers withdraw to Colorado in order to live in Christian fellowship until the final trump, due any day now. An attractive girl leads Clark to the Lower Branch Temple and to Jesse, a Vietnam veteran who is now a 'high-ranch messiah'. As a novelist, Updike often relies on the wearisome trick of someone asking a new character to tell us about himself. Within the rustic temple, sceptical Clark and primitive Scripture-soaked Jesse tell us about themselves. Clark: 'Yeah, well. What was I going to say? Something. I don't want to bore you.' Jesse: 'You will never find Jesse bored. Never, by a recital of the truth. Weary, yes, and sore-laden with the sorrows of mankind, but never bored.' A good thing, too, considering the level of the dialogue. Jesse fulminates with biblical quotes from the likes of Ezekiel, while Clark wimps on and on about the emptiness of gilded life in the Three B's.

The actual events at Waco revealed, terribly, what a paranoid federal apparatus, forever alert to any infraction of its stern prohibitions, was capable of when challenged head-on by non-conformists. How, I wondered, will Updike, a born reactionary, deal with the state's conception of itself as ultimate arbiter of everything, no matter how absurd? Even 'the good child' must be appalled by the slaughter of Jesse and his fellow believers by a mindless authority.

Since we shall witness all this through Clark's eyes, Updike has made him even more passive than his usual protagonists. Too much acid in the Vipers Lounge? Clark does have a scene with Uncle Danny who explains the real world to him in terms that the editorial page of the *Wall Street Journal* might think twice about publishing, before publishing. Danny: 'Vietnam was a hard call. . . . But somebody always has to fight.' (In the case of Vietnam, somebody proved to be poor white and black males.) 'You and I walk down the street safe, if we do, because a cop around the corner has a gun. The kids today say the state is organized violence and they're right. But it matters who's doing the organizing . . . Joe Stalin . . . or our bumbling American pols. I'll take the pols every time.' Thus, straw villain undoes straw hero; neither, of course, relevant to the issue, but Updike–Danny (true empathy may have been achieved at last) is now in full swing: 'The kids today . . . grow long hair . . . smoke pot and shit on poor Tricky Dicky' only because of 'the willingness of somebody else to do their fighting for them. What you can't protect gets taken away. . . .' Hobbesian world out there. Danny does admit

that we got nothing out of Vietnam, not even 'thanks' – one wonders from whom he thinks gratitude ought to come. But, no matter. Danny hates Communism. Hates Ho Chi Minh. Hates those
'Hollywood fatcats and bleeding hearts' who oppose the many
wars. Even so, 'I try to be dispassionate about it. But I love this
crazy, wasteful, self-hating country in spite of myself.' It would
seem that Updike–Danny has not got the point. The people of the
country don't hate the country, only what has been done to it by
those who profit from hot and cold wars and, in the process, bring
to civilian governance a murderous military mentality, witness
Waco.

How does Clark take all this? 'To Clark, Uncle Danny seemed a
treasure, a man from space who was somehow his own. . . .' Clark
has not known many employees of the CIA, for whom this sort of
bombast is the order of the day. That order flows not only through
the pages of the *Wall Street Journal* but throughout most of the
press, where Hume's Opinion is shaped by the disinformation of a
hundred wealthy tax-exempt American foundations such as Olin,
Smith-Richardson, Bradley, Scaife and Pew, not to mention all the
Christian coalitions grinding out a world-view of Us against Them,
the Us an ever-smaller group of propertied Americans and the
Them the rest of the world.

Clark would now be ripe for neo-conhood, but for the fact that
he was never a con or anything at all until he drifted into Jesse's
orbit, already set on a collision course with the US government
which allows no group the pleasure of defiance even in the name
of the One in whose Image we were fashioned. Jesse has been
stockpiling weapons for 'The Day of Reckoning'. Lovingly, Updike
lists the arsenal. Clark suddenly realizes that here, at last, is the
perfect orgasm, something well worth dying for. 'The gun was surprising: provocative like a woman, both lighter and heavier than
he would have thought.' The ultimate love-story of a boy and his
gun, 'ready to become a magic wand'. Disappointingly, at the end,
Updike is too patriotic or too timid to allow federal law-
enforcement officers to destroy the temple along with the men,
women and children that Jesse has attracted to him. Colorado

State Troopers do Caesar's work, unlike Waco where Caesar himself did the deed.

At the end, Clark turns on Jesse and betrays him. In order to save the children from the Conflagration, Clark 'shot the false prophet twice'. Although Clark himself perishes, he dies a hero, who saved as many lives as he could from the false prophet whom he had, for no coherent reason, briefly served. Finally, world television validates Clark's life and end. Who could ask for anything more?

Stendhal's view that politics in a work of art is like a pistol shot at a concert is true, but what is one to do in the case of a political work that deals almost exclusively with true patriot versus non-patriot who dares criticize the common patria? I quoted at length from Updike's *Self-Consciousness*, in order to establish what human material this inhuman novel is based on. I have also tried to exercise empathy, tried to feel, as President Clinton likes to say, the author's pain. Actually, to find reactionary writing similar to Updike's, one must turn back to John Dos Passos's *Mid-century*, or to John Steinbeck's *The Winter of Our Discontent*. But Updike, unlike his predecessor Johns, has taken to heart every far-out far-right piety currently being fed us.

Also, despite what Updike must have thought of as a great leap up the social ladder from Shillington obscurity to 'Eliotic' Harvard and then on to a glossy magazine, he has now, Antaeus-like, started to touch base with that immutable Dutch-German earth on which his ladder stood. Recent American wars and defeats have so demoralized our good child that he has now come to hate that Enlightenment which was all that, as a polity, we ever had. He is symptomatic, then, of a falling back, of a loss of nerve; indeed, a loss of honour. He invokes phantom political majorities, righteous masses. Time to turn to Herzen on the subject: 'The masses are indifferent to individual freedom, liberty of speech; the masses love authority. They are still blinded by the arrogant glitter of power, they are offended by those who stand alone . . . they want a social government to rule for their benefit, and not against it. But to govern themselves doesn't enter their heads.'

Updike's work is more and more representative of that polarizing within a state where Authority grows ever more brutal and malign while its hired hands in the media grow ever more excited as the holy war of the few against the many heats up. In this most delicate of times, Updike has 'builded' his own small, crude altar in order to propitiate – or to invoke? – 'the fateful lightning of His terrible swift sword'.

The Times Literary Supplement
26 April 1996

7
A Note on *The City and the Pillar* and Thomas Mann

Much has been made – not least by the Saint himself – of how Augustine stole and ate some pears from a Milanese orchard. Presumably, he never again trafficked in, much less ate, stolen goods, and once this youthful crime ('a rum business,' snarled the unsympathetic American jurist Oliver Wendell Holmes, Jr) was behind him, he was sainthood-bound. The fact is that all of us have stolen pears; the mystery is why so few of us rate halos. I suspect that in certain notorious lives there is sometimes an abrupt moment of choice. Shall I marry or burn? Shut the door on a life longed for while opening another, deliberately, onto trouble and pain because. . . . The 'because' is the true story seldom told.

Currently, two biographers are at work on my sacred story, and the fact that they are trying to make sense of my life has made me curious about how and why I have done – and not done – so many things. As a result, I have begun writing what I have said that I'd never write, a memoir ('I am not my own subject,' I used to say with icy superiority). Now I am reeling haphazardly through my own youth, which is when practically everything of interest happened to me, rather more soon than late, since I was force-fed, as it were, by military service in the Second World War.

My father once told me, after reviewing his unpleasant period in public office, that whenever it came time for him to make a crucial decision, he invariably made the wrong one. I told him that he must turn Churchill and write his own life, demonstrating what famous victories he had set in motion at Gallipoli or in the 'dragon's soft underbelly' of the Third Reich. But my father was neither a writer nor a politician; he was also brought up to tell the truth. I, on the other hand, was brought up by a politician grandfather in Washington, DC, and I wanted very much to be a politician, too. Unfortunately, nature had designed me to be a writer. I had no choice in the matter. Pears were to be my diet, stolen or homegrown. There was never a time when I did not make sentences in order to make those things that I had experienced cohere and become 'real'.

Finally, the novelist must always tell the truth as he understands it while the politician must never give the game away. Those who have done both comprise a very short list indeed. The fact that I was never even a candidate for the list had to do with a choice made at twenty that entirely changed my life.

At nineteen, just out of the army, I wrote a novel, *Williwaw* (1946): it was admired as, chronologically, at least, the first of the war novels. The next year I wrote the less admired *In a Yellow Wood* (1947). Simultaneously, my grandfather was arranging a political career for me in New Mexico (the governor was a protégé of the old man). Yes, believe it or not, in the greatest democracy the world has ever known – freedom's as well as bravery's home – elections can be quietly arranged, as Joe Kennedy liked to chuckle about.

For someone twenty years old I was well situated in the world, thanks to two published novels and my grandfather's political skills. I was also situated dead centre at a crossroads rather like the one Oedipus found himself at. I was writing *The City and the Pillar*. If I published it, I'd take a right turn and end up accursed in Thebes. Abandon it and I'd turn left and end up in holy Delphi. Honour required that I take the road to Thebes. I have read that

I was too stupid at the time to know what I was doing, but in such matters I have always had a certain alertness. I knew that my description of the love affair between two 'normal' all-American boys of the sort that I had spent three years with in the wartime army would challenge every superstition about sex in my native land – which has always been more Boeotia, I fear, than Athens or haunted Thebes. Until then, American novels of 'inversion' dealt with transvestites or with lonely bookish boys who married un-happily and pined for Marines. I broke that mould. My pair of lovers were athletes and so drawn to the entirely masculine that, in the case of one, Jim Willard, the feminine was simply irrelevant to his passion to unite with his other half, Bob Ford: unfortunately for Jim, Bob had other sexual plans, involving women and marriage.

I gave the manuscript to my New York publishers, E. P. Dutton. They hated it. One ancient editor said, 'You will never be forgiven for this book. Twenty years from now you will still be attacked for it.' I responded with an uneasy whistle in the dark: 'If any book of mine is remembered in the year 1968, that's real fame, isn't it?'

To my grandfather's sorrow, on January 10, 1948, *The City and the Pillar* was published. Shock was the most pleasant emotion aroused in the press. How could our young war novelist . . .? In a week or two, the book was a best-seller in the United States and wherever else it could be published – not exactly a full atlas in those days. The English publisher, John Lehmann, was very nervous. In his memoirs, *The Whispering Gallery*, he writes, 'There were several passages in *The City and the Pillar*, a sad, almost tragic book and a remarkable achievement in a difficult territory for so young a man, that seemed to my travellers and the printers to go too far in frankness. I had a friendly battle with Gore to tone down and cut these passages. Irony of the time and taste: they wouldn't cause an eyebrow to be lifted in the climate of the early sixties.' Nevertheless, even today copies of the book still fitfully blaze on the pampas and playas of Argentina and other godly countries. As I write these lines, I have just learned that the book will at last appear in Russia, where a Moscow theatre group is adapting it for the stage.

What did my confrères think? I'm afraid not much. The fag writers were terrified; the others were delighted that a competitor had so neatly erased himself. I did send copies to two famous writers, fishing, as most young writers do, for endorsements. The first was to Thomas Mann. The second was to Christopher Isherwood, who responded enthusiastically. We became lifelong friends. Through Joseph Breitbach I was told that André Gide was planning to write an 'appreciation', but when we finally met he spoke only of a handwritten, fetchingly illustrated pornographic manuscript that he had received from an English clergyman in Hampshire.

At fourteen I had read Thomas Mann's *Joseph* books and realized that the 'novel of ideas' (we still have no proper phrase in English for this sort of book, or, indeed, such a genre) could work if one were to set a narrative within history. Later, I was struck by the use of dialogue in *The Magic Mountain*, particularly the debates between Settembrini and Naphta, as each man subtly vies for the favours of the dim but sexually attractive Hans Castorp. Later, there would be complaints that Jim Willard in *The City and the Pillar* was too dim. But I deliberately made him a Hans Castorp type: what else would someone so young be, set loose on the world – the City – that was itself the centre of interest? But I did give Jim something Hans lacked: a romantic passion for Bob Ford that finally excluded everything else from his life, even, in a sense, the life itself. I got a polite, perfunctory note from Thomas Mann, thanking me for my 'noble work': my name was misspelled.

Contemplating the American scene in the 1940s, Stephen Spender deplored the machinery of literary success, remarking sternly that 'one has only to follow the whizzing comets of Mr Truman Capote and Mr Gore Vidal to see how quickly and effectively this transforming, diluting, disintegrating machinery can work.' He then characterized *The City and the Pillar* as a work of sexual confession, quite plainly autobiography at its most artless. Transformed, diluted, disintegrated as I was, I found this description flattering. Mr Spender had paid me a considerable compliment; although I am the least autobiographical of novelists,

I had drawn the character of the athlete Jim Willard so convincingly that to this day aging pederasts are firmly convinced that I was once a male prostitute, with an excellent backhand at tennis. The truth, alas, is quite another matter. The book was a considerable act of imagination. Jim Willard and I shared the same geography, but little else. Also, in the interest of verisimilitude I decided to tell the story in a flat grey prose reminiscent of one of James T. Farrell's social documents.

In April 1993, at the University of New York at Albany, a dozen papers were read by academics on *The City and the Pillar*. The book has been in print for close to half a century, something I would not have thought possible in 1948, when *The New York Times* would not advertise it and no major American newspaper or magazine would review it or any other book of mine for the next six years. *Life* magazine thought that God's country was being driven queer by the young army first-mate they had featured only the previous year, standing before his ship. I've not read any of the Albany papers. For one thing, it is never a good idea to read about oneself, particularly about a twenty-one-year-old self who had modelled himself, perhaps too closely, on Billy the Kid. I might be shot in the last frame, but I was going to take care of a whole lot of folks who needed taking care of before I was done.

There were those who found the original ending 'melodramatic'. (Jim strangles Bob after an unsuccessful sexual encounter.) When I reminded one critic that it is the nature of romantic tragedy to end in death, I was told that so sordid a story about fags could never be considered tragic, unlike, let us say, a poignant tale of doomed love between a pair of mentally challenged teenage 'heteros' in old Verona. I intended Jim Willard to demonstrate the romantic fallacy. From too much looking back, he was destroyed, an unsophisticated Humbert Humbert trying to re-create an idyll that never truly existed except in his own imagination. Despite the title, this was never plain in the narrative. And of course the coda *was* unsatisfactory. At the time it was generally believed that the publishers forced me to tack on a cautionary ending in much the same way the Motion Picture Code used to insist that wickedness be punished. This was not true. I had always meant the end of the book to be black, but not as black as it turned out. So for a new edition of the book published in 1965 I altered the last chapter. In fact, I rewrote the entire book (my desire to imitate the style of Farrell was perhaps too successful), though I did not change the point of view or the essential relationships. I left Jim as he was. I had no choice: he had developed a life of his own outside my rough pages. Claude J. Summers, in his book *Gay Fictions*, recently noted that of the characters:

> only Jim Willard is affecting, and he commands sustained interest largely because he combines unexpected character- istics. Bland and ordinary, he nevertheless has an unusually well-developed inner life. Himself paralyzed by romantic illusions, he is surprisingly perceptive about the illusions of others. For all the novel's treatment of him as case history, he nevertheless preserves an essential mystery. As Robert Kiernan comments (*Gore Vidal*), Jim Willard is Everyman and yet he is l'étranger . . . the net effect is paradoxical but appro- priate for it decrees that, in the last analysis, we cannot patronize Jim Willard, sympathize with him entirely, or even claim to understand him. Much more so than the typical character in fiction, Jim Willard simply exists, not as the subject of a statement, not as the illustration of a thesis, but simply as himself.

Recently, I received a note from a biographer of Thomas Mann. Did I know, he asked, the profound effect that my book had had on Mann? I made some joke to the effect that at least toward the end of his life he may have learned how to spell my name. 'But he didn't read the book until 1950, and as he read it he commented on it in his diaries. They've just been published in Germany. Get them.' Now I have read, with some amazement, of the effect that Mann's twenty-one-year-old admirer had on what was then a seventy-five-year-old world master situated by war in California.

Wednesday 22, XI, 50
. . . Began to read the homo-erotic novel 'The City and the Pillar' by Vidal. The day at the cabin by the river and the love-play scene between Jim and Bob was quite brilliant. – Stopped reading late. Very warm night.

Thursday 23, XI, 50
. . . Continued 'City and Pillar'.

Friday 24, XI, 50
. . . In the evening continued reading 'The City and the Pillar'. Interesting, yes. An important human document, of excellent and enlightening truthfulness. The sexual, the affairs with the various men, is still incomprehensible to us. How can one sleep with men – [Mann uses the word *Herren*, which means not 'men' but 'gentlemen'. Is this Mann being satiric? A rhetorical question affecting shock?]

Saturday evening 25, XI, 50
. . . in May 1943, I took out the *Felix Krull* papers only to touch them fleetingly and then turn to *Faustus*. An effort to start again must be made, if only to keep me occupied, to have a task at hand. I have nothing else, no ideas for stories; no subject for a novel. . . . Will it be possible to start [*Felix Krull*] again? Is there enough of the world and are there enough people, is there enough knowledge available? The homosexual novel interests me not least because of the experience of the world and of travel that it offers. Has my isolation picked up enough experience of human beings, enough for a social-satirical novel?

Sunday 26, XI, 50
Busy with [the *Krull*] paper, confusing.
Read more of Vidal's novel.

Wednesday 29, XI, 50
. . . The *Krull* papers (on imprisonment). Always doubts. Ask myself whether this music determined by a 'yearning theme'

is appropriate to my years. . . . Finished Vidal's novel, moved, although a lot is faulty and unpleasant. For example, that Jim takes Bob into a Fairy Bar in New York.

I am pleased that Mann did not find the ending 'melodramatic', but then what theme is more melodramatically 'yearning' than *Liebestod*? In any case, the young novelist who took what seemed to everyone the wrong road at Trivium is now saluted in his own old age by the writer whom he had, in a certain sense, modelled himself on. As for Mann's surprise at how men could sleep with one another, he is writing a private diary, the most public act any German master can ever do, and though he often refers to his own 'inversion' and his passions for this or that youth, he seems not to go on, like me, to Thebes but to take (with many a backward look) the high road to Delphi, and I am duly astonished and pleased that, as he read me, he was inspired – motivated – whatever verb – to return to his most youthful and enchanting work, *Felix Krull*.

Some of my short stories are almost as lighthearted as Thomas Mann in his last work. One of them, 'The Ladies in the Library', is an unconscious variation on *Death in Venice*. Three variations on a theme: Mann's Hans Castorp; then my own, Jim Willard; then a further lighter, more allegro version on Jim in the guise of a character whom Mann appropriately called Felix – Latin for 'happy'.

The Threepenny Review
Summer 1995

8

Anthony Burgess

Though in life Anthony Burgess was amiable, generous and far less self-loving than most writers, I have been disturbed, in the last few years, to read in the press that he did not think himself sufficiently admired by the literary world. It is true, of course, that he had the good fortune not to be hit, as it were, by the Swedes, but surely he was much admired and appreciated by the appreciated and admired.

In my lifetime he was one of the three 'best' novelists to come out of England (all right, the other two are the Swedised Golding, and Iris Murdoch) but he was unlike the whole lot in the sense that one never knew what he would do next. He resisted category.

To me this is a great virtue, and a tiny source of income for him because he was the only writer of my time whose new book I always bought and always read. On or off form, there was always something that he had come up with that I did not know – or even dream of – while his Enderby series are even finer comedies than those by the so much admired E. Waugh.

I was both moved and alarmed that one of his own last reviews in the *Observer* was of my collected essays in which appeared a long piece on his first volume of memoirs: I recalled him personally, with fondness; reported on his life and work; remarked, of the memoir, that he had no sense of humour.

In his review of me he quotes this, remarking that, once, he did have a sense of humour. I almost wrote him to say that I was referring only to the autobiography. Now I know that he had known for some time that he was dying of cancer, no rollicking business.

I cannot think what English book reviewing will do without him. He actually read what he wrote about, and he was always interesting on what he read. He did not suffer from the English disease of envy that tends to make so much English reviewing injurious to the health of literature.

When I first met him in 1964, he was about to be famous for *A Clockwork Orange*. He was, however, truly notorious because he had reviewed, pseudonymously, several of his own books in a provincial newspaper. 'At least,' I said at the time, 'he is the first novelist in England to know that a reviewer has actually read the book under review.'

Shakespeare, Joyce, Roman Empire (of the imagination), Malaysia; the constipated Enderby, whose fine poems were often included in the prose text. He ranged throughout language, a devoted philologist, and throughout music as a composer.

Once his first wife snarled – when it became clear that I was eight years younger than he – that I ought not to have got some Book Club selection when he had written so much more than I. Neither of us quite sober, we began to compare units of production. When it became clear that I was ahead, he said with quiet pomp, 'I am really a composer.' I was left without a single choral work, much less a fanfare, to put in the scales.

At one point when we were both living in Rome, whenever I would be offered a twelve-part television mini-series on the Medici or the Huns, I'd say, 'Get poor Burgess', and so they did. When I made the mistake of using the phrase 'poor Burgess' in an interview, he wrote, 'I can't say that I liked that "poor Burgess" bit. Happily, I left Gore out of the Encyclopedia Britannica on the contemporary novel.' In due course, he transcended Italian television and did, for the RSC, the finest version I have ever seen of

Cyrano de Bergerac. Many parts, not so poor Burgess.

I ended my review of Anthony's autobiography – much of it about how he lost faith in God – by making a play on the title *Little Wilson* (Burgess's real name) *and Big God*. I suggested that the book might better have been called *Little Wilson and Big Burgess*, 'who did it his, if not His, way'.

I saw him a year or two ago. We were being jointly interviewed by BBC Radio. 'Odd,' he said, 'I keep looking at my watch. It's like a tic. I wonder why?' For once, I made no answer.

The Observer
28 November 1993

9
Pride

Is pride a sin at all? The Oxford English Dictionary strikes a primly English note: 'A high or overweening opinion of one's own qualities, attainments or estate', or too clever by half, the ultimate put-down in those bright arid islands where ignorance must be lightly worn.

Apparently, the Romans and the Greeks had other, by no means pejorative, words for it. The quintessential Greek, Odysseus, revelled in being too clever by any number of halves. Of course, neither Greeks nor Romans had a word for sin, a Judaeo-Christian concept that the Germans did have a word for, *Sünde*, which Old English took aboard. Obviously, in any time and place an overweening person is tiresome, but surely laughter is the best tonic for restoring him to our common weeniness. He hardly needs to be prayed for or punished as a sinner. Yet pride is listed as the first of the seven deadly sins, and only recently – by accident, not design – did I figure out why.

Over the years I have taken some . . . well, pride in never reading my own work, or appearing with other writers on public occasions, or joining any organizations other than labour unions. In 1976, when I was elected to the National Institute of Arts and

Letters, I promptly declined this high estate on the ground that I was already a member of the Diners' Club. John Cheever was furious with me: 'Couldn't you have at least said Carte Blanche? Diners' Club is so tacky.' A couple of months ago I declined election to the Society of American Historians – politely, I hope.

James Joyce's 'silence, exile, and cunning' is the ultimate in artist's pride. But for someone politically inclined, that was not possible; even so, one could still play a lone hand, as a writer if not as an engaged citizen. Recently, Norman Mailer asked me if I would join him and two other writers in a reading of George Bernard Shaw's *Don Juan in Hell*. The proceeds would go to the Actors Studio. I would play the Devil, who has most of the good lines.

So, out of Charity – Vanity? – I set to one side my proud rule and shared a stage with three writers and the fading ghost of a very great one; fading because Shaw can appeal only to those who think that human society can be made better by human intelligence and will. I am of Shaw's party; the Devil's, too, I found, as I began to immerse myself in the part.

In a very long speech, the Devil makes an attractive case for himself; he also explains the bad press that he has got from the celestial hordes and their earthly admirers. The Devil believes that the false view of him in England is the result of an Italian and an Englishman. The Italian, of course, is Dante, and the Englishman is John Milton. Somewhat gratuitously, Shaw's Devil remarks that like everyone else he has never managed to get all the way through *Paradise Lost* and *Paradise Regained*. Although I had my problems with the second, the first is *the* masterpiece of our language, and Lucifer, the Son of Morning, blazes most attractively while God seems more arbitrary and self-regarding than ever, eager in His solipsistic pride to hear only praise from the angelic choirs, as well as from Adam and Eve, two mud pies He liked to play with.

It is Milton's conceit that proud Lucifer, a bored angel, tempts Adam and Eve with the only thing a totalitarian ruler must always keep from his slaves, knowledge. Rather surprisingly, the First Couple choose knowledge – well, she chooses it; they lose Eden; go forth to breed and die while Lucifer and his party, expelled from heaven, fall and fall and fall through Chaos and Old Night until they reach rock bottom, hell:

Here we may reign secure, and in my choice
To reign is worth ambition though in hell:
Better to reign in hell than serve in heav'n.

I first heard those words in 1941, spoken by Edward G. Robinson in the film of Jack London's *Sea Wolf*. It was like an electric shock. The great alternative. I can do no other. Bright world elsewhere. To reign and not to serve. To say, No. This was my introduction to Milton and to Lucifer's pride.

I was brought up in a freethinking Southern family where pride of clan could lead to all sorts of folly as well as to exemplary self-sacrifice.

My great-grandfather sat for a whole day on the steps of the courthouse at Walthall, Miss., debating whether to go fight with the rest of the clan in a civil war that he knew could not be won, and for a cause that he despised. Pride required him to fight with his clan; he fell at Shiloh.

Fifty years later in the Senate, his son defied the leader of his party, President Woodrow Wilson, on the issue of whether or not the United States should fight in World War I. The Chamber of Commerce of Oklahoma City sent him a telegram saying that if he did not support the war, he would be an ex-senator. He sent them a telegram: 'How many of your membership are of draft age?' He fell from office, as they had promised.

There is a whiff of sulphur here, perhaps; but there is also the sense that one is the final judge of what must be done despite the seductive temptations and stern edicts of the gods. In the absence of a totalitarian sky-god or earthly ruler, there is the always troubling dictatorship of the American majority, which Tocqueville saw as the dark side to our 'democracy'.

Very much in the family tradition, in 1948, I ran counter to the majority's loony superstitions about sex and fell quite far indeed. (This newspaper's regular daily critic not only did not review the offending novel, *The City and the Pillar*, but told my publisher that he would never again read, much less review, a book of mine: six subsequent books were not reviewed in the daily paper.) But pride required that I bear witness, like it or not, and if the superstitious masses – or great Zeus himself – disapproved, I would go even deeper into rebellion, and fall farther. Understandably, for the cowed majority, pride is the most unnerving 'sin' because pride scorns them quite as much as Lucifer did God.

Significantly, a story that keeps cropping up from culture to culture is that of the man who steals fire from heaven to benefit the human race. After Prometheus stole the fire for us, he ended up chained to a rock, an eagle gnawing eternally at his liver. Zeus' revenge was terrible, but the Prometheus of Aeschylus does not bend; in fact, he curses Zeus and predicts: 'Let him act, let him reign his little while as he will; for he shall not long rule over the gods.'

So let us celebrate pride when it defies those dominations and powers that enslave us. In my own case, for a quarter-century I have refused to read, much less write for, this newspaper, but, as Prometheus also somewhat cryptically observes, 'Time, growing ever older, teaches all things.' Or, as Dr Johnson notes, reflecting Matthew's Gospel, 'Pride must have a fall'; thus proving it was the real thing and not merely the mock.

The New York Times
4 July 1993

Part II

1

George

I grew up in Washington DC. Did I – or anyone so situated – give much thought to the man for whom our city was named? Hardly. The Washington monument, even for me at the age of ten, was of world-class boredom. Mount Vernon on the Potomac was interesting – particularly George's clothes, lovingly displayed. He was a giant, with large hands, feet and a huge rump; also a formidable poitrine due to some sort of syndrome which rendered him Amazonian in appearance and childless – mule-like – for life. But he was a man of great dignity and strength and once when he ordered two soldiers to stop a fight and they went right on, he picked each up by the scruff of the neck and banged the two heads together. Very satisfying. Plainly a dominatrix of the old-fashioned sort.

A condition of my admission to St Albans, a local school, was that I read a biography of Washington. I, who could, even then, read almost anything, was desolate. George Washington. The syllables of that name had the same effect on me that Gerald Ford now does. But I finally got through what was a standard hagiography of the sort that every nation inflicts upon its young in order to make them so patriotic that they will go fight in wars not of their choosing while paying taxes for the privilege. Pre-Watergate, to get people to do such things it used to be necessary to convince the innocent that only good and wise men (no women then) governed us, plaster-of-Paris demi-gods given to booming out, at intervals, awful one-liners like: 'Give me liberty or give me death.' Thus, were we given the liberty to pay our taxes though it might have been nice to have had the freedom to use for the public good some of the money taken from us.

A long time has passed since my school days and my first encounter with George. Currently, incomes are down. Taxes are up. Empire has worn us out and left the people at large broke. In the process, we ceased to have a representative government. In 1996, 51 per cent of those qualified to vote chose not to vote for president. President Clinton was re-elected by 49 per cent of the voters, a minus mandate to put it mildly. And so, George, where are you now when we need you? To which the answer is, which George do you have in mind? Bush or. . . .

The real George Washington, to the extent that we can reconstruct him, was born in 1732 and died in 1799, younger at death than the crotchety Bob Dole was in the late election. When George was eleven, his father died and he was brought up by his half-brother, Lawrence, who had married into the Fairfax family, one of the richest in Virginia. It was Lawrence who owned that fine estate on the Potomac river, Mount Vernon. As George was not much of one for books and school, he became a surveyor at fifteen; he was also land-mad and so, while surveying vast properties, he started investing every penny he could get his hands on in land. Some of it, crucially, along the Ohio river. Meanwhile, the Grim Reaper was looking out for George. Lawrence and his daughter both died when George was twenty, making him the master of Mount Vernon. Now very rich – but never rich enough – he took up soldiering. The colonial governor of Virginia sent him to the Ohio Valley (near today's Pittsburgh) with orders to drive the French from 'American' territory. And so, in 1754, the first of George's numerous military defeats was inflicted upon him by the French. With characteristic Gallic panache, they sent him back home where he was promptly promoted to colonel. But then anyone destined to have his likeness carved on a mountainside can only fall upward. In 1758, George was elected to the Virginia legislature, the House of Burgesses; the next year he married a very rich widow, Martha Dandridge Custis. George was now, reputedly, the first American millionaire.

George and Revolution. As George looked like a general – the unpleasantness near Pittsburgh was overlooked – the second Continental Congress, in a compromise between Massachusetts and Virginia, chose him to be commander-in-chief of the new Continental army whose task it was to free the thirteen American colonies from England. 'No taxation without representation' was the war cry of the rebelling colonists just as it is of the Reverend Jesse Jackson and close to a million disenfranchised blacks in George's city today.

A far less accomplished general than Ethan Allen or Benedict Arnold, George did know how to use *them* well. In 1775, although Boston and New York were in British hands, George sent an army north to conquer Canada – Canada has always been very much on the minds of those Americans inclined to symmetry. When the White House and Capitol were put to the torch in 1814 and President Madison fled into the neighbouring woods, where was the American army? Invading Canada yet again. The dream. The impossible dream.

George moved south to New York where he managed to lose both Long Island and Manhattan to the British who remained comfortably in residence until the French fleet came to George's aid in October 1781 and the British, now bored, bad-tempered, and broke, gave up the colonies. In a moving ceremony, George took over New York City and, as the British flag came down and our flag went up, there was not a dry eye to be seen, particularly when the American soldier, shimmying up the flag-pole to hoist New Glory, suddenly fell with a crash at George's feet. The treacherous Brits had greased the pole.

George went home. He was a world figure. The loose confederation of independent states was now beacon to the world. George farmed. He also invented a plough so heavy that no ox could pull it; he was grimly competing with crafty fellow-farmer Jefferson who had invented the dumb-waiter. Never an idle moment for the Founding Dads. Then Something Happened.

Captain Daniel Shays of Massachusetts, a brave officer in the Revolution, had fallen on hard times. Indeed most of the veterans of the war were suffering from too little income and too many taxes. They had been better off before independence, they declared, and so Shays and his neighbours, in effect, declared war on Massachusetts in 1786 when Shays and several hundred armed veterans marched on the state arsenal at Springfield. Although this impromptu army was soon defeated, Shays' Rebellion scared George to death. He sent agonized letters to various magnates in different states. To Harry Lee: 'You talk . . . of employing influence to appease the present tumults in Massachusetts. I know not where that influence is to be found, or if attainable, that it would be a proper remedy for the disorders. *Influence* is no *government*. Let us have one by which our lives, liberties and properties will be secured, or let us know the worst at once.' There it is. The principle upon which the actual American republic was founded, erasing in the process Thomas Jefferson's astonishing and radical proposal that, along with life and liberty, the citizen has the right to pursue happiness and even – with rare luck – overtake it. George was too hard-headed for that sort of sentimentality. George knew that property must always come first and so, in due course, he got the republic that he wanted, a stern contraption set in place to insure the safety and property of the prosperous few.

After two terms as president (with Alexander Hamilton acting as prime minister), George went home to Mount Vernon in 1796, mission accomplished. Although Madison and Mason (with Jefferson back of them) came up with the mitigating Bill of Rights, that Bill has never won many American hearts. After the Civil War the Fourteenth Amendment made it clear that the rights for United Statespersons also applied to each citizen as a resident within his home State. The Supreme Court, always Georgian save for the Earl Warren lapse in the Sixties, promptly interpreted those rights as essentially applicable to corporations. And so, in death, George won again.

The man? George was dignity personified. The impish Gouverneur Morris was bet ten dollars that he wouldn't dare go up to Washington at one of Lady (they called her that) Washington's levees and put his hand on George's shoulder. Morris did; collected his bet; then said, 'I don't think that I shall do this a second time.' In his last address as President, George warned against foreign adventures and also *permanent* alliances with foreign nations while, as rarely as possible, trusting to *'temporary* alliances for extraordinary emergencies'. In his worst nightmares, George could never have dreamed of just how many 'extraordinary emergencies' his forty-odd successors would be able to cook up.

George and posterity? He is ever-present in our decaying institutions. Iconography? The movies have generally ignored him while his biographies tend to be dull because the biographers are too busy defending his principles while pretending that we live – or are supposed to live – in a democracy, an absolute non-starter from the beginning.

George today? A year or two ago a wealthy friend (so rich that he never handles actual cash) picked up a dollar bill that someone had left on a table and said, with wonder, 'When did George Bush put Barbara's picture on the money?' Barbara Bush and George are lookalikes. In the end, as it was at the beginning, it *is* all about money as George knew from the start.

2

FDR: Love on the Hudson

For nearly twenty years I lived at Barrytown on the east bank of the Hudson, upriver from the villages of Hyde Park, Rhinebeck, and Rhinecliff. Technically, I was a River person, since I lived in a River house built in 1820 for a Livingston daughter; actually, I was an outsider from nowhere – my home city of Washington, DC, being as close to nowhere as any place could be, at least in the minds of the River people. *The* Mrs Astor, born Caroline Schermerhorn, boasted of having never been west of the Hudson – or was it her drawing room at Ferncliff which *looked* west upon the wide Hudson and the Catskill mountains beyond? The River road meandered from some spot near Poughkeepsie up to the old whaling port of Hudson. Much of it had been part of the original Albany Post Road, not much of a post road, they used to say, because it was easier to take mail and passengers by boat from New York City to Albany. Even in my day, the Hudson River was still a splendidly convenient boulevard.

The area entered our American history when the Dutch patroons, centred upon New Amsterdam, began to build neat stone houses north of their island city. Of the Dutch families, the grandest was called Beekman. Then, in war, the Dutch gave way to the English, some of whom were actually gentry though most were not. But the river proved to be a common leveller – or raiser up. The newcomers were headed by one Robert Livingston, who had received from James II the 'Livingston Manor' grant that included most of today's Dutchess and Columbia counties. Other wealthy families began to build great houses on the east bank of the river, making sure that their Greek Revival porticoes or mock Gothic towers would make a fine impression on those travelling up or down river. The Dutch co-existed phlegmatically with the new masters of what was no longer New Amsterdam but New York; they also intermarried with the new Anglo ascendancy.

By the middle of the last century, all in a row from Staatsburg north to the Livingston manor, Clermont, there were the houses of Roosevelts, Vanderbilts, Astors, Delanos, Millses (theirs was Mrs Wharton's House of Mirth), Chanlers, Aldriches, Montgomerys. The Dutch Roosevelts of Hyde Park were fifth cousins to President Theodore Roosevelt (of Long Island). They had also intermarried not only with the Beekmans but with the Delanos. In fact, for Franklin Delano Roosevelt, his Beekman heritage was a matter of great pride, rather like an Englishman with a connection to the Plantagenets, the one true legitimate, if fallen, dynasty. So it was with Franklin's cousin, Margaret (known as Daisy) Suckley; although a member of a good River family she, too, exulted in her Beekman blood and now in Geoffrey C. Ward's engrossing study, *Closest Companion*, of the two cousins and their . . . love affair? the joy that they take in their common Beekman heritage is absolute proof that although President Roosevelt wanted to inaugurate 'the age of the common man', it was quietly understood from the very beginning that a Beekman connection made one a good deal more common than any other man and, thus, democracy had been kept at bay.

I remember Daisy well. She was a small, pleasant-looking woman in her sixties, with a charming, rather secretive smile. She had a soft voice; spoke very little. Unmarried, she lived in her family house, Wilderstein, having sold off an adjacent River house,

Wildercliff, to the critic and Columbia professor F. W. Dupee. I would see her at the Dupees and at Mrs Tracy Dows's but only once at Eleanor Roosevelt's Hyde Park cottage (the ladies did not really get on); I knew that she was the President's cousin (Eleanor's too) and that she had been with Franklin the day he died in Georgia. One thought of her as a poor relation, a useful near-servant, no more. By and large, there was not much mingling of the River cousinage. As the Astor family chieftain, Vincent, put it, 'No Visititis on the Hudson.' Even though – or because – they were all related, most seemed to be on amiably bad terms with the rest. Only Daisy, wraith-like, moved from River house to River house, a benign presence. Now Ward has read her letters to Franklin as well as Franklin's letters to her, and Daisy has become suddenly very interesting as Ward, politely but firmly, leads us onto history's stage.

Did Daisy and Franklin have an affair? This is the vulgar question that Ward is obliged to entertain if not answer. But what he is able to demonstrate, through their letters and diaries, is the closest friendship of our complex mysterious President, who kept people in different compartments, often for life, never committing too much of his privacy to anyone, except his Beekman cousin and neighbour, quiet Daisy.

It is no secret that Ward has already written by far the best study* of Franklin Roosevelt that we are ever apt to get. Along with his scholarship and wit, the last rather rare in American biography, Ward shared with Roosevelt the same misfortune, polio – he, too, spent time at Warm Springs, Georgia, a spa that Roosevelt had founded for himself and others so struck. Polio was the central fact of Roosevelt's mature years. He could not walk and, towards the end, could no longer even fake a steel-braced upright step or two where useless leg muscles were compensated for by strong arms and whitened knuckles, as he clutched at the arm of a son or aide.

The first fact of Franklin's entire life was his adoring mother,

---

* *Before the Trumpet: Young Franklin Roosevelt, 1882–1905* (Harper and Row, 1985), and *A First-Class Temperament: The Emergence of Franklin Roosevelt* (Harper and Row, 1989).

Sara Delano Roosevelt, known to the River as Mrs James. She adored him, he adored her. He always lived in *her* house on the River where she was chatelaine, not his wife and cousin, Eleanor. By 1917, the Franklin Roosevelt marriage effectively ended when Eleanor discovered that he was having an affair with her social secretary, Lucy Mercer. Eleanor's ultimatum was swift; give up Lucy or Eleanor will not only divorce Franklin but allow Lucy the added joy of bringing up *his* five children. Since Franklin already had the presidency on his mind, he gave up Lucy while Eleanor, with relief, gave up their sexual life together. Gradually, husband and wife became like two law partners. He did strategy and major court-room argument; she went on circuit. I never detected the slightest affection – as opposed to admiration – for Franklin in the talks that I had with Mrs Roosevelt during the last years of her life. She had been profoundly shaken to find that Lucy was present that day at Warm Springs when he had his terminal stroke. Worse, she discovered that he had been seeing her for years, often with the connivance of Daisy. Eleanor at the graveside was more Medea than grieving widow.

A number of 'new' aspects of Franklin's character emerge from those previously unpublished letters and diaries, many not even known of until now. One is his almost desperate need for affection from a woman (or amiable company from a man like Harry Hopkins) and how little he got of either. Until his mother's death, he relied on her for comfort. When she was gone he was either alone and depressed in the White House or surrounded by people for whom, despite his failing strength, he had to be unrelievedly 'on' or, as he put it, 'Exhibit A'.

Most Rooseveltians are either Franklinites or Eleanorites. Since I never knew him, I saw him largely through my family's eyes – that is to say, as a sinister, rather treacherous, figure who manoeuvred us into war – while I got to know Eleanor as a neighbour and, later, as a political ally when I ran for Congress in the District. Now I begin to see how Eleanor must have looked to Daisy and, perhaps, to Franklin, too. The portrait is forbidding. She is forever on the move, on the firm's behalf, of course, but there are hints that she would rather be anywhere than at his side. Daisy is almost always careful to praise Eleanor's good works. But there are times when Daisy grows exasperated with a wife who is never there to look after an invalid husband who, by 1944, is visibly dying before their eyes. On February 8, 1944, Daisy notes in her diary: 'I said he should either take a rest or a short drive, every afternoon. He said he hated to drive alone. I said he should ask Mrs R. He laughed: "I would have to make an appointment a week ahead!"'

Eleanor also saw to it that Franklin would never have a decent meal in the White House:

> The P. [President] & all the men came back about 7.45; all enthusiastic about their supper. The P. told them at supper that in W. H. he never had such good beef stew, carrots, macaroni, home baked bread, butter, & coffee! Poor Mrs [Henrietta] Nesbitt, the W. H. housekeeper!

Ward comments:

> Mrs Nesbitt was a Hyde Park caterer whom Eleanor Roosevelt had hired to manage the White House kitchens. FDR disliked her and detested her pallid cooking, but was unable to get rid of her. She was evidently as imperious as she was inept; when the President sent her a memorandum detailing his dislike of broccoli, she ordered the chefs to serve it to him, anyway. 'It's good for him,' she said. 'He *should* like it.'

Daisy concedes, 'His wife is a wonderful person, but she lacks the ability to give him the things his mother gave him. She is away so much, and when she is here she has so many people around – the splendid people who are trying to do good and improve the world, "uplifters" the P. calls them – that he cannot relax and really rest.' But then, confronted with the disastrous news of his first thorough medical check-up in the spring of 1944 – enlarged heart, congestive heart failure, hypertension – Eleanor said that she was not 'interested in physiology'. Like Mary Baker Eddy, she felt such things were weaknesses of the mind.

The Beekman cousins began their close relationship when he invited her to his first inauguration as president. Daisy was enthralled and wrote her cousin; thus, the long correspondence began; later, they would travel together. Daisy was what used to be called, without opprobrium, a spinster. Of the two boys and four girls at Wilderstein only one girl was to marry. Their mother, still alive in the Thirties, loathed sex and, as Ward puts it, 'invariably wept at weddings at the thought of the awful things awaiting the bride.' Daisy showed no interest in marriage and, presumably, none in sex. By 1933 the Suckley fortunes were at a low ebb; the eldest brother had invested badly but then matters stabilized and she had her small income and could still live at home. In due course, she was put in charge of the Roosevelt Library at Hyde Park. She was intelligent but not clever; drawn to quack doctors, numerologists, astrologists; she also *knew* that the ghost of Abraham Lincoln was constantly aprowl in the White House.

Daisy's first 'date' with Franklin was in September 1934. He took her for a drive to Eleanor's get-away cottage, Val-Kill. There is rather a lot in her diaries of *little* me and the President *himself* at the wheel.

By November Franklin is writing, 'You added several years to my life & much to my happiness.' By early 1935, when the New Deal is in crisis with Huey Long, the Supreme Court, Dr Townsend, Franklin writes her, 'I need either to swear at somebody or to have a long suffering ear like yours to tell it to quietly!'

For the remaining ten years of Franklin's life, Daisy provided that ear. The letters to her have not all survived but hers to him are complete as well as her diary. She came to know many secrets. She was on hand when Churchill came to Hyde Park. Daisy was not quite temperance but Churchill's constant whisky drinking awed her. When they visited Franklin's blue-haired cousin, Laura Delano, something of a card, the Prime Minister asked for his usual whisky while the wilful Laura, a devotee of complex sugary drinks, gave him a daiquiri to drink. Not noticing what was in the glass, Churchill took a sip and then, to Laura's horror, spat it out at her feet. Even in my day, a decade later, Laura would look very stern at the mention of Churchill's name. Interestingly, for those clan-minded River families, so like the American South, Daisy was closer to Eleanor in blood than to Franklin – fourth cousin to her, sixth to him.

If anything 'happened', it would have begun during August 1933 when they took shelter from a storm on what they called Our Hill. The spinster and the sickly polio victim seem unlikely as lovers, though, a year earlier at Warm Springs, Elliot Roosevelt assured my father that the President was very active sexually, particularly with his secretary Missy LeHand. But that Franklin and Daisy were in love is in no doubt and that, of course, is the point. They were already discussing a cottage atop Our Hill for after the presidency, or even before, if possible. It should be noted that Missy Lehand's family thought that the house on Our Hill was to be for Missy and Franklin and I suspect that he might even have mentioned it as a getaway to his last love, Crown Princess Martha of Norway, who came to stay during the war, causing Missy to retire (and promptly die) and Daisy to note with benign malice, 'The Crown Princess hasn't much to say, but as the P. talks all the time anyway it didn't make much difference. It is strange, however, that a person in her position, & with so much natural charm, has no *manner*! Even in her own home . . . she leaves the guests to take care of themselves. . . .'

Daisy reads Beverly Nichols for hints on how to do up the house-to-be. Franklin thinks his own tastes are too simple for 'B. Nichols' (how thrilled that silly-billy would have been to know that he was read and reread by the Leader of the Free World). Meanwhile, history kept moving. Re-election in 1936. Again in 1940. The Allied armies are finally beginning to win, and the President's body is gradually shutting down. It is poignant to observe Daisy observing her friend in his decline. She tries to feed him minerals from one of her cranks. (Analysts found nothing harmful in them, and nothing beneficial either.) She puts a masseur on to him who tells him he'll soon be walking. So eager is Franklin for good news that he claims to have been able to move a little toe.

Daisy never forgets that she is River, not Village. But Franklin the politician must speak for Village, too. She applauds his efforts at educating the national Village folk 'because so many people in our class still object to more than the minimum of education for the mass of the people' as 'they lose the sense of subservience to – shall I say? – us.' It is plain that neither Beekman cousin ever had much direct experience with Villagers.

Daisy records a very odd conversation with the President's eldest son, James, on January 26, 1944 (the war is ending):

> At lunch, Jimmy talked about the young, uneducated boys who are learning that you kill or get killed, etc., etc., and may prove to be a real menace if, at the end of the war, they are suddenly given a bonus, and let loose on the country – He thinks they should be kept in the army, or in C.C.C. camps or something like that, until jobs are found for them, or unless they are put back to school – He says many are almost illiterate.

Fear of class war is never far from the River mind. Happily, Franklin was ready with the GI Bill of Rights which sent many Villagers to school, while his heir, Harry Truman, compassionately put the country on a permanent wartime footing, thus avoiding great unemployment. Curiously, River's fear of Village was to come true after Vietnam when the Village boys came home to find that they had been well and royally screwed by a Village, not a River, government. The rest is – today.

At the time of the 1944 election, the infamous fourth term (decried by many Roosevelt supporters), Franklin was dying. But he pulled himself together for one last hurrah; submitting to heavy make-up, he drove in the rain in triumph through Manhattan. He was now sleeping much of the day. Harry Hopkins, his closest man friend, was also dying and so, in effect, the war was running itself to conclusion. It was Daisy's view that Franklin wanted to stay in office long enough to set up some sort of League of Nations and then resign and go home to the River. Incidentally, in all the correspondence and diaries there is not one reference to Vice-President Truman.

Daisy's last entries are sad, and often sharp, particularly about Eleanor's abandonment of her husband. After some logistic confusion at the White House, she writes, 'Mrs R. should be here to attend to all this sort of thing. The P. shouldn't have to – and it has to be done.'

Apparently, Franklin was always prone to nightmares. (Like Lincoln in a similar context?) One night he called for help with 'blood curdling sounds'. He thought a man was coming 'through the transom', and was going to kill him. He asked to see a screening of *Wilson*, a fairly good film of obvious interest to Franklin as Woodrow Wilson's heir and fellow Caesar; by the picture's end, and Wilson's physical crack-up, the President's blood pressure was perilously high; and there were no beta blockers then.

The Yalta meeting wore him out and both Churchill and Stalin noted that their colleague was not long for this world. But he knew what he was doing at the meeting. Eleanor told me that when he got home – they met briefly before he went to Warm Springs – she chided him for making no fuss over leaving Latvia, Lithuania and Estonia in Russia's hands. The *Realpolitik* member of the firm told her that Stalin would not give them up without a war. 'Do you think the American people, after all they've gone through, would fight for those small countries?' Eleanor sighed, 'I had to agree that he was right again.'

The deviousness of Franklin, the politician, was a necessity, increased no doubt by whatever psychic effect his immobility had on him. One of the reasons he tossed his head this way and that was not only for emphasis but to command attention – after all, he could never get up and walk out of a room – and his constant chattering was also a means to disguise what he was up to while holding everyone's attention. Of the two, Eleanor was more apt to be brutal. It was a disagreeable surprise to me, an Eleanorite, to read:

> Mrs R. brought up the subject of the American fliers who came down in Arabia, & were mutilated & left to die in the desert. She insisted that we should bomb all Arabia, to stop such things. The P. said it was an impossible thing to do, in the first place, as the tribes are nomadic, & hide in secret places etc. Also, Arabia is a huge desert etc. Besides, it would be acting like the Japanese, to go & bomb a lot of people, who don't know any better. . . . I put in one word, to the effect that we have lynching in this country still, but we don't go & bomb the town where the lynching occurs – Harry Hopkins joined Mrs R. – but their point seemed to me so completely illogical that I restrained myself, & kept silent!

One is struck by what such awesome power does to people and how it is the 'compassionate' Eleanor who wants to kill at random and the Artful Dodger President who does not.

Finally, Franklin's obsessive stamp collecting pays off. He knows his geography. Unlike subsequent presidents, he knows where all the countries are and who lives in them. He is also aware that the war with Japan is essentially a race war. Who will dominate the Pacific and Asia, the white or the yellow race? As of June 1944, race hatred was the fuel to our war against Japan, as I witnessed first-hand in the Pacific. Yet Franklin, Daisy reports, is already looking ahead:

> In regard to the Far East in general which means the yellow race, which is far more numerous than the white, it will be to the advantage of the white race to be friends with them & work in cooperation with them, rather than make enemies of them & have them eventually use all the machines of western civilization to overrun & conquer the white race.

Today, such a statement would be denounced as racist if not, indeed, an invocation of the Yellow Peril.

Last speech to Congress to report on Yalta. I saw the newsreel at an army hospital in Alaska. The President spoke, seated; apologized for not standing but he said the weight of his metal braces was now too much. Never before had he publicly referred to his paralysis. The voice was thick, somewhat slurred. It was plain that he had had a stroke of some sort. Then Franklin and Daisy were off to Warm Springs where they were joined by Lucy Mercer Rutherfurd and a painter friend. Laura Delano was also on hand. The River was rallying around him. Then, while being painted, he slumped and said, 'I have a terrific pain in the back of my head.' As he was carried into the bedroom, Laura alone heard him say, 'Be careful.' After fire, he most feared being dropped. Eleanor came and history resumed its course, and Mr Truman does get a mention, when he is sworn in as president.

Toward the end Daisy was always there – closest companion – to feed him and watch him as he dozed off, to talk of the River and, doubtless, of Our Hill, though it had been plain for some time that he would never live there. I should note she signed her letters to him 'M' for Margaret, her real name, or simply 'YM', 'Your Margaret'. He signed his letters 'F.' All in all, an unexpectedly sweet story in a terrible time, when, along with wars and depressions and dust bowls, Villages became cities and the River polluted and one Beekman cousin petrified into history while the other, Daisy, simply faded, smiling, away. Ward has made FDR's story something no one else has managed to do, poignant, sad.

The New York Review of Books
11 May 1995

3

Truman

An English paper asked a number of writers to meditate, briefly, on their heroes or villains. My villain, I wrote, is a perfectly nice little man called Harry S. (for nothing) Truman. A worthy senator, he had been casually chosen by our Augustus, Franklin D. Roosevelt, to be vice-president in 1944. Some months later, Augustus joined his imperial ancestors Jefferson, Polk, Lincoln, and cousin Theodore in Valhalla (just above Mount Rushmore). Truman was now master of the earth, a strange experience for a failed farmer, haberdasher, and machine politician from Missouri.

Roosevelt, the late conqueror, had not bothered to tell his heir that we were developing an atomic bomb or what agreements he had made about the post-war world with the barbarian chieftain and ally, Stalin. Truman had to play it by ear. The whole world was now his: what to do with it?

Lately, as the American empire bumps to an end – too many debts, insufficient military enemies – Truman and the empire are being mythologized at an astonishing rate. A recent biography of Truman emphasized his grit, and his miraculous re-election against terrible odds.

At no point in the hagiographies of Truman does anyone mention what he actually did to the United States and the world. First, he created the National Security State. He institutionalized the Cold War. He placed us on a permanent wartime footing. He started that vast haemorrhage of debt which now is more than $4 trillion and growing by $1 billion each day. Why did he do this? First, the good reason. When the Japanese, much provoked by us, attacked, we had not got out of the Depression that followed the crash of 1929. The Roosevelt New Deal of the Thirties had been palliative, but not a solution. There was still great unemployment and the spectre of violent social change. War gave us full employment. War removed our commercial rivals and put an end to the colonial empires of our allies, empires we quietly took over in the name of 'self-determination', democracy and Grandma Moses, an icon of the day.

Truman and his advisers from both political parties decided that they would, in effect, declare war on a vile religion known as Communism and its homeland, the Soviet Union. The demonization of the Soviet Union started in 1947, when they were no threat to the American empire and its clients. They were indeed unpleasant masters to their own people and to those buffer states that we allowed them to keep after the War. We thought they were unduly paranoid about being invaded, but a nation that has been three times invaded from the West might be forgiven a bit of nervousness.

Although the United States has not been invaded since the British burned down Washington, DC in 1814, Truman and company deliberately created a siege mentality. The Russians were coming, they proclaimed. To protect us, the National Security Act was passed in 1947. Thus, government was able to regiment the American people, keep the allies on a tight leash, and lock the Russians up in their northern cage. In 1950 the American republic was quietly retired and its place taken by the National Security State, set up secretly and outlined in a document not to be made public for 25 years, the National Security Council Memorandum 68. War and Navy Departments were combined into a single 'Defense' department while the CIA, an unconstitutional secret police, was invented. The NSC-68 established the imperial blueprint that governed the world until the recent crack-up of the Soviet Union, which happened *not* as a result of our tactics of ongoing wars, and an arms race that they could not afford, but was due to the internal fragility of an artificial state which was, in a sense, a crude mirror of our own, now falling apart, as well, through debt and internal ethnic wars.

Truman's blueprint made seven points. First, we were never to negotiate with the Soviet Union in any honest way. Two, we were to develop the hydrogen bomb. Three, build up conventional forces and reinstate the draft. Four, increase taxes to pay for this – in 1954 I earned $100,000 and paid $90,000 to the peace-time government of the US. This is the only thing that Ronald Reagan, equally hit in the same town, Hollywood, and I ever had in common. Five, mobilize through the media all Americans to fight Communism – Truman instituted 'loyalty oaths', a nice totalitarian gimmick that Joseph McCarthy would have a lot of fun with. Six, control the Allies with Nato, hence our military presence to this day in Europe. Seven, propagandize the Russians through misinformation, and so on. Since 1950 the US has been compulsively at war (hot) in Korea and Vietnam and Iraq; (tepid) Panama, Nicaragua, El Salvador, Guatemala; and (cold) Iran, Angola, Chile, Grenada. Also, the interference through our secret police in European elections, starting with April 1, 1948 when the CIA ensured the election of the Christian Democrats in Italy, through the harassment of Harold Wilson's Labour government in the Sixties, to various crimes in every continent. . . .

I shall stop here. Deliberately, the thirty-third president of the United States set in train an imperial expansion that has cost the lives of many millions of people all over the world. Now we are relatively poor, unloved, and isolated, with a sullen polity ready for internal adventures. Thanks a lot, Harry.

The Independent Magazine
3 October 1992

4
Goin' South: Clinton–Gore I

As I write these lines, nothing less than earthly intervention (by Perot?) can prevent the Clinton–Gore team from assuming, as the Chinese say, the mandate of Heaven come November.

They are, at first glance, Huckleberry Finn and Tom Sawyer, and the sight of them in shorts, like a pair of ducks waddling down rustic lanes, reminds us that they are not natural athletes, like the ancient, long-limbed Bush. Also, attractive Huck seems to have Tom's conniving character, while Tom seems to have no specific character at all. But at least we will be rid of Ichabod Crane (Bush) and his little pal Penrod (Quayle) who can now go home to Indiana.

In many ways, this has been the most interesting election of my lifetime because, unexpectedly, the people at large have become aware that the political system functions no better than the economic one, and they are beginning to suspect, for the first time, that the two are the same. When this awful connection is made, we will be seeing many more Perots and Dukes and worse, if possible, crawling out from under the flat rocks of the republic as the tremors grow more violent.

Since what is wrong with us is no longer cyclic but systemic, I suspect that more than half the electorate won't vote in November [it was four years later that they didn't vote] even though, paradoxically, they are more than ever worried about the economy. Yet they are bitterly aware that if there are solutions, no candidate has mentioned even one. Certainly the record and rhetoric of such a highly conventional, professional team as Clinton–Gore do not suggest that there will be a new dawn. Worse, the potential Clinton Cabinet, as guessed at by the press, lacks all vitality, much less new ideas. [It proved to be a gorgeous ethnic–sexual mix or mess, a sinking Noah's Ark of correctness.]

Even so, for the next hundred or so days after the election, we shall be reading in the press about the vigorous new team in Washington. Hopeful notes will be struck. The Sunday electronic zoo will honk and twitter over who is the *real* number three at State; meanwhile, a tax bill will be sent to Congress. Slightly higher taxes will be requested for the rich (Congress will say no: too little too late, if not too much too early). There will be no increase in the tax rate on corporate profits because, for all practical purposes, corporations are tax-exempt. In 1950, 38 per cent of federal revenues came from a tax on corporate profits. Today, corporations provide only 10 per cent. Corporations will not be taxed because they don't want to be taxed, and so they are not taxed, thanks to the Congresses and presidents that their political contributions have bought. After all, 90,000 lawyers and lobbyists are in place in Washington, DC, not only to exempt their corporate employers from taxation but also to make sure that they can 'legally' avoid those frivolous federal regulations that might require them, let us say, to cease poisoning their customers. Meanwhile, the Vice-President is the head of something called the President's Council on Competitiveness, which sees to it that any corporation can evade any disagreeable governmental regulation or standard in the interest of 'competitiveness'.

The new president will be applauded when he attacks waste at the Pentagon. Everyone is praised for attacking waste. But no one ever does anything about it because no one ever can. Although there have been no declared wars since 1945 (except those of our own invention), the United States has a total war economy, and we shall go right on building aircraft carriers and Seawolf submarines until all the money's gone. Over the years, the Pentagon has seen to it that there is a significant 'defence' planet in each congressional district; that is why most congressmen will always say no to cutbacks because of the Effect on the Economy.

In any case, Clinton–Gore, as southern conservatives, are wedded from birth to the military. Partly this is due to the hawkish nature of the southern states. During Reconstruction, politics and the army were about the only careers open to the ambitious southerner. Even for the unambitious, military service was often the only way out of poverty. The fact that southerners traditionally keep their congressional representatives in office longer than other regions means that they end up with those committee chairmanships that deal with the military, and so the South's great source of revenue has always come from 'defence'. Since expenditure on war is what got us into our present mess, one would think that the military budget – and its ominous twin, the interest that we must pay on $4 trillion of debt – should have been the centrepiece of the campaign.

But Clinton–Gore never got close to the subject, and they will not address it in office. Bush himself wisely kept the campaign focused on the sacredness of the foetus, hard to upstage in a country where, according to the good Dr Gallup, 47 per cent think that God created Man one afternoon out of some convenient mud, while 40 per cent think that God may have taken a bit longer to put the finishing touch on what, after all, is His self-portrait. Only 9 per cent believe in Darwinian evolution and science. So with folks like that out there, perhaps it is better to talk about abortion and adultery and who spells Jennifer with a *G* and who spells it with a *J*, and what can this *mean*?

It is far too late for the United States, in any foreseeable future, to remain in the same economic league as Western Europe and Japan.* But we have one great opportunity, which only crafty Dick Nixon ever truly grasped – Russia. Although we don't have much money left to give them, a lively president and a few corporate magnates with no more than average IQs could start making deals to develop Russian oil and other resources. This would generate the money for the Russians to buy our consumer goods, which, in turn, would make us prosperous again. Naturally, this will require intelligence and planning, two things our corporate governing class has not been capable of since 1945. But the opportunity is superb. Until two years ago, it looked as if West Germany had landed the Russian account, but then their union with East Germany threw them off course. That leaves us and Canada as Russia's friendly industrialized neighbours in the Northern Hemisphere. H. L. Mencken noted many years ago that the 'Russians were like the Americans. They, too, were naturally religious and confiding; they, too, were below the civilized average in intelligence; and they, too, believed in democracy, and were trying to give it a trial.' The time has come for an economic union.

Our allies are deeply disturbed by the intensity of the sick religiosity that the United States is currently experiencing (due more to television preachers than to the Good Book). Obviously, a people who cannot deal with the natural sciences is not going to do very well in the twenty-first century, when religion will play hardly any part, at least in Western Europe and Asia, our competition.

Of course, it's not considered nice to criticize someone else's religion; yet this particular election has been based almost entirely on religion, and it is now clear just how our single-party system (with two right wings, one called Democratic, one called Republican) will end. The country is now splitting into the Party of God, whose standard-bearer the godless Bush so ironically tried to be, and the Party of Man, which represents, in theory, observance of religion-free laws and a limitation of the state's control of the private lives of the citizenry. In the primaries, only Jerry Brown

* Helmut Kohl's effort to build a Fourth Reich on a European German-based currency has been a temporary boost to the US dollar while the Japanese now regroup, in the shadow of China Redux – whatever the next centres, the US will not be central.

grasped the necessity of a party of the people at large, while only Pat Buchanan grasped the true potency of God's Party.

Although Clinton–Gore are essentially Party of God politicians, they moderated their views and did not too piously defend the sacred foetus on the sensible ground that most women, even Godly ones, resent God's ministers' regulating their gynaecologic works. After all, the reproductive system that God devised for both men and women is ridiculous enough as it is – certainly, any competent plumber could have done a better job; yet to pretend that the Great Baron Frankenstein in the Sky's sexual handiwork is evil (as in original sin) is truly evil; and that is where the present conflict between the two evolving parties is taking place, and the ultimate confrontation, as ol' Ross Perot would say, ain't gonna be pretty.

Meanwhile, we have numerous elections but no politics. Each candidate must hustle corporate money and then put together as many groups as he can to win. After all, once elected, he does not have to serve any voters, on the ground that if he pleases one group he'll alienate another, so why rock the boat? But he does have to serve Lockheed or Boeing or Exxon or the American Israel Public Affairs Committee and all the other corporations or lobbies that pay for him.

The office of vice-president is now the preserve of the Israeli lobby, and Gore will continue the Quayle tradition. After all, in the 1988 presidential primaries, Gore's campaign was largely paid for by the lobby, whose point man was the ineffable *New Republic* publisher, Marty Peretz (who boasted in *Spy* magazine that he'd written 'Al's' speech at the Democratic Convention). The alliance between a Pentagon-oriented southern politician (Gore has never voted against any appropriation for war) and the Israeli lobby was a not-unnatural one in the days of the Cold War. But no longer. Imagine if a Roman Catholic lobby were in place to siphon off billions of federal dollars to bail out the truly broke Vatican, while covertly supporting the terrorism of, let us say, the Irish Republican Army. I don't think the Godly (non-Catholic) would like this, while the Manly would be in court. Once selected by Clinton, Gore made his first speech to AIPAC, where he grovelled without shame. He was there to get money for services rendered; and on offer. Happily, the new Israeli prime minister, Rabin, has just given the American Israeli lobby hell on the ground that their crude buying of senators in order to pit the legislative against the executive branch might start a backlash among even the densest goyim. Henceforth, the Israeli command post will be not the Senate but the vice-president's office.

What to do? The logical and intelligent solution would be to go back to Philadelphia and make a new Constitution with a stronger Bill of Rights, a weaker executive, a disciplined Supreme Court (the original court mucked about with admiralty suits rather than trimesters, and they were much, much happier in their modest work). A parliamentary system might be more workable than our current – that word again – gridlock. Yes, I am quite aware that no ruling class has ever abolished or even reformed itself, so there is not much chance for us to invoke the great powers invested in We the People, who are ultimately sovereign, if we could ever again meet in Congress assembled and make a new charter. But if the times get too bad and a dictator does not take over, I suggest exercising the Philadelphia Option, not only in memory of Benjamin Franklin but of W. C. Fields, Philadelphia's other great son, whose screen performance as Mr Micawber in *David Copperfield* was a prescient impersonation of Uncle Sam today.

In a sense, the great cancer of our system, the defence budget, will go into remission when the Japanese and the Germans are no longer buying our Treasury notes. But what then? Here, Clinton is making a bit of sense. Public works of the Rooseveltian sort could stave off revolution, which was exactly what the United States was facing in 1933, as I observed firsthand. Then came the New Deal. People got jobs. Roads. Conservation. Dams. When Roosevelt was told that he might well be the most popular president in American history, he said, 'If I'm not, I will be the last.'

For the present, in the pursuit of the Numero Uno job, Clinton has worked himself into a number of contradictory binds. But then so did Roosevelt who promised, in Philadelphia (again), that if elected president he would balance the budget. In 1936, up for re-election and on his way back to Philadelphia, he turned to Sam Rosenman, his speech-writer, and said, 'Well, what do I say now about the deficit?' Rosenman was serene: 'Deny you were ever in Philadelphia.'

Although no public jobs can be created and no bridges repaired as long as all that money goes for unworkable Rube Goldberg Star Wars systems, not to mention cost overruns and plain corruption, Clinton will have to overcome his natural southern affinity for all things military. Conversion is the name of the only game we have left. Conversion from war to peace. Instead of Seawolf submarines, he must build bullet trains (my advice to Jerry Brown, who dramatized it on television and won the Connecticut primary). The same workforce that now builds submarines has the same technology to build trains. This would not reduce the deficit, but then nothing ever will.

Clinton has a chance to take a deep breath and start building and repairing the country. If this is done rapidly and intensely – the way Roosevelt did in the Thirties, with fair success; and in the Second War, with great success – then we shall start generating that famous cash base Perot keeps nattering on about.

In any event, the only alternative to such a programme is social chaos. Clinton's greatest asset is a perfect lack of principle. With a bit of luck, he will be capable, out of simple starry-eyed opportunism, to postpone our collapse. After all, Franklin Delano Roosevelt was equally unprincipled. On the other hand, he had the aristocrat's self-confidence, and he was a master of manipulation. Clinton's nervous eagerness to serve his numerous betters is not reassuring because, as he tries to manipulate them, they often, cold-bloodedly, manipulate him. But as Huck Finn with Tom's cunning, he may get himself – and us – through. Like Roosevelt, Clinton has a lot of energy, and an eye on the main chance: If he has only a bit of FDR's luck, we may ride out the storm. But 'fasten your seat belts', as Bette Davis so memorably warned. It is going to take real slickness to get us past the deadly reef of true faith up ahead, so dangerously set in that sea of debt created by the few who could not resist ripping off the many in the name of Freedom,

Democracy and a Supreme Being as personally revealed to good Dr Gallup. We must wish Clinton luck. After all, if he fails, *he* will be the last president.

GQ
November 1992

5
Bedfellows Make Strange Politics

All's fair. Presumably in love and war, not to mention in the American electoral process as it becomes more and more surreal. For those who laughed all the way through Bob Woodward's situation comedy *The Agenda*, *All's Fair* will give even greater delight. For one thing, this is a him-and-her comedy, worthy of early Hepburn and Tracy. *She* is Mary Matalin, a darkly handsome Croatian from Chicago, with a sense of humour. *He* is James Carville, a Louisiana Cajun, with a sense of humour. Picture Susan Sarandon and John Malkovich together for the first time.

No expense must be spared in this production, any more than any expense was spared in the great election of 1992 that pitted George Bush against Bill Clinton and then, for comic relief, added Pat Buchanan and Ross Perot, two choleric below-the-title character actors, good for cutaways when the stars needed a rest. Director? Preston Sturges, if alive, might have had too much gravitas. The Zucker brothers *et al.*, who gave us *Airplane!* and *Naked Gun*, are a bit too much on the nose. If I were the producer – now I'm just spitballing, this is early on – but I'd like to turn *All's Fair* over to Oliver Stone and tell him to make the hardest-hitting *serious* film that he can about the degradation of the democratic dogma. The result, I promise you, will be not only hilarious but good citizenship in spades.

This is the story of Mary Matalin, political director of George Bush's campaign for re-election to the Presidency that he so much adorned ('Read my lips, no capital gains taxes'), and James Carville, who acted in the same capacity for Bill Clinton, the Comeback Kid. Love interest? This is the beauty part, as S. J. Perelman would say: Mary and James are in love before the campaign begins; then, after the election, they get married and settle down on television, where each now glows, he a 'liberal' star, she a 'conservative' one. Conflict? How can two professional politicians maintain their personal relationship in a campaign that grows more and more dirty as those magical days until November's first Tuesday fly by? It is not easy.

This is a political *Pillow Talk*, with alternating points of view. First, *James*. He gives his view of an event. Then *Mary*. She gives hers. They are often fascinating – sometimes deliberately, some-times inadvertently – as they discuss the mechanics of election. James and Mary? There is something numinously biblical about their names: James, brother of our Lord, Bill, and Mary Magdalene . . . Matalin, who has a star-struck crush on George Bush, surely a unique condition.

Each was already a successful political operator when they met in 1991. She had worked on Bush's winning Presidential campaign. He had worked on a number of senatorial and guber-natorial campaigns, mostly successful after he teamed up with Paul Begain, now of the White House. Each is intrigued by what he's heard about the other. 'I like to know people who do politics for a living,' says Mary, upfront as always. He is equally curious about her, although she notes, dryly, that according to James's sisters, until he met Mary he had not been seen in the company of a female more than 18 years of age. On their first date they quarrel about politics. Not to worry. Like most professionals who 'do' politics, neither is an ideologue. She lashes out at lefties like Albert Gore (known to Bush as Ozone Man) for having written such Marxist nonsense as: the automobile is damaging the environment.

Politically, James the populist openly prefers Bob Casey, the son of a coal miner in Pennsylvania, as governor, to a patrician like William Scranton; and that's about it for deep political thoughts.

Mary's first impression of James: 'I took a look at him . . . a squinty-eyed, bald-headed skinny guy. He was wearing skin-tight jeans and a little muscle-man shirt with a green turtleneck collar. I'll bet any amount of money that he doesn't remember what I was wearing.' *James:* 'I know she had her hair the way I don't like it.'

In the spring of 1991, Bush of Mesopotamia looks to be unbeatable. Such Democratic power-houses as Lloyd Bentsen decide that it is impossible to beat him and choose not to run. Then two things happen. First, John Heinz, Senator from Pennsylvania, is killed in a plane crash. Next, Governor Casey, in violation of every law of American politics, appoints the man best qualified to be a senator, Harris Wofford. A special election is called. Enter James, campaign director. A long shot, Wofford is elected on universal health care. An issue is born. Also a political star: James is now in a position to audition Democratic candidates for the 1992 election. He turns down Senators Bob Kerrey and Tom Harkin. He takes on Clinton. He meets Mary, who has a strong sense of professional hierarchy. James is strictly a statewide operator while she is Presidential. When she learns that James has leapt above his humble station, she goes, as they say in the book, ballistic. How can what is now a couple be on opposing sides in a Presidential election? Grimly, Mary thinks, 'If I didn't get [the job] because of Carville I'd have to kill him.' But she gets it.

The media are mildly bemused by the situation. But then, like Wall to Pyramus and Thisbe, the media, which now keep them physically apart, bring them together. They are forever waking up in the morning – each in his own bed far from the other – to see the face of the beloved on the morning news. They are all over television, and thus two media stars are born. He is effective but she is splendid, with her dark cobra eyes and her secret smile to camera that tells us: I can't believe what I'm hearing. Give me a break.

There is a new vocabulary in play. James and Mary are professional 'spin masters'. James gives the press credit for this resonant phrase: 'The word "spin", I think, means what political strategists do when we go out and put our candidate in the most favourable light. That's what spin is. Well, la-di-da, guess what? They're right. . . . Why don't the media just admit the truth about themselves that they're way more into self-justification than information?' There is a lot of talk about 'body language' (Woodward likes this phrase, too) though no explanation of what is meant, other than Gerald Ford falling down. Needless to say, James and Mary are cautious on the subject of the media (a plural noun becomes disagreeably singular as it means, paradoxically, more and more outlets). They must live with media; exploit media; die with media.

James: 'No one understands the power of the media in this country. I went into this campaign believing they were powerful. I didn't know. The power they have is staggering. . . . They like to think of themselves as learned and insightful and thoughtful and considered. They claim the mantle of truth. Hell, truth is they make initial snap judgments and after that all of their time . . . is spent on nothing but validating their original judgment.' Also noted is the media's fragmentation, best demonstrated by 'the emerging power of CNN . . . a very, very important player in Presidential campaigns. . . . It used to be that the Associated Press had the real effect on campaign coverage. *The New York Times*, *The Washington Post* and the other majors are all morning papers, while the AP serviced afternoon papers with the first take on breaking campaign events. . . . But there are fewer and fewer afternoon papers in the country, and CNN is on all day, every day. . . . They don't have a lot of viewers but, hell, as long as you have a hundred reporters looking at you and they are filing stories, you don't need to have numbers to have influence.'

Finally, there is the actual election of 1992. James steers Clinton through primaries fraught with drama. Events from the past keep slowing down what Bush used to call the Big Mo (momentum). All our old friends make a final (presumably) appearance.

Gennifer Flowers (*Mary:* 'God, if that's Clinton's taste in women . . .'). Clinton plays golf at an unintegrated club (*James:* 'Someone close to the body' should have checked out the club. The Body is the phrase for the Candidate, like the central puzzle in a murder mystery). Interesting odd facts like: Why does television spend so much time photographing Clinton when he jogs? In case he has a heart attack. Remember Jimmy Carter's eyes rolling upward during a marathon?

James dismisses Jerry Brown as 'a nut' who is far too pessimistic for a happy people. He also glosses over Brown's primary victory in Connecticut where, for the first and last time, the defense budget was challenged with a brand-new thought – conversion from a militarized to a peacetime economy: make bullet trains in the same factories where submarines are made. Kerrey is a war hero, attractive in every way, but he has no 'message'. The others don't matter. The nomination is won. En route, Jesse Jackson is sandbagged, ostensibly because of a black singer rapping about killing whites, but largely because the Jackson image is still too radical for the sacred centre where the votes are.

Incidentally, words like 'liberal' and 'conservative' and 'radical' mean absolutely nothing in this text, any more than they do in American politics. The only radical note struck in the campaign was by Pat Buchanan when he prescribed a religious war for us. This certainly promises to liven up future elections – should any be held, of course. If *All's Fair* has a subtext, it is that the cost of electing one of two – or even three – essentially interchangeable candidates is not only too high but potentially divisive when Cross confronts Satanic condom.

Mary has a harder time than James. An incumbent President does not expect to have to fight in primaries, but suddenly there is Crossfire Pro-Cross Pat Buchanan, with his lullaby of hate and his 20 per cent of the Republican vote. As if that were not enough bother, Ross Perot pays for a series of budget lectures on prime time. Not since Robert Benchley's 'Treasurer's Report' has anyone given so much pleasure to so many with sheer numbers galore.

*

Mary, who has not only been there but knows a thing or two, does have one enthusiasm that passeth all understanding. *Mary:* 'I picked up the phone and heard the unmistakable voice. Honest to God, my mouth went dry and my palms got sweaty. . . . No one, myself included, could believe it was actually him.' The Pope? Who on earth – or in heaven – could that voice belong to? 'He was incredibly deferential and respectful. Didn't want to bother me, but was wondering, if it wasn't too much trouble, could he get a copy of the "hypocritical Democrats" fax. . . . To my even greater amazement and pleasure, he did a whole monologue to my notorious fax.' Did you guess who? Rush Limbaugh. (Tim Robbins is interested.)

Rush had got interested in the campaign as it started to go very 'negative'. Apparently, Clinton had gone to Moscow as a student and the KGB had turned him into the Manchurian Candidate. He had also written a letter explaining why he disapproved of the Vietnam War, easily the *most* distinguished and honest statement of his career thus far. But as Bush drops in the polls, the decision is made to play dirty, school of Lee Atwater, Mary's guru, whose recent death had left the campaign singularly lacking in Willie-Horton-style ads. Little Miss Mary Mischief is thrilled: 'No one had really been happy with the option of just doing positive Bush because we didn't think we'd break through. And besides, going negative puts everybody in a mischievously productive and creative mood.' All sorts of tricks and treats are then offered an electorate that, according to James, has no real grasp of any political issue other than the economy and how it directly affects them. In fact, James concludes that, between the knee-jerk party-line voters and the indifferent majority, elections are decided by between 3 and 7 per cent of the electorate. Get *their* attention and approval and you win.

Neither hero nor heroine quite agrees on what happened at the end. The dull look of the economy should have been enough to eject an incumbent President, but Mary thinks that Bush was done in, ultimately, by Lawrence E. Walsh, the independent counsel, who, on October 30, 1992, produced sufficient smoking revolvers to convince 3 to 7 per cent of American voters that Bush was up to his ears in the Iran-contra capers of the Reagan era. If, as the Bush campaign kept chattering, the election was based on 'trust' (I think the word they meant was 'plausibility'), then Bush lost on October 30. A *Time* magazine poll reported that 40 per cent thought Clinton was lying about his draft status, but 63 per cent thought Bush was lying about Iran-contra. That did it, somewhat helped by the debates, where Clinton came through as 'caring' while Bush looked at his watch (Mary is angry that the public thought this was a sign of boredom at the debates, when it was really a signal to the questioner to cut off a long-winded Clinton answer), and the small but imperfectly formed Perot failed to get onto the high stool assigned him: he managed the first rung but not the second and so ended up leaning, oddly, against – what else? the impossible dream. Of such stuff is our little history made.

Mary is shattered by Bush's defeat. James is more thrilled at not losing than winning, although 'I always fall in love with my candidate.' A last meeting with the Clintons. Falstaff with Henry the King. Everything is changed. Prince Hal is no more. James will not serve in the Administration. There is a fond farewell, then James goes home to Mary.

James still checks in at the White House, as Woodward reports. Mary is now prime-time, big-time television. Mr and Mrs Clinton are currently suffering the trials of Job. George Bush is alone with his memories, of which, perhaps, the most vivid he describes to Mary: They are aboard his campaign train through Ohio and Michigan.

'He called me into the back car, had something he wanted to tell me.

'"I've been mooned. I've been mooned!"

'"Oh, my God."

'He thought this was incredibly funny. "Yes, an entire family. Mother, father and children. Can you imagine?"'

One can imagine very easily. But it was not the good man from Kennebunkport, Texas, who was being so honoured. Rather, it was the system that he and Bill and James and Mary represent. Moonie power is bound to prevail in the end – or so we optimists believe as we wait, impatiently, for the James and Mary film, 'The Mooning of the President'.

The New York Times Book Review
18 September 1994

6

Bubba Rules: Clinton–Gore II

Four years ago, I wrote that 'nothing less than earthly intervention (by Perot?) can prevent the Clinton–Gore team from assuming, as the Chinese say the mandate of Heaven.' Now history seems ready to repeat itself: Clinton will defeat Dole, whose original choice for a vice-presidential running mate, I can now reveal, was God. Why not? God has expressed no preference for either party, and on abortion, not even Pat Buchanan can instruct Him in those uterine mysteries the far right so furiously celebrate in the eldritch caverns of Eleusis, Mississippi. But God had other fish to fry.

In 1992 I compared Arkansas Clinton and Tennessee Gore to Huck Finn and Tom Sawyer, which was how they were presenting themselves to the folks. Actually, Clinton (Yale Law School) is plainly avatar to the Artful Dodger, while Gore (Harvard) is wealthy heir to a dour political dynasty. But each presents himself as an old-style southern moderate, while each has that haunted look of the southern lad who knows, as he enters middle age, that no amount of jogging and dieting will prevent him from one day becoming unelectably fat.

Usual question: What are the Clintons really like? Here is William Jefferson Clinton (né Blythe) on the subject recently:

'Hillary was born 40, and she'll always be 40. . . . I was born 16, and I'll always be 16.' So he has engagingly remained. There is a famous picture of him at about that age, shaking President Kennedy's hand at the White House. The boy Clinton is radiant. 'How,' one can imagine him thinking, if not daring to ask, 'do you get laid around here?' In a candid mood, the thirty-fifth president could have had a lot of tips for the forty-second. After all, at heart, Kennedy was a sophisticated 19-year-old with a ravenous sexual appetite, while Jackie was as old as Mother Nile. For some, power is quite enough. For Mrs Thatcher, to be alone with her boxes was, surely, world enough and time. But Clinton seems almost in the Kennedy class of innumerable brief encounters with that majority of the electorate which, appreciatively, favours him by an astonishing 24 per cent over Dole, while with the male minority he barely holds his own. Women like men who like women, no matter how exasperating. When there was a rumour that Hillary had flung a lamp at her husband, a White House aide solemnly acknowledged that this was true. 'Not only did she throw it,' he said, 'she hit him with it, and we have buried him in the Rose Garden. We never thought you people would notice.'

Clinton's disposition is also highly mercurial. One of Clinton's most useful aides is the small but exquisitely formed George Stephanopoulos. When the First Magistrate is in a rage, he seizes his youthful adjutant and begins to hurl him around the room. As the stoic youth ricochets off the wall like Buster Keaton, he gamely serves his president until the storm is passed and they can move more serenely on to some seminar, at which they will eat lots of fried things together.

As Clinton moves – majestically now – through his campaigning, he seems sure of his re-election. Certainly, this time around, the earthly Perot poses no threat to anyone except perhaps the Dole–God dream ticket, and even then, a well-aimed thunderbolt could send him scurrying back to his home planet, Texas.

Thunderbolts of human rather than divine construction are on all our minds these days. Foreigners find mystifying the amount of mayhem permitted in the United States despite ever more draconian laws against something loosely called terrorism. There is now one gun for each of the country's quarter billion citizens. As yet, each man, woman and child has not got his gun, but that day of perfect equality is bound to come. After all, according to one of the most powerful buyers of politicians, the National Rifle Association, 'Guns don't kill people, people kill people.' Meanwhile, the gun lovers have now learned how to blow up federal buildings with only farm detritus, while easily manufactured pipe bombs can cause a good bit of havoc in a public park. Clinton, after choking up on television at the thought of terrorism's innocent victims, rushes to join Congress in making laws intended to remove the protecting shield of the Bill of Rights from any citizen tagged as a potential 'terrorist'. But no candidate dares explain to the American people *why* the country is apparently spinning into chaos, because to do so would be to confess that there are, in effect, two governments of the United States. There is the visible (official) one, which is powerless to do anything about the economy short of waging – but never declaring – a war, preferably on a very small country, like Panama. Then there is the invisible government, the actual ownership of the country – currently (and uncharacteristically) at sea almost as much as its employees in Congress. Could it be that times *have* changed?

Our traditional panacea, the undeclared war, is less profitable than it used to be, and the wartime economy that Harry Truman and company imposed on the United States in 1950 is now some $5 trillion in debt – which does not stop 77 per cent of the country's before-tax income from going to the 1 per cent that owns most of the wealth. Some 39 million Americans now live in poverty of a sort unknown to other First World countries; and despite happy cries from the Clinton administration at each job created by the fast-food emporia, the median income of the famous middle class (some 65 per cent of the whole) has dropped 13 per cent since 1973, when the wives of workers were first obliged to take jobs just to maintain the family budget. As one woman happily observed on television the other day, 'Oh, Clinton's right when he says there are plenty of jobs out there. Fact, my husband and I have four jobs between us, and we're still broke.'

Although the stunning increase in the wealth of the few – the core of the invisible government – and the increase in the poverty of the unrepresented many have been precisely noted by the Congressional Budget Office, no politician will explain *how* we mislaid what was once a fairly egalitarian, highly prosperous society. As the people at large are instinctively aware that their visible government neither represents them nor regards them benignly, they have pretty much stopped voting.

The American takes it for granted that his moral fibre is never to be weakened by health care, education of the people at large or, indeed, anything at all except Social Security, a moderately profitable independent trust fund set up in 1935. Unfortunately for the American, thanks to the expense of the all-out cold–hot war on the Great Satan of the North Pole, the fund is for all practical purposes empty. Dolorous representatives of the Pentagon now tell us that it was wasteful 'people programmes' that used up the money – even though, in the interest of an arcane rite called 'balancing the budget', what small amounts that did go to the poor in the way of job training and welfare have just been cut back by Clinton, always one step ahead of a Congress that has, since 1992, been in the hands of zealous reactionaries in thrall to the foetus and the flag as well as at angry war with those who do not have money. It does not take the ghost of a Marie Antoinette to realize that when the few declare war on the many, the millinery business is headed for bad times.

Does Clinton know what he's doing? (Even the invisible government's chief media spokesman, *The New York Times*, termed the reduction-of-welfare bill that he signed 'odious'.) As the most intelligent politician on the American scene, yes, he knows pretty much what is wrong, but he is not about to do anything that might cost him a single vote.

Clinton has learned to play the dull, reactive media like the virtuoso he is, and Dole, if not God, can't think what to do about him. No matter what new bêtise the Right comes up with, Clinton has got there at least a day early and has made their issue his.

Currently, everyone hates (when not raping or corrupting on the Internet) teenagers. What is to be done with these layabouts? This is a crucial Republican–family-values issue, the result of all that money (practically none, in fact) *thrown* at the poor, who, by nature, are lawless, drugged, sexy, violent. But before the Doleful could get around to a death penalty for pubescent vagrants, Clinton struck. Curfews for teenagers, he proclaimed. Whoever said 'freedom to assemble' applied to anyone with acne? Uniforms to be worn at school, particularly those whose students come from families with not enough money to buy ordinary clothes, much less brown or beige shirts. Then, before Dole had picked himself up off the greensward, Clinton called for a national registry of sex offenders *and* a crackdown on fathers who do not pay for their children, two groups that could well overlap. All Dole could gasp was, 'Character. Integrity. Or whatever. That's what it's about. America.'

Clinton struck again. No more violence on television (the freedom to censor is the hallmark of a democracy). No teenage sex, much less smoking. Since there isn't any public money left (military procurement still burns up about $250 billion a year for that big war with China – gotta be ready), Clinton is now turning to the states and cities to help him with his programmes in a joint crusade to go 'roaring into the twenty-first century, united and strong.' Meanwhile, Dole is on his knees, communing with Him, who might have been his copilot.

On the Friday before the Democratic Black Tuesday of 1994 that saw the election of Republican majorities in both houses of Congress, I had dinner with Hillary Clinton, her aide Maggie Williams and three other guests. We had been invited to the White House (I'd met Mrs Clinton when she visited Ravello, an Italian town where I live part-time), but as I have no fond memories of the *Executive Mansion*, I proposed a hotel across the street. Mrs Clinton was delighted to come out. Maggie Williams was grimly funny about the hazards of life in the White House. A few weeks earlier, a small plane had been crashed – deliberately? – into the building.

'So just as soon as I had finished explaining for the hundredth time to my mother that an airplane can fall on top of you just about anywhere, and she was getting to believe me, this man comes along and sprays the front of the White House with a machine-gun.'

'You should apply for combat pay,' I said to Mrs Clinton.

'What about pay? I've never worked so hard in my life.'

We all knew that the Tuesday vote was going to be bad for the Democrats, so we avoided the subject. Talked about Washington in general. About Eleanor Roosevelt, whom I'd known and she was fascinated by. Then I began to probe, tactfully, I hope: How well did the Clintons understand just what they were up against? Did they know who actually owns and is rather idly ruling the United States – a very small class into which Bush had been born and trained and they had not. So, Who? What? How? I gave an example of poignant concern. In 1992 the country, by a clear majority, wanted a national health service. But insurance companies, in tandem with the medical-pharmaceutical axis, have always denounced any such scheme as Communist, and so the media, reflecting as it must the will of the ownership, had decreed that such a system is not only unworkable but un-American. As our people are never allowed more than one view of anything, Mrs Clinton failed to get the administration's health plan through Congress. But worse was to befall her and the president. The always touchy ownership of the United States felt that it had been challenged by what were, after all – despite such lofty 'visible' titles as 'president' – mere employees. If the Clintons could not be got rid of in an election, they could at least be so blackened personally and politically that they would no longer be taken seriously. So, to this punitive end, the ownership spent hundreds of millions of dollars on television advertisements 'proving' that under the Clinton plan each citizen would lose his own doctor and become a cipher in a computer (which he is pretty much anyway, thanks to the FBI, etc.), while its authors were guilty of everything from murder to ill-grooming.

As an old Washingtonian, I mentioned some of the ways in which great corporate entities destroy politicians. 'It will never be on the issues. It will always be something unexpected. Something personal. Irrelevant. From long ago. Then they will worry it to death.'

'That's certainly true.' Mrs Clinton was grim. 'No story *ever* ends around here. Even when it's over.'

I was about to suggest that if there was to be a war (as there is) between hated insurance companies and a popular plan, why not target the insurance companies publicly as the enemy and go on the attack? But Paul Newman, another guest, saved Mrs Clinton from the golden treasury of my hindsight: 'Get Gore to tell you about the day the horse ran away with Eartha Kitt. . . .'

Like a pair of dusty Ronald Reagans, we told Hollywood stories of the 50s. She brightened considerably. 'I wish I'd been there. Back in those days. You make it sound so interesting.' She has beautiful manners. She asked about the Roosevelt years, and I told her how Mrs Roosevelt delicately one-upped those who attacked her. 'No, I'm not angry,' she would say with her gentle half smile. 'Only a little . . . sad.' I told her, too, that until the war there was practically no security. The president would drive himself along nearby country roads.

Mrs Clinton shook her head, amazed. 'I was talking to one of the Secret Service men about security the other day, and he said that as far as they were concerned, they'd be happier if we lived in a bunker and travelled the streets in a tank.'

I, amazed in turn, asked, 'Was he joking?'

She gave us her dazzling blue-eyed smile, said, 'Good night', and made her way back to the White House, where painters had been hard at work hiding the machine-gun's bullet marks.

Meanwhile, whither the republic? The election: Should the various inept business dealings of the Clintons back in Arkansas become a serious issue, the many millions of dollars that Dole has acquired over the years while serving the great corporations in the Senate will suddenly become an issue so large that even the highly conservative media will be forced, as in the case of Watergate, to report who paid how much to which campaign for what favour in return.

But this sort of thing usually ends in a stalemate. In 1960 Kennedy's sex life and an allegedly annulled first marriage could not be used by the Nixonites because the Kennedyites would then bring up all the money that the billionaire plane maker Howard Hughes had funnelled to the Nixonites. 'It's so funny,' Jackie Kennedy once said, 'all the money we – and they – spend digging up all this dirt, and then no one ever uses any of it.' She sounded a bit wistful at the thought of so much frivolously wasted money that she might have liked.

The financial state of the union will never, in 1996, be addressed. In 1992 Clinton vowed he would cut back the Pentagon budget. He did get rid of a lot of manpower, but the real government promptly set him straight on weapons procurement; yet even they must have been mildly embarrassed when their members of Congress insisted on giving the Pentagon a billion or two more dollars than the bottomless pit had actually asked for. Clinton spoke nobly of a reform of the way that the few can buy elections under the current rules. Now, as a beneficiary of the ownership's largesse, he is silent. They may fear and loathe him, but they always hedge their bets and always pay for both candidates; later, at the dark of the moon, they collect their ton of flesh from the winner.

Although much of the election will be about Important Moral Issues like abortion, prayer in school and the status of 'gays', *terrorists* will be the word most sounded in the land from now until November. Until recently, *terrorist* has been a code word for the Muslim world, which does not love Israel, whose lobby in Washington controls Democratic presidents on Middle East matters. Republican presidents are less vulnerable, but even they must placate the lobby. More worrisome, *terrorist* has now become a word used to describe those lumpen Americans who have come to hate a government that builds more prisons than schools, intrudes on their private lives through wiretaps and other forms of surveillance, and puts in prison for life young people caught a third time with marijuana.

Death sentences for terrorists is the current cry. Public executions are being mooted. Autos-da-fé! 'Tonight we have who Mr

Dole hoped would be the Republican vice-presidential candidate on our programme. Welcome, Governor God.'

'Actually, Larry, just God will do. Or Ms God. As you know, I have never sought public office.'

'That's very interesting. Now, *briefly*, please, what is your informed view of the autos-da-fé, the public burning of heretics?'

'Well, Larry in our private capacity, we always felt—'

'I'm sorry, our time is up.'

Speaking of God – and who does not, often, in what we call God's country? – as part of the predeath plea bargain with the Almighty, R. M. Nixon has been allowed to give us his views on the candidates from beyond the grave through the medium of a former assistant, Monica Crowley, writing in the pages of *The New Yorker*. The undead Nixon is in great form. He describes a number of chats he had with Clinton just before Nixon moved his office to the sky, accompanied by a Secret Service detail glumly immolated on a ghat covered with ghee in order to guard him upstairs.

Nixon thinks the world of Dole. As of 1992, he thought him 'the only one who can lead ... by far the smartest politician – and Republican – in the country today.' Nixon was thinking then of how to defeat the Foetus Folk with a sensible candidate. Nixon finds Clinton intriguing. He is touched – and relieved – when Clinton rings him and chats at length. Later they meet. Clinton is worried about the economy. Nixon – who learned in 1974 all about the invisible government when one of its members, Katharine Graham of *The Washington Post*, deftly flushed his presidency – notes that 'history will not remember him for *anything* he does domestically. The economy will recover; it's all short-term and, let's face it, very boring.' The old trickster knows that economic power is kept forever out of the reach of the corporate ownership's chosen officeholders. Leave the economy alone and they'll leave the president alone to have the most fun a president can ever have, which is to fight a big war, as Lincoln or the Roosevelt cousins did.

According to Crowley, Nixon thinks Clinton's main fault is 'mistaking conversation for leadership, and personal interaction for decision making.' Nixon himself preferred making state visits abroad to doing just about anything at all at home. What he ever did on these trips, beyond photo ops with Mao and company, is vague. He does admit, a bit sadly, about Clinton, 'He loves himself, though, and that comes across.' Finally, 'He could be a great president. . . . But I doubt it. It's clear that this guy can be pushed around. . . .' Two years later, it would appear that it is the Artful Dodger who is doing the pushing and the dodging and the joyous stealing of any and every policy his opponents might favour.

I shall give myself the last word here, as I did in 1992 when I predicted that Clinton would beat Bush, as he will beat Dole in 1996, barring the detonation of some rustic honey wagon in his path. 'Clinton's greatest asset,' I wrote then, 'is a perfect lack of principle. With a bit of luck, he will be capable, out of a simple starry-eyed opportunism, to postpone our collapse. After all, Franklin Delano Roosevelt was equally unprincipled.' My ironic compliments were, of course, misunderstood in media-land where I was accused of calling both FDR and Clinton crooks, which they were – and are – but no more than any other politicians in a society whose elections are as corrupt as ours. Actually, I was paying each the high compliment of being a nonideological pragmatist, unlike the true believer, who will destroy the world or, failing that, brings us Auschwitz or the Great Depression. What is needed in a time of class and race wars is a quick-witted, devious, soothing leader, always sufficiently nimble to stay a step or two ahead of a polity that, if it is going anywhere, is heading down the economic scale, jettisoning, in its dizzy progress, our sacred 'inalienable rights'.

Finally, no matter how great Clinton's plurality or majority, *he* now knows, even if we don't, that he will not be allowed to do much of anything at home. He doesn't find economics as boring as Nixon did, because he knows more about such things. But Clinton might find it wise, once re-elected, to reverse some of the astonishing notions that he has recently put forward in order to pre-empt reactionary opponents.

I ended my piece in 1992 with 'We must wish Clinton luck. After all, if he fails, *he* will be the last president.' Many thought this melo-dramatic – the office will go on, even if the country should find its eventual niche somewhere between Argentina and Brazil. But I meant 'last' in the sense that if the half of the people who now don't vote are joined by too many more, then the high office is itself irrelevant, something that Clinton sensed when he declared, in a fit of pique, that despite the new Republican Congress of 1994, the president is *not* irrelevant, which means the thought is very much in his mind.

Meanwhile, let us give Clinton his proper due. Lincoln to one side, he does better funerals than any American president in our increasingly murderous history. This is no small thing. After all, who would care about Pericles today had he not given a sublime funeral oration – as reported by General Thucydides, Retired – in which he reminded the Athenians that an empire like theirs, no matter how larcenously acquired, is a very dangerous thing to let go? Ditto now, as Perot would say.

GQ
October 1996

7
R.I.P., R.M.N.

On April 23 I was awakened early in the morning by a call from BBC Radio. Richard Milhous Nixon had met his terminal crisis peacefully in the night. Sternly the programme's host told me that both former Prime Minister Edward Heath and Henry (never to be former, alas) Kissinger had referred to the thirty-seventh President as a 'towering figure'. I said to the host that the first would have had a fellow feeling for another leader driven from office, while Kissinger's only claim to our attention was his years in service as Nixon's foreign policy valet. Otherwise, Henry would now be just another retired schoolteacher, busy at work on *Son of Metternich*.

So John Kennedy and Richard Nixon (Congress, class of 1946) are now both gone – paladin and goblin, each put back in the theatrical box of discarded puppets and, to a future eye (or puppetmaster), interchangeable. Why not a new drama starring Jack Goblin and Dick Paladin? In their political actions they were more alike than not if one takes the longest view and regards the national history of their day as simply a classical laboratory example of entropy doing its merry chilly thing. In any case, as I wrote in 1983, 'We are Nixon; he is us.'

Much is now being made, among the tears for a man whom only

a handful of Americans of a certain age remember, of Nixon's foreign policy triumphs. He went to Moscow and then détente. He went to Beijing and then saw the Great Wall. Other presidents could have done what he did, but none dared because of – Nixon. As pictures of Johnson and Mao come on the screen, one hears that solemn baritone: 'I am not saying that President Johnson is a *card*-carrying Communist. No. I am not even saying that his presence on that wall means that he *is* a Communist. No. But I question. . . .' As Nixon had been assigned the part of *the* Nixon, there was no other Nixon to keep him from those two nice excursions, ostensibly in search of peace.

After I heard the trumpets and the drums, and watched our remaining Librarians – the high emeritus rank that we bestow on former presidents (a witty one because now no one does a whole lot of reading) – I played a film clip of Nixon in his vice-presidential days. For some reason the soundtrack is gone. A silent movie. An official banquet of some sort. Nixon remembers to smile the way people do. Then a waiter approaches him with a large, sticky dessert. At that moment, Nixon leans over to speak to his partner on the left, frustrating the waiter's effort to serve him. The waiter moves on. Nixon sits back; realizes that his dessert has been given to the man on his right. He waves to the waiter, who does not see him. Now the Nixon face is beginning to resemble that of the third English king of his name. Eyes – yes, mere slits – dart first left, then right. The coast is clear. Ruthless Plantagenet king, using his fork like a broadsword, scoops up half the dessert on his neighbour's plate and dumps it on his own. As he takes his first taste of the dessert, there is a radiance in his eyes that I have never seen before or since. He is happy. Pie in the sky on the plate at last. R.I.P., R.M.N.

The Nation
16 May 1994

8

Kopkind

Most establishment American journalists tend to be like their writing and so, duly warned by the tinkle of so many leper-bells, one avoids their company. On the other hand, after reading from beginning to end *The Thirty Years' Wars*, I realized why it was that I so liked Andrew Kopkind and always read his bulletins from the political front, which were also, endearingly, bulletins from his own life as well, which ended much too soon last October.

Born in 1935, Andy was a decade my junior. Since we were like-minded in so many ways that decade should not have made much difference, but it did in the sense that he was always somewhat exotic to me. The Sixties never meant much to me but they were everything to someone his age. I was – and am – the Forties–Fifties, shaped by the second war and Dr Kinsey, 'radicalized' by Korea and Joe McCarthy. Even so, the slight sense of strangeness I felt about him and his generation only made his take on matters of mutual interest attractively aslant.

To read what Kopkind calls *Dispatches and Diversions of a Radical Journalist 1965–1994* is to be given a deliberately eccentric tour of the American empire's slow deterioration as well as that of its mirror-image on the chilly steppes which so perversely cracked from side to side – seven years' bad luck (and maybe seven more) as my grandmother used to say. I say eccentric because I always thought that I had first met Andy at the Democratic convention in Chicago 1968, but now I read that he had only touched base there for a moment or two. Then, before Mayor Daley could shout Sheeney! at Senator Ribicoff, Andy had gone to the real action: Czechoslovakia, where he observed the Russian invasion and Dubcek's fall. While I was anticipating with excited horror Nixon's coming victory, Andy was writing from Prague: 'One of these days – when the "German problem" is solved – the Czechs will find a new way out of the Soviet sphere and others will follow. Beyond that, Russia has discredited leftist parties and the left in general for years to come. And within the Warsaw Pact countries, and perhaps even in Russia, Czechoslovakia has already become an embryonic "Vietnam".' It took twenty years for Andy to be proved right, during which time he did his best to shore up 'the left' in our own essentially apolitical land.

A generality about the sort of journalist Kopkind was. Unlike the overwhelming majority of the breed, he did not go in for Opinions, the daily ashen bread of the Sunday TV zoo and of those columnists who appear in such papers as *Time* and *Newsweek*, recycling the sort of mindless received opinion that dissolves before one's eyes into its original constituent parts – blurred ink, glossy paper. He had opinions, of course, but he didn't offer them until he had first proved, through detail, his reasons for holding them. Most American journalists who 'do' politics cannot resist getting to know the Players. Walter Lippmann was typical of an earlier generation, the disinterested wise man who remained aloof, chiselling great thoughts on marble columns. Actually a casual trawl through FDR's library at Hyde Park shows how eager Walter was for White House invitations and interviews. At least today's media chorus are all openly bought as they rush to White House to help with a speech, then off to newsroom to praise their own work, then onto television where now they condescend – no doubt, rightly – to mere senators and Cabinet members. Who can forget, a few elections ago, the egregious Phil Donahue wagging a minatory finger in the faces of a clutch of presidential candidates? This is no way to keep separate first and fourth estate, but then, in so tight and collusive a system, it is to no one's real interest to draw a line.

Happily, Andy did not collude, he drew a line: kept his eye steadily on the obscure who might or might not be making a revolution in the national consciousness if not in the streets. How to explain him? He started life in conventional middle-class New Haven. Father, a Republican District Attorney. There was Yale nearby, the Vatican of reactionary politics not to mention nursing mother to OSS and CIA. But Andy had the good luck to have, as he put it, a 'commie pinko rabbi'. He avoided Yale; went to Cornell as a pre-med student. Like me, he was exposed young to the *New Statesman*, a paper that once had the power not only to enlighten but to convert the susceptible to socialism. Medicine was abandoned for writing; then two and a half years at the London School of Economics, trying to be a 'classy' English journalist. Then home for a stint at *Time* magazine at the height of its 'unleash Chiang' mania: *Time*'s founder-owner, Henry Luce, once confided to me that 'the true mission of the United States in the twentieth century is the Christianization of China'. It's a wonder we've almost made it, unkilled, to the goal-post.

Unlike so many Jewish left-leaning journalists of that period, Kopkind never bought into Jewish nationalism, which means wholehearted support of Pentagon, Christian right as well as of those legions of anti-Semites who support Israel in order to benefit, if not from Rapture at Armageddon, military procurement. He regarded Israel as any other polity.

After some police trouble in California (he had been caught practising same-sexuality, which is not only an abomination in the eyes of the Lord but, rather more important, in those glazed mica-like orbs of Henry Luce), Kopkind was obliged to turn 'straight' with the aid of a psychiatrist paid for by *Time*. Despite prayers to Freud as well as the numerous ritual dances and dietary observances necessary to achieve that state of heterosexual grace which has made the United States a thigh-slapping joke in the Western world, *he failed to Mature*. At 29 Kopkind left *Time*.

Time at Berkeley. Some writing for *The New Republic* before it became press office for the Israeli Embassy. Then, early 1965, the march on Selma in Alabama. This was the beginning of the latest but, alas, so far unconcluded phrase of the black attempt to achieve parity in a society where whiteness is compulsory if one wants to be a full citizen. Suddenly, there was an eruption of radical political activity – SNCC, SDS – and Kopkind plunged in: 'I was still the journalist, but I was part of the movement too. The genie was out of the bottle', and for the next thirty years the genie was on duty.

It is odd to note the change of words over the years; in 1965, Negro starts to change to black. The times really seemed to be changing with Jack Kennedy murdered and Martin Luther King moving, in triumph, to the same slaughterhouse that awaits all agents of change in our imperial history. Kopkind is more kindly than not with such enemies of change as the ADA liberals: 'It is hard for liberals, traumatized by both Stalinism and McCarthyism, to understand the new left's attitudes about communism.' That is to riot in understatement. The radical activist takes far more fire from the liberal establishment that so loyally upheld the right of the United States to be in Vietnam than ever it will from the likes of George Wallace.

In due course, after the April 17, 1965, March on Washington to End the War in Vietnam, the movement splintered and the war went on for another decade, making it possible for a radical movement to pick up the pieces. But no such movement has ever, thus far, been able to get through to – much less rationalize – our society. As for promoting economic justice. . . . That's really un-American. To understand why it is not possible to do anything is the burden of Kopkind's genie-hood. Meanwhile, he hates the absurdities of official rhetoric: 'The best that can be said about the domino theory is that it works in reverse. The deeper America's involvement in Vietnam becomes, the less effective is its deterrence value. It is one thing to lose a war with 17,000 advisers and quite another to lose it with 125,000 battle troops' (this was written in 1965); 'to win it (whatever that means) with a land army of half a million would be worst of all. That kind of victory is the death of policy, not the foundation of it.'

He quotes Carl Oglesby (president of SDS), who 'accused the liberals of underpinning the elements of the very system that the New Left attacked: the military and industrial "corporatism" that keeps . . . the poor alive but powerless and, in the end, still poor.' Plainly, we live under a malign star: thirty years later this analysis still describes our estate.

The genie hovers over the Watts riots and notes the obvious: there is more fire to come. In 1966 he was one of the few who thought that 'mini-star' Reagan would beat Pat Brown and become governor of California because Reagan's 'philosophical line is an entirely incomprehensible jumble of every myth and cliché in American life.' But there are the odd small victories along the downward way: the House Un-American Activities Committee takes a well-earned hit. 'The kids' were out in force, mocking the committee. Not only did no one take the Fifth, no one showed anything but contempt of Congress. One youth said, 'I will not answer that question on the grounds that it nauseates me and I might vomit all over the table.' Times a'changing? Well, they did change, in this instance. No more HUAC.

Kopkind's pieces for the *New Statesman* are brief but elegant. In *The New Republic* he is more thorough but not as lively. In *Ramparts* he now has an unmistakable voice; read a sentence or two and you knew who wrote them. For a time, he pins his hopes on Senator Robert Kennedy, but even in *The New York Review of Books* (Bobby-enthralled as of 1967), Kopkind suspects that there is not much substance behind the rhetoric; that he is not an 'insurgent', since the official liberal line was that Bobby is in place to 'save' the system the way that the New Deal 'saved' the system. But Kopkind sees that this wouldn't work even if there was a system worth saving. He has radically grasped the point: top-down reforms are bound to fail. 'It is not Kennedy's fault that he can do no other; it is his situation.' This is generous. He does not note Kennedy's presumably deep conviction 'that we have every moral right to be in Vietnam.'

There are crucial moments when Kopkind was not on the spot.

The two Kennedy assassinations are not recorded, only referred to. The rise of Nixon happens in the margins of his prose. But he keeps a close eye on those in the ranks (down-top) who are for civil rights and an end to war and to the militarized state. Along the way he makes a disturbing sketch of Allard Lowenstein's politics and death, bringing together Kopkind's two central themes – radicalism of politics (we must go to the *roots* of our distress) and same-sexuality, which tormented Al, or so Kopkind thought. Al's first political campaign was, briefly, for me in 1960. I found him bright but consumed with a sort of ambition that I don't think Andy could have imagined, so alien was it to his own serenely balanced communal nature. Al realized that without a sacrifice of his true nature on the altar of Family, he could not be president or even an influence on one. He was not tortured by *who* he was but by *what* he had to do in order to rise. He married (happily, I am told) but continued to burn; and was burnt, as it were, to death. Also, there is the troubling possibility that overwrought ambition had made him a double agent or, as Kopkind puts it, 'Lowenstein was part of a cultural and ideological nexus that sanctioned covert operations and mounted public movements against radicalism at home and abroad.' If so, his radical death was grimly ironic.

May 1968 finds Kopkind in North Vietnam. He is impressed by how well people are coping with enforced decentralization. He captures the differences: 'Our questions often made no "sense" to the Vietnamese because they assumed a context of issues in our own society, not theirs.' If only McNamara had had the slightest of clues! He captures the spirit of the Republican convention at Miami Beach (it is here, I think, that we met). 'The party found its perfect hero in Barry Goldwater because he expressed the inevitability of human defeat; now its choice of Miami Beach . . . completes the metaphor.' He did not share my sudden vision, as the born again and yet again R. M. Nixon lurched forward to accept the nomination, that here was our thirty-seventh President and that we hadn't seen nothing yet. In the fall of that crucial year, Kopkind goes to Cleveland to visit white blue-collar Wallaceland.

Again he zeroes in on the real people as opposed to the PR simu-
lacra at Miami Beach. One worker muses aloud: 'Humphrey –
everything good . . . but he's too easy on race, that's a minus. (Boy,
am I making myself out a racist?) Wallace – I only like him 40% . . .
but the fact that he won, or got a lot of votes, would get people
together. So I'm for Wallace. . . . But you know, sometimes I'm not
sure why I vote for someone. Does that make sense?' It did to
Henry Adams and it does to our current landslide Republican
Congress, elected by only one-third of the electorate: Two-thirds
thought that it made sense to give up on a system from which they
are excluded.

Here comes (and there goes) Gene McCarthy. 'Are we in the
middle of a revolution?' is the title of one of Andy's pieces from
the front. 'Those who hold steadfastly to the old values are true
conservatives; those who only sense the new are worried liberals;
those who see the whole pattern very clearly are radicals, and
they don't know what to do about it.' This is Sartre's *No Exit*
Americanized. It was also Sartre who once observed that the
bourgeois theatre will put up with the most harshly accurate
depiction of the human case, as long as there is no hint that a
solution might exist. What is is and must ever be.

Americans land on the moon and the war goes on. Woodstock
. . . and the war goes on. Judge Julie Hoffman versus Abbie
Hoffman *et al.*, at Chicago . . . and the war . . . Weathermen . . . *Sgt*
Pepper . . . Black Panthers murdered by the state. . . . But Andy is
tiring now.

At the beginning of 1970 he withdraws to a sort of commune in
Vermont. Where 'I was taking a lot of acid.' He also met John
Scagliotti and, as they say, 'came out', though I never suspected for
a moment that he had ever been in, but then I've always been
closet-blind. Andy and John remained together until the end.
Happily, Andy did not retire, though, for a time, there was a hiatus
'when I stopped writing and I stopped doing politics the same day.
I couldn't figure any of this out. I couldn't figure out who I was,
and what I was doing this for and this movement that seemed to
have gone completely out of control, disappeared into a million

crazy bits.' Gradually, he started to 'do' writing and politics again but in a less urgent style since the disparity between what the United States thinks it is and what it actually is is now too great to be reconciled. One can only chip away at the edges. 'I was lucky, too: I learned enough to make myself permanently and constitutionally unable to accept America and its internal and external empires.' So, at the end, he was to make not a separate peace with our evil empire but a separate war, the best that any of us can do in what Jack Kennedy used to croon, 'this twilight time' – presumably before midnight comes up like thunder over DC's Federal Theme Park.

In Andy's last years, he was much involved with sexual politics – as I write these words I cannot believe just how absurd a country has to be to insist on so categorizing its inmates. Cunnilingus over here ... buggery to the right ... frottage on the floor ... keep moving. Bisexuals, stop it! Right now.

But Andy charges in. Present, as he puts it, 'at the creation'. 'There were millions of homosexuals before Stonewall, of course, but there was no coherent, self-aware gay community.' This is more or less true, but one wonders what sort of country needs a 'gay community'? Although there are prohibited sexual acts (for everyone) in Catholic Mediterranean countries, no one is shocked or even interested in the fact that the shepherd Silvio likes to bugger young Mario (at least, when the ewes are menstruating) nor does Silvio's pleasure in Arcadia – young Mario's too – prevent either from being good or bad family men, something that the old culture expected them to be but did not fuss about if they decided not to breed. Anglo-Saxon attitudes were – and are – more crazed and punitive: particularly when sex becomes an exercise in control; hence, sexual politics, alas. Hence, some of Andy's best writing as he describes the lunatic bleatings of the Pentagon generals and psychically challenged Congresspersons, most of whom, as kids say nowadays, have 'seen Dorothy', and given her a big kiss – in Oz if not Kansas.

The last time Andy rang me, officially – that is, as journalistic quarry – it was for a magazine piece that he was doing on Tim

Robbins. Tim had produced and directed and starred in the film *Bob Roberts*, in which I appeared. He had also written the script, the lyrics for the songs and, as I recall, organized the catering for cast and crew. Andy's usual opening was always reassuring. 'Don't worry. This interview's absolutely pointless,' my favourite kind. 'I'm doing this piece for one of these magazines . . . you know, they pay you all this money for stories about Mike Ovitz and they look like those giveaway magazines you get on airlines.' We both went on journalistic auto-pilot. But suddenly, trying to explain what made the youthful Robbins tick, I heard myself say, 'I suppose it's just natural *wu-wei*.' Andy's voice became alert. 'What's that?' I chided him for having read so little Lao Tzu. I then gave an English approximation: 'passive achievement'. The archer who isn't worried about going for the gold can pick up his bow and hit the bull's eye easily. If he strains – is jittery – he will miss. 'Tim has natural *wu-wei*.' And so, I thought, as I hung up, do you. In due course *wu-wei* appeared, for the first and last time, in an airline-type magazine, two shrivelled small words between the Gucci and the Lancôme ads.

Although the perhaps mythical sage Lao Tzu meant *wu-wei* as a goal for the individual, he does see its application to the state. In *The Way of Acceptance*, he observes: 'The more the people are forbidden to do this and that, the poorer they will be. The more sharp weapons the people possess, the more will darkness and bewilderment spread through the land. The more craft and cunning men have, the more useless and pernicious contraptions will they invent.' Even using homely fertilizer. 'If I work through Nonaction the people will transform themselves.' So either Andy Kopkind *wu-wei* or – *Oklahoma OK!*

The Nation
12 June 1995

PART III

1

How We Missed the
Saturday Dance

Duke Ellington on the jukebox: 'Missed the Saturday dance, heard
they crowded the floor, duh duh duh-duh. . . .' I can almost carry
a tune but I can't remember the words to any song, including the
inspired lyrics of our national anthem. But this song, and those
notes, have been sounding in my head for over half a century, ever
since I heard them at a dance hall near the army camp where I was
stationed.

Just out of Exeter, I had enlisted in the army at 17. That was a
year after George Bush, just out of Andover, enlisted in the navy.
Most important, my best friend from a Washington, DC, school
enlisted in the Marine Corps. He had been 'safe' at Duke: he had
a contract to be a professional baseball player when the war was
over. But he thought that he should go fight too. He became a
scout and observer for the Third Marine Division in the Pacific. He
saw action at Guam. He was assigned to 'Operation Detachment'
and shipped out to Iwo Jima, where the Japanese were entrenched
in tunnels beneath that bleak island's surface.

On February 19, 1945, the Marines landed on Iwo Jima, after a
long, fairly futile aerial bombardment. The Japanese were out of

173

reach belowground. On D-Day plus nine, elements of the Third Division landed on the already crowded island, eight square miles of volcanic ash and rock. Like the skull of some prehistoric brontosaurus, Mount Suribachi looms over the five-and-a-half-mile-long island. Lately, I have been watching closely each frame of an old newsreel that now seems so long ago that it might as well be a series of Brady stills from Antietam except for the fact that it is still as immediate to me as yesterday, even though I was not there but on another Pacific island, far to the north in the Bering Sea. It took a month to win the island. Twenty thousand Japanese were killed; 6,821 American troops, mostly marines, were killed. On D-Day plus ten, 1 March, 1945, at 4:15 a.m., Pvt. James Trimble was killed instantly by a grenade. He was 19 years old. Bush and I survived.

It is somehow fitting that our generation – *the* war generation, as we think, perhaps too proudly, of ourselves – should be officially as well as actuarially at an end with the replacement of George Bush by a man who could be his – our – son. I say fitting because our generation, which won in battle the American Empire, is somehow nicely epitomized by the career of Bush, who served with energetic mindlessness the empire, always managing, whenever confronted with a fork in the road of our imperial destiny, to take, as did his predecessors, the wrong turning.

Elsewhere, I have noted that the American Golden Age lasted only five years; from war's end, 1945, to 1950, the Korean War's start. During this interval the arts flourished and those of us who had missed our youth tried to catch up. Meanwhile, back at the White House, unknown to us, the managers of the new world empire were hard at work replacing the republic for which we had fought with a secret national security state, pledged to an eternal war with communism in general and the Soviet Union in particular. It is true that Harry Truman and our other managers feared that if we did not remain on a wartime footing we might drift back into the Great Depression that had not ended until the Japanese attacked us at Pearl Harbor, and everyone went to war or work. It is part of the national myth that the attack was unprovoked. Actually, we had been spoiling for a war with Japan since the beginning of the century. Was the Pacific – indeed Asia – to be theirs or ours? Initially, the Japanese preferred to conquer mainland Asia. But when it looked as if we might deny them access to Southeast Asian oil, they attacked. Had they not, we would never have gone to war, in the Pacific or in Europe.

I was born eight years after the end of the First World War. As I was growing up, it was well-remembered that we had got nothing out of that war in Europe except an attack on the Bill of Rights at home and, of course, the noble experiment, Prohibition. Young people often ask me, with wonder, why so many of us *enlisted* in 1943. I tell them that as we had been attacked at Pearl Harbor, we were obliged to defend our country. But I should note that where, in 1917, millions of boys were eager to go fight the Hun, we were not eager. We were fatalistic. In the three years that I spent in the army, I heard no soldier express a patriotic sentiment, rather the reverse when we saw the likes of Errol Flynn on the screen winning freedom's war, or, even worse, John Wayne, known to us by his real name, Marion, the archetypal draft-dodging actor who, to rub it in, impersonated a Flying Tiger in the movies.

Although we were not enthusiastic warriors, there was a true hatred of the enemy. We were convinced that the 'Japs' were sub-human; and our atrocities against them pretty much matched theirs against us. I was in the Pacific Theatre of Operations where the war was not only imperial but racial: the white race was fighting the yellow race, and the crown would go to us as we were the earth's supreme race, or so we had been taught. One of the ugliest aspects of that war was the racial stereotyping on both sides. In Europe we were respectful – even fearful – of the Germans. Since blacks and women were pretty much segregated in our military forces, World War II was, for us, literally, the white man's burden.

So while the Golden Age had its moment in the sun up on deck, down in the engine room the management was inventing the 'Defense' Department and the National Security Council with its secret, unconstitutional decrees, and the equally unconstitutional CIA, modelled, Allen Dulles remarked blithely, on the Soviets'

NKVD. We were then, without public debate, committed to a never-ending war, even though the management knew that the enemy was no match for us, economically or militarily. But, through relentless CIA 'disinformation', they managed to convince us that what was weak was strong, and that the Russians were definitely coming. 'Build backyard shelters against the coming atomic war!' A generation was well and truly traumatized.

The Korean War put an end to our title as invincible heavyweight military champion of the world. We might have maintained our mystique by avoiding this eccentric war (we did call it a 'police action'), but by then we had so exaggerated the power of the Soviet Union in tandem with China that we could do nothing but reel from one pointless military confrontation to another.

Unfortunately, Kennedy was less cynically practical than those who had presided over what Dean Acheson called 'the creation' of the empire. Kennedy actually believed – or pretended to believe – their rhetoric. He liked the phrase 'this twilight time'. He believed in the domino theory. He believed in 'bearing any burden'. He invaded Cuba, and failed. He turned his attention to Asia, to 'contain China' by interfering in a Vietnamese civil war where a majority had already voted for the communist Ho Chi Minh, who, quoting Jefferson, asked Eisenhower to make Vietnam an American protectorate. But, as Ike explained in his memoirs, this wasn't possible: they were *Communists*.

In June 1961 Kennedy began the fastest build up militarily since Pearl Harbor; he also rearmed Germany, setting off alarm bells in the Soviet Union. They spoke of denying us land access to our section of Berlin. Kennedy responded with a warlike speech, invoking 'the Berlin crisis' as a world crisis. In response, Khrushchev built the wall. It was as if we were, somehow, willing a war to turn sad twilight to incandescent nuclear high noon.

The missile crisis in Cuba was the next move, with us as the provocateurs. Then, with the Vietnam War, we not only took the wrong road, we went straight around the bend, fighting the longest war in our history in a region where we had no strategic interest unless we were to openly declare what the management, then and now, does truly believe: the United States is the master of the earth and anyone who defies us will be napalmed or blockaded or covertly overthrown. We are beyond law, which is not unusual for an empire; unfortunately, we are also beyond common sense.

The only subject, other than the deficit, that should have been discussed in the late election was the military budget. Neither Bush nor Clinton came anywhere close. Eventually, we shall be unable to borrow enough money to preen ourselves in ever weaker countries, but until then, thanks to the many suicidal moves made by that imperial generation forged in the Second World War, our country is now not so much divided as in pieces.

The latest managerial wit has been to encourage – by deploring – something called 'political correctness', this decade's Silly Putty or Hula Hoop. Could anything be better calculated to divert everyone from what the management is up to in recently appropriating, say, $3.8 billion for SDI than to pit sex against sex, race against race, religion against religion? With everyone in arms against everyone else, no one will have the time to take arms against the ruinously expensive empire that Mr Clinton and the unattractively named baby boomers have inherited. I wish them luck.

There are those who sentimentalize the Second World War. I don't. There can be no 'good war'. We set out to stop Germany and Japan from becoming hemispheric powers. Now, of course, they are economic world powers while we, with our $4 trillion of debt, look to be joining Argentina and Brazil on the outer edge. All in all, the famed good, great war that gave us the empire that we then proceeded to make a mess of was hardly worth the death of one Pvt. James Trimble USMCR, much less the death of millions of others.

I have just listened to the original Duke Ellington record. Here are those lyrics that I always forget.

'Missed the Saturday dance, heard they crowded the floor, couldn't bear it without you, don' get around much anymore.' All in all, it's a good thing for the world that with Bush's departure *we* don't get around much anymore. Somalia–Bosnia is the last of our hurrahs, produced by CNN and, so far, sponsorless. Maybe now, without us, Clinton's generation will make it to the Saturday dance that we missed. And let's hope that the floor won't prove to be too crowded with rivals in trade if not in love, death.

Newsweek
11 January 1993

2

In the Lair of the Octopus

In 'Murder as Policy' (April 24), Allan Nairn notes, accurately, that the 'real role . . . of all US ambassadors [to Guatemala] since 1954 [has been] to cover for and, in many ways, facilitate American support for a killer army.' Nairn's report on the capers of one Thomas Stroock, a recent viceroy, is just another horror story in a long sequence which it was my . . . privilege? to see begin not in 1954 but even earlier, in 1946, when, at 20, a first novel just published, I headed south of the border, ending up in Antigua, Guatemala, where I bought a ruined convent for $2,000 (the convent had been ruined, let me say in all fairness, by earthquake and not by the Guatemalan military or even by the US embassy).

Guatemala was beginning to flourish. The old dictator, Ubico, an American client, had been driven out. A philosophy professor named Arévalo had been elected president in a free election. A democratic socialist or social democrat or whatever, he had brought young people into government, tamed the army and behaved tactfully with the largest employer in the country, the American company United Fruit.

Easily the most interesting person in – and out – of the town was Mario Monteforte Toledo. Under 30, he was a thin, energetic intel-

179

lectual who wrote poetry. He had a wife in the capital and an Indian girlfriend in Antigua, and when he came to visit, he and I would meet and talk, and talk.

Mario was President of the Guatemalan Congress and was regarded by everyone as a future president of the republic. In politics he was vaguely socialist. I, of course, reflecting my family's politics, was fiercely Tory. We had splendid rows.

Scene: patio of my house. Overhanging it the high wall of the adjacent church of El Carmen. Under a pepper tree, near an ugly square fountain like a horse trough, we would sit and drink beer. He told me the gossip. Then, after a ritual denunciation of the rich and the indifferent, Mario started to talk politics. 'We may not last much longer.'

'We . . . who?'

'Our government. At some point we're going to have to raise revenue. The only place where there is any money to be raised is *el pulpo*.' *El pulpo* meant the Octopus, also known as the United Fruit Company, whose annual revenues were twice that of the Guatemalan state. Recently workers had gone on strike; selfishly, they had wanted to be paid $1.50 a day for their interesting work.

'What's going to stop you from taxing them?' I was naïve. This was long ago and the United States had just become the Leader of the Lucky Free World.

'Your government. Who else? They kept Ubico in power all those years. Now they're getting ready to replace us.'

I was astonished. I had known vaguely about our numerous past interventions in Central America. But that was past. Why should we bother now? We controlled most of the world. 'Why should we care what happens in a small country like this?'

Mario gave me a compassionate look – compassion for my stupidity. 'Businessmen. Like the owners of United Fruit. They care. They used to pay for our politicians. They still pay for yours. Why, one of your big senators is on the board of *el pulpo*.'

I knew something about senators. Which one? Mario was vague. 'He has three names. He's from Boston, I think. . . .'

'Henry Cabot Lodge? I don't believe it.' Lodge was a family

friend; as a boy I had discussed poetry with him – he was a poet's son. Years later, as Kennedy's Ambassador to Vietnam, he would preside over the murder of the Diem brothers.

As we drank beer and the light faded, Mario described the trap that a small country like Guatemala was in. I can't say that I took him very seriously. With all the world, except the satanic Soviet Union, under our control it was hardly in our national interest to overthrow a democratic neighbour, no matter how much its government irritated the board of directors of United Fruit. But in those days I was not aware to what extent big business controlled the government of our own rapidly expiring Republic. Now, of course, everyone knows to what extent our subsequent empire, with its militarized economy, controls business. The end result is much the same for the rest of the world, only the killing fields are more vast than before and we make mischief not just with weak neighbours but on every continent.

Mario had given me the idea for a novel. A dictator (like Ubico) returns from an American exile as the Octopus's candidate to regain power. I would tell the story through the eyes of a young American war veteran (like myself) who joins the general out of friendship for his son. The more I brooded on the story, the more complexities were revealed. *Dark Green, Bright Red*. The Greens, father and son, were the Company, and dark figures indeed, haunting the green jungles. Bright Red was not only blood but the possibility of a communist taking power.

'No novel about – or from – Latin America has ever been a success in English.' As of 1950, my publisher was right.

Four years after the book was published, Senator Lodge denounced Arévalo's popularly elected successor, Arbenz, as a communist because, in June 1952, Arévalo had ordered the expropriation of some of United Fruit's unused land, which he gave to 100,000 Guatemalan families. Arévalo paid the company what he thought was a fair price, their own evaluation of the land for tax purposes. The American Empire went into action, and through the CIA, it put together an army and bombed Guatemala City. US Ambassador John Peurifoy behaved rather like Mr Green in the novel. Arbenz resigned. Peurifoy wanted the Guatemalan Army's chief of staff to become president, and gave him a list of 'communists' to be shot. The chief of staff declined: 'It would be better,' he said, 'that *you* actually sit in the presidential chair and that the Stars and Stripes fly over the palace.'

Puerifoy picked another military man to represent the interests of company and empire. Since then, Guatemala has been a slaughterground, very bright red indeed against the darkest imperial green. Later, it was discovered that Arbenz had no communist connections, but the 'disinformation' had been so thorough that few Americans knew to what extent they had been lied to by a government that had now put itself above law and, rather worse, beyond reason.

Incidentally, I note that the disinformation still goes on. In the April 9 *New York Times* (a 'recovering' newspaper in recent years), one Clifford Krauss airily says that Guatemala's Indians have been regularly screwed for 400 years, so what else is new? He gives a tendentious history of the country – purest Langley boilerplate, circa 1955 – but omits the crucial 1931–44 dictatorship of Jorge Ubico.

I must say I find it disconcerting to read in 1995 that 'by surrounding himself with Communist Party advisers, accepting arms from Czechoslovakia and building a port to compete with United Fruit's facilities, Arbenz challenged the United States at the height of the cold war.' God, to think that such evil ever walked the Central American night! 'President Eisenhower's CIA organized a Guatemalan [*sic*] invasion force and bombed Guatemala City in 1954.'

Dark Green, Bright Red was just reissued in England. Reviewing it in the *Evening Standard*, the journalist Patrick Skene Catling writes, 'I wish I had read this prophetic work of fiction before my first visit to Guatemala in 1954. Gore Vidal would have helped me to understand how John Peurifoy . . . was able to take me up to the roof of his embassy to watch . . . the air raids without anxiety, because he and the CIA knew exactly where the bombs were going to fall.'

A final note – of bemusement, I suppose. I was at school with

Nathaniel Davis, who was our Ambassador in Chile at the time of Allende's overthrow. A couple of years later Davis was Ambassador to Switzerland and we had lunch at the Berne embassy. I expressed outrage at our country's role in the matter of Chile. Davis 'explained' *his* role. Then he asked, 'Do you take the line that the United States should never intervene in the affairs of another country?' I said that unless an invasion was being mounted against us in Mexico, no, we should never intervene. Davis, a thoughtful man, thought; then he said, 'Well, it would be nice in diplomacy, or in life, if one could ever start from a point of innocence.' To which I suppose the only answer is to say – Go! Plunge ever deeper, commit more crimes to erase those already committed, and repeat with Macbeth, 'I am in blood / Stepped in so far that, should I wade no more, / Returning were as tedious as go o'er.'

The Nation
5 June 1995

3
With Extreme Prejudice

Article I, Section 9 of the Constitution requires government agencies to submit their budgets at regular intervals to Congress for review. Neither the CIA not the DIA does this.* Occasionally, at the dark of the moon, they will send someone up to the Hill to disinform Congress, and that's that. After all, to explain what they actually do with the money that they get would be a breach of national security, the overall rubric that protects so many of them from criminal indictments. Although most Americans now think that the CIA was created at Valley Forge by General Washington, this unaccountable spy service was invented less than half a century ago, and since that time we have been systematically misinformed about the rest of the world for domestic policy reasons (remember Russia's outstanding economic surge in 1980?). Intelligence is an empty concept unless directly related to action. In a war, knowledge of the enemy's troop movements is all-important. In peacetime, random intelligence-gathering is meaningless, when not sinister.

Since our rulers have figured that one out, they have done their

* Central Intelligence Agency, Defense Intelligence Agency.

best to make sure that we shall never be at peace; hence, the necessity of tracking enemies – mostly imaginary ones, as the Pentagon recently revealed in its wonderfully wild scenarios for future wars. Since Communism's ultimate crime against humanity was to go out of business, we now have no universal war to conduct except the one against drugs (more than $20 billion was wasted last year on this crusade). As there is now no longer sufficient money for any of these 'wars', there is no longer a rationale for so many secret services unless the Feds really come out of the closet and declare war on the American people, the ultimate solution: after all, one contingency plan in Ollie North's notebook suggested that in a time of crisis, dusky-hued Americans should be sequestered.

I would suggest that the State Department return to its once-useful if dull task of supplying us with information about other countries so that we might know more about what they'd like to buy from us. The hysterical tracking down of nuclear weapons is useless. After all, we, or our treasured allies, have armed all the world to the teeth. We have neither the money nor the brains to monitor every country on earth, which means, alas, that if some evil dictator in Madagascar wants to nuke or biologically degrade Washington, DC, there's not much we can do about it. Certainly, the CIA, as now constituted, would be the last to know of his intention, though perhaps the first to get the good of his foul plot. I would abandon all the military-related secret services and I would keep the FBI on a tight leash – no more dirty tricks against those who dislike the way that we are governed, and no more dossiers on those of us who might be able to find a way out of the mess we are in, best personified by the late J. Edgar Hoover and best memorialized by that Pennsylvania Avenue Babylonian fortress that still bears his infamous name.

The Nation
8 June 1992

4
Time for a People's Convention

November 18, 1991. Despite jet lag, I find myself half-asleep, making a speech in a nineteenth-century auditorium in Pittsburgh. I stand behind a lectern at stage left, blinded by film and television lights. At stage right stands the youthful 'Bob Roberts', played by Tim Robbins, who is also the director and writer of this film (as yet untitled). We are fictional characters. I am the incumbent liberal Senator from Pennsylvania; he is the challenger. 'Bob' is a self-made millionaire turned pop singer, now turned politician. He is a sort of David Duke but without the luggage of a lurid past. He will win the election.

I have a weird sense that I have done all this before. Certainly, the hall is familiar, even to the entire text of the Gettysburg Address in giant gold letters above the stage. Then I realize that 'I' have been through all this some weeks earlier. Only I was Harris Wofford and 'Bob Roberts' was Dick Thornburgh and they, too, spoke in the same hall. That time Wofford won: this time he – 'I' – lose. Then as my peroration resounds, I realize that I have never actually been in Pittsburgh before and that my familiarity with the hall is because of CNN – or was it C-Span?

Once I had finished my work as supporting 'actor', I moved on to Dartmouth where I spent a week in Hanover, New Hampshire, chatting with faculty and students. But, again, unreality kept breaking in. My first morning in Hanover, I looked out the bedroom window and for a moment I thought I was back at my old school, Exeter, from which I had graduated a half-century earlier, unless a recurrent nightmare runs true to course, in which case I did *not* graduate but have spent fifty dusty years trying, unsuccessfully, to make up a failed math test. Once awake, I found that my old friend *déjà vu* was back in town as a half-dozen hopeless presidential candidates were going through their quadrennial paces. In 1982 I had run against one of them, Jerry Brown, in California and lost a Senate primary election. Now he was making my old speeches. Should I warn him not to? No. Meanwhile, New Hampshire is in deep depression – shops out of business, banks failed, real estate belly-up, and everywhere the newly unemployed, looking for work where there is none.

From Dartmouth to Miami, and a firsthand look at the collapse of Pan American in its capital city. Local television devoted a great deal of time to the 7,500 workers suddenly let go, while stunned passengers crowded the ticket counters in order to read the scribbled message: 'All Pan Am flights cancelled' – forever. I thought of the arrogant Juan Trippe, who had founded the airline at about the same time that my father was founding what was to become TWA, now near bankruptcy. I am definitely dreaming, I decided, and drove on to Key West, which I had not seen since my last visit to Tennessee Williams, thirty years earlier. German and French families crowded Duval Street, taking advantage of the cheap (ever cheaper as I write) dollar. I felt like a ghost who has been granted a day's visit to the future. I split for limbo, my home city of Washington, DC, where I am due to address the National Press Club.

The usual efforts had been made to block my appearance but, as usual, they had failed. Apparently I am 'outrageous', a word never exactly defined, though – from what I can tell – it appears to mean that as I say what I think about our political system and as I think a lot more about it than any of our journalists who are paid to present an irreal picture of these bad times, I cause a degree of outrage if not, as I would hope, rage.

This is the third time in thirty years that I have talked to the press club. Before me, my father addressed the club; before him, my grandfather. In a way, this is a family affair, but lately the family's hometown seems to have fallen apart. That morning I had strolled from the Willard Hotel toward the Capitol. Burnt-out buildings were just off Pennsylvania Avenue; burnt-out people were on the avenue – and elsewhere, too. It was like the spring of 1932, when jobless veterans of World War I marched by the thousands on the capital and made a camp at the Anacostia Flats. They wanted a bonus. On June 17, I drove with my grandfather to the Senate. They stoned his car. Ever since, I have always known that the famous 'it' which can't happen here will happen here, and last month as I walked through my home city, 'it' seemed ever closer to hand, and we are now in a prerevolutionary time. Hence, the emphasis in the media on the breakup of the Soviet Union and Yugoslavia, or of anything other than the breakdown, if not breakup, of the United States and its economy. Just now, a month later, I watched on television as angry workers stormed through the streets of what I took to be Moscow until CNN identified the city as New York and the workers as members of one of our few labour unions – construction workers, I think, protesting lack of work, hope.

Like a ghost – but this time from the future – I tried to explain to the press club what it is they do that they don't know they do. I quote David Hume: The Few are able to control the Many only through Opinion. In the eighteenth century, Opinion was dispensed from pulpit and schoolroom. Now the media are in place to give us Opinion that has been manufactured in the boardrooms of those corporations – once national, now international – that control our lives.

Naturally, this sounded to my audience like the old conspiracy theory. Later, I was asked if I actually thought that Kay Graham and Larry Tisch really told the news departments of *The Washington Post* and CBS what to tell us. I said, Yes, of course, they do on occasion, but in everyday practice they don't need to give instructions because everyone who works for them thinks exactly alike on those economic issues that truly matter. I even mentioned the unmentionable, the ruling class. I noted that those members who were not going to inherit money are sent like Bush to Andover and me to Exeter – two schools for the relatively brainy. Those who will inherit money (e.g., the late Nelson Rockefeller) go to Groton or St Paul's, where, in order not to grow up to become dissolute wastrels, they will be taught useful hobbies, like stamp or people collecting. This sort of education insures that everyone so educated will tend to think alike. The few who break ranks are – what else? – outrageous. In any case, the indoctrination of the prep schools alone is usually quite enough to create a uniformity of ruling-class opinion when it comes to the rights of property. Since our corporate state is deeply democratic, there are always jobs available to middle-class careerists willing to play the game.

Almost forty years ago, I heard Secretary of State John Foster Dulles say that of course our foreign policy (as outlined in the then-secret National Security Council Memorandum 68) would lead to an arms race with the Soviet Union but that, as we were richer, they would cave in first. Dulles was right. They did. But he had not taken into account the economic cost to us or, worse, that in the process we would lose the old Republic and its Constitution, so revered by its current destroyers. Political decadence occurs when the forms that a state pretends to observe are known to be empty of all meaning. Who does not publicly worship the Constitution? Who, in practice, observes it at all? Congress has only two great powers under the Constitution: the power to declare war and the power of the purse. The first has been relinquished to the Executive; the second has drowned in a red sea.

The Supreme Court is no longer the Executive's equal. Rather, it is the Executive's tool. The White House's open coaching of the unqualified Clarence Thomas for a place on the Court made it dramatically clear that the Court now acts as a nine-member legal council to the Executive, its principal function the validation of Executive decrees. The current Court has also displayed a startling dislike of the American people, and the joy with which the nine nullities chop away at our Bill of Rights is a marvel to behold. But then the hatred of those *inside* the fabled Beltway for those *outside* has now – what else? – created a true hatred on the part of the Many for the Few who govern them, or appear to govern, since the actual decision makers – and the paymasters – are beyond anyone's reach, out there in the boardrooms of the world.

In the absence of true political debate, we have what I think of as the Sunday menagerie on television. Here journalists and politicians gaze at one another through the bars of received Opinion and chatter about 'process', a near-meaningless word in these parts. Recently I watched Richard Darman, the budget director, gabble to Messrs Evans and Novak about the deficit. To my amazement, the defence budget was actually mentioned by Evans. Apparently the Brookings Institution had daringly suggested that if a few hundred dollars were cut, we would still be able to support with our swift nuclear sword the 'democracy' of Tonga. But although the defence budget continues to be the cancer that is killing our body politic, it may not be dealt with at any length by the media, and Darman was swift to create the necessary diversion: 'Entitlements!' he moaned right on cue. 'If only we could get *them* on the table.' He shook his head in despair at the trillions of dollars that we waste on free dentures and on the financing in luxury of profligate unwed mothers.

Now it is wonderfully ironic for anyone to complain about what the zoo calls 'people programmes' because, wasteful or not, there aren't many. But no one can point this out on television because both journalists and politicians are hired by the same people and behind those people is the corporate wealth of the country, which requires that the budget be faked. The famous entitlements consist largely of disbursements for Social Security, and although Social Security contributions are always counted as part of the federal revenue, they are not. Social Security is a separate trust fund whose income and outgo have *nothing* to do with the actual budget. So why does the government like to pretend that Social Security payments are part of its annual revenue? Because if you take those payments *out* of the budget, everyone would realize that perhaps three-quarters or more of the federal income, over the years, has been spent on 'defence' or war-related matters or on servicing the debt on money borrowed for war.

If Social Security payments are not counted as revenue, Bush is currently spending $1.1 trillion a year, while taking in only $726 billion from taxes. The real national debt is about $4 trillion; in 1980 it was a mere $1 trillion. It is true that the Pentagon itself gets less money these days than it used to, but debt service, foreign aid, nuclear energy and payments to the true victims of our wars, the veterans, still account for most federal expenditures and deficits.

From time to time it is shyly suggested that taxes be raised – for individuals but never for corporations. To those who maintain that our political life is not controlled by corporations, let me offer a statistical proof of ownership – the smoking gun, in fact. In 1950, 44 per cent of federal revenues came from individual taxpayers and 28 per cent from a tax on corporate profits. Today, 37 per cent comes from individuals and only 8 per cent from the corporations (see John McDermott, 'The Secret History of the Deficit', August 21/28, 1982). Once Bush's only fiscal notion becomes law and the capital gains tax is eliminated, the work of corporate America will be complete, and the ownership will have ceased to support the United States. Naturally, should a badly run company like Chrysler go bust, the American people will be expected to pay for managerial mistakes. In any case, let it be solemnly noted that during the forty years of the national security state, corporate America not only collected most of the federal revenue for 'defence' but, in the process, reduced its share of federal taxes by twenty percentage points. Was this a conspiracy? No. They all think alike. Yes. They all think alike.

Since it is unlikely that Japan and Germany will forever continue to buy our Treasury bonds, how will the ownership pay for itself? Well, we could always renege on servicing the debt, but as Richard Nixon would say, *that would be the easy way* (and will, alas, be taken). The sublime way, which will be taken by the next administration, will be to sell off that 31 per cent of the United States that is held by the federal government in our name.* This fire sale will be highly popular with the buyers but it will be odd for Americans to have so little real estate to call their own.

When I was at the press club three years ago Opinion makers were mildly interested in overruns at the Defense Department. There was to be an investigation, and John Tower would be in place to make sure that nothing untoward was discovered. But Dick Cheney got the job instead, and there have been no meaningful investigations on his watch.

Meanwhile, the much discussed savings and loan 'bailout' is not possible. In current dollars and including service-connected veteran benefits, the cost of World War II was about $460 billion. The estimated cost of bailing out the S&Ls will be at least $500 billion. So, as *The Wall Street Journal* recently noted, the S&L bailout will cost $40 billion more than World War II. As for the state of the banks . . . well, it would appear that we have been robbed.

It is a commonplace that half of those qualified to vote for president don't vote; also that half the adult population never read a newspaper. No bad thing, all in all, assuming that they *could* read a newspaper, which is moot as our public schools are among the worst in the First World while our prison population, symmetrically, is the highest, surpassing the *ci-devant* Soviet Union. Naturally, we lead the First World in the execution of criminals or 'criminals'.

Every four years the naïve half who do vote are encouraged to believe that if we can elect a really nice man or woman President everything will be all right. But it won't be. Any individual who is able to raise $25 million** to be considered presidential is not going to be much use to the people at large. He will represent oil, or aerospace, or banking, or whatever moneyed entities are paying for him. Certainly he will never represent the people of the country, and they know it. Hence, the sense of despair throughout the land as incomes fall, businesses fail and there is no redress.

* A good chunk of Utah oil land was sold off in 1996.
** In the election of 1996 a billion dollars apiece was spent by Clinton and Dole. This is Rome during the fall.

Before the national security state was invented, we had something called 'representative government'. It did not work awfully well but at least there was some sense that, from time to time, something might be done about a depression – the sort of thing that cannot be done by a system in which most public revenues are earmarked for weaponry and war and secret police forces and, of course, the servicing of trillions of dollars' worth of debt.

'When we suffer, or are exposed to the same miseries *by a government*, which we might expect in a country *without government*, our calamities is [*sic*] heightened by reflecting that we furnish the means by which we suffer. Government, like dress, is the badge of lost innocence; the palaces of kings are built on the ruins of the bowers of paradise.' I quote from *Common Sense*, by Thomas Paine. How do we get rid of this bad government? There is certainly no road back to Eden in any society. Even if we could return, our own Eden was a most serpentine affair, based as it was on the enslavement of Africans and the slaughter and deportation of an indigenous population.

But until 1950, when our ramshackle world empire was institutionalized as the national security state, we *were* improving ourselves, and the generality took part in government while Opinion was not so cynically and totally manipulated as now. Since we cannot pay for the empire any longer, we shall soon be coming home – but to what? Our 'inalienable' rights are being systematically alienated. Never has an American government been so busy interfering with the private lives of its citizens, subjecting them to mandatory blood, urine, lie-detector tests. Yet the war on drugs has nothing at all to do with drugs. It is part of an all-out war on the American people by a government interested only in control. As this grows more evident, I suspect that we shall begin to see an organized resistance to so tyrannous a state. Meanwhile, as we have neither political parties nor, indeed, politics, only issueless elections, I see only one peaceful way out of this corpse of a Republic, this literally bankrupt national security state.

Article Five of the Constitution describes two methods whereby it may be amended or otherwise altered. One way, and so far the only way yet taken, is by a vote of two-thirds of both houses of Congress. The amendment is then sent for ratification by the state legislatures. The *second* procedure is very interesting indeed – in fact, one might almost call it democratic.

Two-thirds of the state legislatures can request a constitutional convention, which Congress must then convene. Unlike us, the founders did not worship their handiwork. Many thought the original Constitution was bound to fail. Thomas Jefferson wanted to hold a constitutional convention at least once a generation because, as he said, you cannot expect a man to wear a boy's jacket. As it turned out, the jacket has been so reshaped over the past two centuries that it is now a straitjacket for the people at large and satisfying to no one except those who gain election – and profits – from a most peculiar institution.

In recent years there have been several movements to convene a constitutional convention. These efforts have been the work of single-interest groups usually on the far right. One group wants to forbid abortion to every woman. Another wants a balanced budget embedded in the Constitution. What *is* interesting is that in the 1970s and 1980s thirty-two state legislatures voted in favour of such a convention; but many of them cautiously noted that no subject other than a balanced budget, say, could be discussed.

In 1967, Senator Sam Ervin was so intrigued by Article Five that he researched the subject and explained the mechanics of such a convention in S.2307. He came to the conclusion that, as *We the People* are the true *de jure* sovereign of these states, *We the People* cannot be held by anyone to any single issue once we convene *our* convention. If we so choose, the entire Constitution could be rewritten. At this point I part company with the American Civil Liberties Union, who, for once, are more pessimistic about the people than I. The first thing *they* will get rid of is the Bill of Rights, the liberals moan. To which the answer is, first, I don't think the people are suicidal and, second, what is the difference between losing those rights at an open convention as opposed to a gradual loss of them behind the closed doors of the current Supreme Court?

It is true that we are a less homogeneous and less educated people than the 3 million original inhabitants of the thirteen colonies. But I cannot believe that our convention would do away with our liberties while granting more power, say, to the Executive to fight wars that in the end harm only *us*. I am aware that the people at large have been kept ignorant by bad schools and by the dispensers of false Opinion. That is true. That is a problem. But ignorance is not stupidity. And self-interest, as both Hamilton and Madison agreed, is a great motor to the state, properly checked and balanced.

In any case, we are now faced with the fury of those who have been deprived for too long of decent lives. It takes no unusual power of prophecy to remark that they will not be apathetic forever. 'If it be not now, yet it will come. The readiness is all.' Rather than be *un*ready for anarchy, I submit that we must sit down and in an orderly way rethink our entire government as well as our place in the world.

The founders' last gift to us is the machinery to set things right. Article Five. Let us use it.

Thus, I ended my speech to the National Press Club – outrageously, of course.

The Nation
27 January 1992

5

The Union of the State

Over the years I have written quite a lot about the state of the Union. Now, in the interest of novelty, I'd like to discuss the *Union of the State*. I have always tried to say something so obvious that no one else has noticed it. For instance, I once suggested that we criminalize most firearms, and legalize most drugs. This would put an end to the now eternal War on Crime that, we are told, is devastating our alabaster cities and not doing the amber waves of marijuana much good either. I realize, of course, that vested interests are now too great for us to do anything of an intelligent nature in this – or almost any – regard. The National Rifle Association will never wither away as long as there is a single Congressman left to be paid off or a child unarmed.

Our violence and murder rate are unique in the First World. This may be a negative uniqueness but it is all our own, and to be cherished; at least we are number one at something other than indebtedness. We now have over a million people in prison and another couple of million on probation or parole; why not just lock up half the population and force the other half to guard them? That would solve crime; it might also entice Amnesty International to start whining here at home. After all, 58 per cent of those in our

federal prisons are there for drug offences. Most are not dangerous to the public, and even though our over-kindly government
thinks they are dangerous to themselves, they should still be
allowed to pursue their constitutional, if unhealthful, happiness in
freedom. Certainly they do not deserve to be confined to a prison
system that a Scandinavian commission recently reported to be
barbarous for a supposedly First World country.

Unfortunately, the rulers of *any* system cannot maintain their
power without the constant creation of prohibitions that then give
the state the right to imprison – or otherwise intimidate – anyone
who violates any of the state's often new-minted crimes. Without
communism – once monolithic and on the march – our state lacks
a Wizard of Oz to terrify all the people all the time. So the state
looks inward, at the true enemy, who turns out to be – who else?
the people of the United States. In the name of correctness, of
good health or even of God – a great harassment of the people-at-
large is now going on. Although our state has not the power to
intimidate any but small, weak countries, we can certainly throw
most Americans in prison for violating the ever-increasing list of
prohibitions. Will this change for the better with a change of
Congress or President? No. Things are going to get a lot worse
until we apply the state's new white hope to the state itself: Three
strikes, you're out. How then to 'strike out' the state? I have an
idea.

Kevin Phillips recently attacked – in *Time* – Washington, DC, a
beautiful city, built, if not on a hill, at least on what, in 1800, was a
quite attractive swamp. He quoted Jefferson's warning that when
every aspect of government is drawn to Washington – he meant the
city, not the general – Washington, in his words, would become 'as
venal and oppressive as the government from which we separated'.
(This was England, by the way, not the Disney studio so recently
and bloodily thrown back at Bull Run.)

Phillips tacitly acknowledges that the people have no representation within the Beltway, unlike the banks or insurance
companies. Consequently, officeholders and their shadow, the
media, are equally disliked by a vast majority. Unfortunately, the

people are without alternative. That is what makes the situation so volatile and potentially dangerous. Think what might have happened had Ross Perot possessed the oily charm of Charlton Heston. Certainly, it is plain that when a people comes to detest the political system in which it is entrapped, that system will not endure for long.

I've always been mystified at how obtuse politicians and the media are. Every politician of consequence, for the last quarter-century, has run against Washington, against lobbyists, against insiders, against Jefferson's 'venal and oppressive' ruling class – or, to be precise, the representatives of our actual rulers, who circle the globe like Puck with all the swift anonymous speed of a fax laden with campaign money. It is very hard, one would think, to live with so total a contradiction. For instance, both Carter and Reagan campaigned against Washington, and both won. Neither understood why people voted for him. Neither made the slightest attempt, even cosmetically, to curb Jefferson's tyrannous capital. The two new employees forgot their speeches and went right on doing business as instructed by those huge economic forces that govern earth.

Can someone like Clinton make a change? I don't see how. We would like health care of the sort every civilized nation has but we can never have a rational system as long as insurance companies are allowed to benefit. The people may want affordable health care, but they are not going to get it in the United States of America as now constituted.

Phillips has come up with an old notion of mine: devolution, the dictionary word for breaking up the Union into smaller, more manageable units. He would move much of the government away from Washington, I suppose to inconvenience the 800,000 lawyers who will then be able to deduct as legitimate travel expense the weary weekly journey from cozy Montgomery County to sky-topped Denver. He would move various departments permanently to other states and rotate the capital from this to that city. He would like an amendment to the Constitution 'setting up a mechanism for holding nationwide referendums to permit the citizenry

to supplant Congress and the President in making certain cat-
egories of national decisions.' Like declarations of war? Could he
be *that* radical? Along with this bit of major surgery on the body
politic, he has some useful Band-Aids. But no more. Nevertheless,
I am well-pleased that what I've been proposing for so long has
now gone mainline. So let me go a bit further out.

In 1992 I switched on CNN and heard Jerry Brown – in New
Hampshire – giving pretty much a speech that I had given for the
National Press Club [see 'Time for a People's Convention'] on how
to restore power to its only legitimate source, We the People. As
Jerry and I had not spoken since I ran against him in the
California Senate primary in 1982, I was pleasantly surprised and
praised him publicly for his wisdom, while blessing him for his
plagiarism, no matter how belated. He rang me in Italy. Yes, it was
my speech. Unlike Joe Biden, he is an honest man. And did I have
anything more? And would I come to New Hampshire? I said, yes,
I had more, but, no, I would forgo the winter wonderland of New
Hampshire, currently known as Dole Land.

However, thanks to CNN and the fax machine, I could monitor
his campaign and send him my thoughts immediately. So a number of suggestions of mine entered the primary campaign. The
principal notion was conversion from war to peace. Find a defence
plant that's closing and say that it should be kept open but converted to peacetime, using the same workforce and technology.
Brown did just that in Connecticut. He told the soon-to-be-
dismissed makers of Seawolf submarines that if he became
President, they would be making not submarines but bullet trains.
At 5 in the morning I got a call from political operator Pat Caddell.
'We won!' he said. 'We won Connecticut.' Then they – not we – lost
New York.

Meanwhile, Perot grabbed my *We the People* as the strange device
for his eccentric banner. I felt very odd, watching CNN in Italy,
and hearing at least three candidates using my lines.

Jerry was headed for Pennsylvania after New York and, as the
game was up, I said why not propose something really useful:
launch a new idea that might take a few years to penetrate but

when it does, might save us all.

Here is the gist of what I wrote him. I started with the eternal problem of what we do about income tax. As the people at large get nothing much back from the money that they give the government – Social Security is not federal income – why not just eliminate the federal income tax? How? Eliminate Washington, DC. Allow the states and municipalities to keep what revenue they can raise. I know that tens if not hundreds of thousands of lobbyist-lawyers and hired media gurus will have a million objections. But let us pursue the notion.

Why not divide the country into several reasonably homogeneous sections, more or less on the Swiss cantonal system? Each region would tax its citizens and then provide the services those citizens wanted, particularly education and health. Washington would then become a ceremonial capital with certain functions. We shall always need some sort of modest defence system, a common currency and a Supreme Court to adjudicate between the regions as well as to maintain the Bill of Rights – a novelty for the present Court.

How to pay for what's left of Washington? Each region will make its own treaty with the central government and send what it feels should be spent on painting the White House and on our common defence, which will, for lack of money, cease to be what it is now – all-out offence on everyone on earth. The result will be no money to waste either on pork or on those imperial pretensions that have left us $4.7 trillion in debt. Wasteful, venal, tyrannous Washington will be no more than a federal theme park administered by Michael Eisner.

Will the regions be corrupt, venal, etc.? Of course they will – we are Americans! – but they will be corrupt on an infinitesimal scale. Also, more to the point, in a smaller polity everyone knows who's up to no good and they can police themselves better than the federal government ever could – even if it had ever wanted to.

All over the world today centrifugal forces are at work. In a bloody war in the old Yugoslavia and parts of the old Soviet Union, and in a peaceful way in the old Czechoslovakia. Since history is nothing but the story of the migration of tribes, we must now note that the tribes are very much on the move again, and thanks to modern technology we can actually watch Bengals and Indians overflowing each other's borders.

Racially, the composition of Europe has changed more in the past fifty years than in the previous 500. Whether this is good or bad is irrelevant. It is. Now, here at home, people fret about invasions from the Hispanic world, from Haiti, from the boat people of Asia. But, like it or not, we are changing from a white, Protestant country, governed by males, to a mixed polity, and in this time of change there is bound to be conflict. The fragmentations that we see everywhere are the result of a *dislike* for the nation-state as we have known it since the bloody nation-building of Bismarck and Lincoln.

People want to be rid of arbitrary capitals and faraway rulers. So let the people go. If our southern tier is to be Spanish and Catholic, let it be. But also, simultaneously, as we see in Europe, while this centrifugal force is at work – a rushing away from the centre – there is also a centripetal one, a coming-together of small polities in order to have better trade, defence, culture – so we are back, if by change, to our original Articles of Confederation, a group of loosely confederated states rather than a *United* State, which has proved to be every bit as unwieldy and ultimately tyrannous as Jefferson warned. After all, to make so many of Many into One you must use force, and this is a bad thing, as we experienced in the Civil War. So let us make new arrangements to conform with new realities.

I will not go so far as to say that we shall ever see anything like democracy at work in our section of North America – traditionally we have always been a republic entirely governed by money, but at least, within the regions, there will be more diversity than there is now and, best of all, the people will at last have the sensation that they are no longer victims of a far-off government but that they – and their tax money – are home at last.

The Nation
26 December 1994

6

Mickey Mouse, Historian

On June 3, 1996 *The Nation* showed in a foldout chart how most of the US media are now owned by a handful of corporations. Several attractive octopi decorated the usually chaste pages of this journal. The most impressive of these cephalopod molluscs was that headed by Disney-ABC, taking precedence over the lesser Time Warner, General Electric–NBC and Westinghouse Corporation calamari, from which dangle innumerable tentacles representing television (network and cable), weapons factories (G.E. aircraft engines and nuclear turbines) and, of course, G.N.A. and other insurance firms unfriendly to health care reform.

As I studied this beast, I felt a bit like Rip Van Winkle. When last I nodded off, there was something called the Sherman Anti-trust Act. Whatever happened to it? How can any octopus control so much opinion without some objection from . . . from whom? That's the problem. Most members of Congress represent not states or people but corporations – and octopi. Had I simply dreamed John Sherman? Or had he been devoured by Dragon Synergy? Little did I suspect, as I sighed over this latest demonstration of how tightly censored we are by the few, that, presently, I would be caught in the tentacles of the great molluscs Disney–ABC and

General Electric–NBC, as well as the Hearst Corporation, whose jointly owned cable enterprise Arts & Entertainment had spawned, in 1995, something called The History Channel.

'It all began in the cold,' as Arthur Schlesinger Jr so famously began his romantic historical novel *A Thousand Days*. Only my cold was London, where, for Channel Four, I wrote and narrated three half-hour programmes on the American presidency, emphasizing the imperial aspects latent in the office from the beginning, and ending, currently, with our uneasy boast that we are the last great global power on the ... well, globe. 'The one indispensable nation', said President Clinton – or did he say 'disposable'?

The programmes were well received in Britain. The History Channel bought the US rights. In ninety-minute form my view of the imperial presidency was to be shown just before the 1996 political conventions. But then, from the tiny tentacle tip of The History Channel, synergy began to surge up the ownership arm, through NBC to its longtime master General Electric; then ever upward, to, presumably, the supreme mollusc, Mickey Mouse himself, Lord of Anaheim. *Great Mouse, this programme attacks General Electric by name. Attacks American imperialism, which doesn't exist. Bad-mouths all that we hold sacred.* Oh, to have been a fly on the castle wall when word arrived! The easy solution, as Anaheim's hero-President, R. M. Nixon, might have said, would have been to kill the programme. But craftier minds were at work. *We'll get some 'experts' like we do for those crappy historical movies and let them take care of this Commie.*

So it came to pass that, unknown to me, a G.E. panel was assembled; it comprised two fly-weight journalists from television's Jurassic Age (Roger Mudd, Sander Vanocur) and two professors, sure to be hostile (one was my old friend Arthur Schlesinger Jr, about whose client, J.F.K., I am unkind; the other was someone called Richard Slotkin). I was not invited to defend myself, nor was anyone else. As a spokesperson for The History Channel put it, 'Vidal is so *opinionated* that we had to have real experts on.' *The Nation*'s recent warning about the danger of allowing the corporate few to make and control mass opinion was about to be dramatized at my expense.

Fade in: Roger Mudd. He is grim. He wears, as it were, not so much the black cap of the hanging judge as the symbol of his awful power, *Mickey Mouse ears*. He describes my career with distaste. Weirdly, he says I had 'social ambitions at the Kennedy White House and [*non sequitur*] ran for Congress' but lost. Actually, I ran for Congress before Kennedy got to the White House. Also, in upstate New York, I got some 20,000 more votes than J.F.K. did as head of the ticket. During my campaign, Bobby Kennedy came to see me at Saugerties Landing. It was, appropriately, Hallowe'en. 'Why,' he snarled, 'don't you ever mention the ticket?' 'Because I want to win,' I said, imitating his awful accent. That started the feud.

Mudd reports that I am 'acerbic, acid-tongued', don't live in the United States (except when I do), and the viewer is warned beforehand that this is only my 'bilious look' at American history and our presidents, whom Mudd says that I describe variously as incompetent, avaricious warmongers. This is – warmongering to one side – slanderously untrue. Then, Mickey Mouse ears atremble with righteous indignation, he reassures us that, at programme's end, *real* historians will set the record straight. And so, muddied but unbowed, I fade in.

I begin in a sort of mock-up of the White House TV room. I say a few mildly bilious words about current politics.

He who can raise the most money to buy time on television is apt to be elected president by that half of the electorate that bothers to vote. Since the same corporations pay for our two-party, one-party system, there is little or no actual politics in these elections. But we do get a lot of sex. Also, he who subtly hates the blacks the most will always win a plurality of the lilywhite-hearted. The word 'liberal' has been totally demonized, while 'conservative', the condition of most income-challenged Americans, is being tarnished by godly pressure groups whose symbols are the foetus and the flag. As a result, today's candidates are now rushing toward a meaningless place called 'the centre', and he who can get to the centre of the centre, the dead centre, as it were, will have a four-year lease on this studio.

I then trace the history of our expansionist presidents from Jefferson's Louisiana Purchase to Bush of Mesopotamia's Gulf War, produced by Ted Turner's CNN, a sort of in-house TV war. I end the programme in front of the Vietnam Memorial. We have come a long way, I say, from Jefferson's Declaration of Independence to 'the skies over Baghdad have been illuminated.' Then Mudd, more than ever horrified by what he'd seen and heard, introduces a TV journalist called Vanocur, who introduces Professors Schlesinger and Slotkin. It's very clear, says Vanocur, that Vidal doesn't like America. Arthur's response is mild. Well, let's say he is disappointed in what's happened.

At the beginning of Mudd's first harangue, I must say I did wonder what on earth had caused such distress. It was clear that neither cue-card reader had any particular interest – much less competence – in American history; but then, I had forgotten the following aria:

Our presidents, now prisoners of security, have been for a generation two-dimensional figures on a screen. In a sense, captives of the empire they created. Essentially, they are men hired to give the commercials for a state which more and more resembles a conglomerate like General Electric. In fact, one of our most popular recent presidents spent nearly twenty years actually doing commercials for General Electric, one of our greatest makers of weapons. Then Mr Reagan came to work here [in the White House], and there was the same 'Russians are coming' dialogue on the same Teleprompter, and the same make-up men.

The G.E. panel, carefully, made no reference to their fellow pitchman Reagan, but they found unbearable my suggestion that we have been surpassed, economically, by Asia. I noted that:

As Japan takes its turn as world leader, temporarily standing in for China, America becomes the Yellow Man's Burden, and so we come full circle. Europe began as the relatively empty, uncivilized Wild West of Asia. Then the Americans became the Wild West of Europe. Now the sun, setting in our West, is rising once more in the East.

This really hurt Mudd, and he couldn't resist noting that Japan's standard of living is lower than ours, a factoid that, presumably, magically cancels our vast debt to them. He reminds us that we have also been hearing a lot of bad economic news about other countries; but then we always do, lest Americans ever feel that they are being short-changed by a government that gives its citizens nothing for their tax money and companies like General Electric billions for often useless weapons and costly overruns. Approvingly, Mudd tells us that 'industrious immigrants' are rushing to our shores. Well, those we have helped to impoverish south of the Rio Grande do come looking for work, particularly from countries whose societies we have wrecked in the name, often, of corporate America (United Fruit in Guatemala, I.T.T. in Chile), or they come from Southern Asia, where our interferences dislocated millions of people, some of whom unwisely boated to our shores, lured by our generous minimum wage, universal health care and superb state educational system.

Mudd's mouse squeak becomes very grave indeed as he tells us how the defence budget has been slashed to a mere fraction of what it used to be and must be again if we are ever to keep the peace of the world through war. Yet today we outspend the military budgets of Western Europe and Japan combined. Although there have been large cuts in personnel as military bases are turned over to the real estate lobby, outlays of the sort that benefit Mudd's employers still run to nearly $300 billion a year.

The two historians were less openly protective of General Electric and military procurement. Schlesinger doesn't find much in the way of historical distortion. But then what motive would I have had to neglect what Jefferson liked to call 'true facts'? I am neither political publicist nor hagiographer, and I know the country's history as well as most people who have dedicated a generation to its study.

Schlesinger does say that I misquote Jefferson's Declaration of Independence. That must sound pretty serious to the average viewer. It also sounds pretty serious to me that Arthur doesn't realize I was quoting, accurately, the original preamble, not the one edited and published by Congress. Jefferson – and I – preferred his first version, of which only a fragment still exists but, luckily, later in life he re-created the original: 'All men are created equal and independent.' Congress cut the 'and independent'. Then: 'From that equal creation, they derive rights inherent and inalienable.' Congress (looking ahead to the Rev. Pat Robertson and all the other serpents in our Eden?) changed this to 'They are endowed by their Creator with certain inalienable rights.' The introduction of a Creator has done our independence no good.

Early on, I observe that 'an adviser to President Truman announced "What is good for General Motors is good for America." The adviser was president of General Motors, of course.' Arthur correctly notes that Charles Wilson was not a member of Truman's Cabinet but of Eisenhower's. Nevertheless, he was a significant *adviser* to Truman. Unfortunately, his famous advice to Truman got edited out of my final programme. Here it is. In 1944 Wilson gave his rationale for a permanent militarizing of the economy: 'Instead of looking to disarmament and unpreparedness as a safeguard against war – a thoroughly discredited doctrine – let us try the opposite: full preparedness according to a continuing plan.' This was to be the heart of the National Security Act of 1947, and the new nation in whose shabby confines we still rattle about.

Arthur does catch me in one 'error'. Tyler, not Polk, annexed Texas, three days before Polk took office. Schlesinger also says that I am wrong about Jackson being 'big business'. But in 1836, Jackson broke up the Second Bank of the United States, a useful if imperfect financial instrument, one-fifth owned by the United States, which he replaced with numerous small banks often run by crooked cronies. The financial panic of 1837 was the result. I call that big business on the largest scale. I've never thought our Harlequin historian quite understood the financial mischief set in train by his romantic protagonist whose 'age' he wrote of in an entertaining book.

It is a little late in the day to turn Lincoln into an abolitionist, but the G.E. panel saw an easy way of making points by piously declaring how much great-hearted Lincoln hated slavery. But I had already noted, 'He disliked slavery but thought the federal government had no right to free other people's property. In this case, 3 million African-Americans at the South.' It should be noted – yet again – that American history departments are now bustling with propagandists revising Lincoln so that he will appear to be something quite other than the man who said that if he could preserve the Union by freeing all the slaves, he would do so, or freeing some and not others, he would do so, or freeing none at all he would free none for the Union's sake. But for General Electric, blushing bride of Mickey Mouse, the image of Lincoln cannot remain half Disney and half true.

At one point, Slotkin accuses me of dealing in hindsight. But that, dear professor, is what history is, and you and I and even Arthur are historians, aren't we? It is true that I refused election to the Society of American Historians; but I am no less a historian than those who are paid to keep the two essential facts of our condition from the people at large: the American class system (there is no such thing, we are flatly told) and the nature of the US empire (no such thing, either). Apparently, it is perfectly natural for a freedom-loving democracy, addicted to elections, to have bases and spies and now FBI terrorist fighters and drug hounds in every country on earth. When Vanocur tries to get Theodore Roosevelt off the imperialist hook, Schlesinger does mutter that the great warmonger did believe in 'a vigorous foreign policy'. Then Arthur makes a slip: T.R. was really only interested in our 'domination of the Western Hemisphere'. Well, certainly half a globe is better than none. But then, as T.R. said, 'No accomplishment of peace is half that of the glories of war.'

Schlesinger notes that, if Jefferson and John Quincy Adams were to return today, they would be surprised that we had not annexed Canada, Cuba and other Western properties. For the G.E. panel such continence is proof that there is no such thing as a US empire. Well, it is true that after two failed invasions, Canada escaped us; even so, we have a naval base on Canadian soil (at Argentia), and Canada plays its dutiful if irritable part in our imperium, economically as well as militarily. Cuba was, in effect, our brothel during the Batista years; now, for trying to be independent of us, it is embargoed while we maintain on the island, as always, the military base of Guantánamo.

Toward the end of their 'discussion', one of the Mouseketeers mocks the notion that big business is in any way responsible for a US empire that does not exist. The G.E. panel, to a man, then proceeds to ignore this key section of my script:

> T.R.'s successor, Woodrow Wilson, invaded Mexico and Haiti in order to bring those poor people freedom and democracy and good government. But stripped of all the presidential rhetoric, the flag followed the banks.
>
> The President was simply chief enforcer for the great financial interests.
>
> Many years later, the commanding general of the US Marine Corps, General Smedley Butler, blew, as it were, the whistle, not just on Wilson, but on the whole imperial racket.

I had showed some fine newsreel footage of Butler, of Marines in Haiti, Taiwan, the streets of Shanghai. I did an imitation of his voice as I spoke his actual words:

> 'I spent most of my time being a high-class muscle man for big business, for Wall Street and for the bankers. In short, I was a racketeer, a gangster for capitalism. I helped make Mexico safe for American oil interests in 1914. Made in Haiti and Cuba a decent place for the National City Bank boys to collect revenues in.'

In later years, Butler also set up shop in Nicaragua, the Dominican Republic and China, where in 1927 the Marines protected Standard Oil's interests.

Vidal as Butler: 'The best Al Capone had was three districts. I operated on three continents.'

Needless to say, General Butler is a permanent nonfigure in our imperial story.

Slotkin began to paraphrase exactly what I had been saying – modern empires are not like the old-fashioned sort where you raise your flag over the capitol of a foreign country. From 1950 on, I demonstrated how the domination of other countries is exercised through the economy (the Marshall Plan after World War II) and through a military presence, preferably low-key (like NATO in Western Europe) and politically through secret police like the CIA, the FBI, the DEA, the DIA, etc. Currently, the empire is ordering its vassal states not to deal with rogue nations (the Helms–Burton bill).

Although the Soviet Union went out of business five years ago, we still have bases in Belgium, Germany, Greece, Italy, the Netherlands, Portugal, Spain, Turkey. In Britain we have seven air force and three naval bases. In 1948, Secretary of Defense Forrestal installed two B-29 groups in the English countryside; it would be a good idea, he said, to accustom the English to a continuing US military presence. To create and administer a modern empire you must first discover – or invent – a common enemy and then bring all the potential victims of this ogre under *your* domination, using your secret services to skew their politics as the CIA did, say, to Harold Wilson's Labour Party.

Today, elsewhere, we have military presences in Bermuda, Egypt, Iceland, Japan, Korea, Panama, the Philippines, Saudi Arabia, Kuwait, etc., not to mention all over the United States and our territories as well as two bases in Australia, a mysterious CIA unit at Alice Springs. If all this does not constitute an empire I don't know what does. Yet we must not use the word, for reasons that the G.E. panel never addressed. At one point, Vanocur pretended that I had said the American people were eager for conquest when I said the opposite. Our people tend to isolationism and it always takes a lot of corporate manipulation, as well as imperial presidential mischief, to get them into foreign wars. Sadly, Schlesinger confirmed that this was so.

Slotkin thought that I had been saying that the late nineteenth-century presidents were creatures of big business when what I said was that big business was off on its rampage and that the presidents, between Lincoln and Theodore Roosevelt, were dimly accommodating.

Then the question of why I was so evil was gravely addressed. Mouse ears were now on the alert. Schlesinger noted that I had headed the America First chapter at Exeter in 1940 and that I still seemed to be an isolationist. Vanocur said isolationists were right-wingers. Schlesinger countered that many, like Norman Thomas (and me), were on the left. Mud, as it were, in hand, Vanocur said that isolationism is 'tinged with anti-Semitism', but that did not play. Schlesinger did note, with a degree of wonder, that there are those who do not seem to understand how our future is inextricably bound up in the politics of all the other continents. This might have been a good place to start an enlightening debate. Had I been included, I might have said that unless the nation is in actual peril (or in need of loot – I am not angelic) there is never any reason for us to engage in foreign wars. Since George Washington, the isolationist has always had the best arguments. But since corporate money is forever on the side of foreign adventure, money has kept us on the move, at least until recently.

I said that Stalin drastically disarmed after the war. Arthur rightly pointed out that so did we: pressure from the isolationist masses forced the government to let go millions of G.I.s, including me. But two days after the announcement of Japan's surrender, Truman said (August 17, 1945) that he would ask Congress to approve a programme of universal military training – in peacetime! He made the request, and got his wish. We rearmed as they disarmed. Briefly.

Between May and September 1946, Truman began the rearmament of our sector of Germany while encouraging the French in their recolonization of Indochina, as well as meddling militarily in China and South Korea. The great problem of living in a country where information and education are so tightly controlled is that very little news about our actual situation ever gets through to the consumers. Instead we are assured that we are so hated by those envious of our wealth and goodness that they commit terrorist acts against us simply out of spite. The damage our presidential and corporate imperialists have done to others in every quarter of the world is a non-subject, as we saw in August, when my realistic overview accidentally appeared on an imperial network and a panel of four was rushed into place to glue mouse ears back on the eagle's head.

Vanocur then affects to be mystified by why I saw so many terrible things about the Disneyland that pays him his small salary. But I thought I had made myself clear. I am a patriot of the old Republic that slowly unravelled during the expansionist years and quite vanished in 1950 when the National Security State took its place. Now I want us to convert from a wartime to a peacetime economy. But since the G.E.-style conglomerates that govern us will never convert, something will have to give, won't it?

When the egregious Vanocur wondered why I had done this programme, Arthur said, 'To entertain himself – and to entertain the audience.' That was disappointing but worthy of the Dr Faustus of Harvard Yard.

I did not report on my country's disastrous imperial activities with much amusement. All I wanted to do was tell a story never told before on our television – and never to be told again as long as the likes of G.E. and Disney are allowed to be media owners and manipulators of opinion.

What to do? Break up the conglomerates. That's a start. And then – well, why not go whole hog – what about a free press, representative government and. . . . Well, you get the picture.

The Nation
30 September 1996

7
US out of UN – UN out of US

The first American Secretary of Defense, James V. Forrestal, on July 15, 1949, in the name of NATO, the Four Freedoms and the pursuit of happiness, accomplished the first successful invasion of England since the Normans when he sent two groups of B-29s to the UK, observing privately to President Truman that it would be a good idea 'to accustom the English' to the ongoing presence of the American air force. Less than a year later, suffering from nervous exhaustion, he put down his copy of Sophocles' *Ajax* and jumped out of a hospital window, leaving behind not only his annotated *Ajax* but the outward visible sign of American occupation, our English bases.

A busy half-century now draws to a close. Along the way, in 1989, the Evil Soviet Empire surrendered to our goodness. Now, as the self-styled Sole Global Nuclear Power, we fire commands rapidly at friend and foe alike. President Clinton, responding gleefully to Congress's targeting of 'terrorist nations', has warned the entire world that if any foe or ally dares do business with Libya and Iran and Iraq, much less leprous Cuba, we shall . . . well, like Lear, we'll do something or other. Don't worry. Are we not the SGNP?

Currently American conservatives (whatever that word now

means) are calling for a *new* imperialism. In the pages of the latest *Foreign Affairs* William Kristol and Robert Kagan (aesthetically, one wants a third 'K') tell us that 'Today's lukewarm consensus about America's reduced role in a post-Cold War world is wrong.' They like simple declarative sentences. So here's one for them. The largest debtor nation on earth has no choice but to reduce its imperial role. No money. The Ks are Reaganites and see the former President as a sort of American Bismarck, although it was as General Custer that he made his mark in movie history, which seems to be their only history, too. The Ks are in the grip of a most unseemly megalomania. 'American hegemony is the only reliable defence against a breakdown of peace and international order.' Tell that to the Asians.

The Ks also say that as we have never been so well off, we can afford to spend an additional $60–80 billion a year on war. This is nonsense. (The style is contagious.) They want a Reaganesque military build-up of great profit to aerospace industries and no one else. Their high-minded line is that there are bound to be many, many more exciting wars for us to fight and win. They seem to believe that our Declaration of Independence was not just for us but a blueprint for the whole world, which is longing to be American. The truth seems otherwise. Hearken to the howls from our allies as the radiant Oval One, from his ever-more Byzantine capital, tells others with whom they may not trade.

One must at least give the 'conservatives', as represented by the Ks, a mark for trying to find something for the United States to do now that the world has settled down to its usual mess of tribal rivalries and trade wars. The British, after the Suez debacle, were given to quoting Dean Acheson – a creator of the Global Empire – to the effect that Britain had lost an empire but had yet to find a role. In answer, J. B. Priestley wrote a wise meditation on the royal coat-of-arms – suggesting that now that the days of the lion were done, why not turn to the unicorn, a mythical elegant beast suggestive of magic and art? And so a considerable flowering in the arts lasted for at least a generation. We have no comparable heraldic lineage, only the bald-headed American eagle, so reminiscent of General

Eisenhower when he tried to give up smoking.

The Ks want the eagle to be brought back to life, claws clutching thunderbolts, the odd olive branch. Apparently, earth is American and we must govern all of it for the good of the human race. But the other nations did not elect us leader post-1989. Rather, Western Europe comes slowly together. Japan prepares for a new metamorphosis while China, 'the sleeping giant' that Napoleon said only a fool would awaken, is already an American creditor. The old order is gone for ever and the brief hegemony of the white race is drawing to an unmourned close.

The Ks seem to be living in a world that never really existed outside the movies or American political rhetoric. They find 'the Europeans and the Japanese supportive of [our] world leadership role'. Not this week nor, indeed, for some years now has the United States been looked to as an upholder of international law and order. When requested to go before the tribunal at The Hague to explain alleged crimes against Nicaragua, the US refused to accept the jurisdiction of a court that we had helped set up. Also, whenever the fit is upon the Oval One, he feels perfectly free to bomb Gaddafi's family or invade Panama killing quite a few Panamanians as he kidnaps their leader and then puts him on trial in an American court that has no jurisdiction over him. Such a model of international roguery is hardly eligible to fill the Ks' notion of a benign world hegemon. What they actually hanker after is Caesarism, no bad option if you are really stronger militarily and economically than everyone else but, alas, aside from the power to nuclearize the planet, Uncle Sam, he dead.

The Declaration of Independence is sometimes thought by old-fashioned European conservatives to be a liberal document. Here, I think, they mix it up with the French Rights of Man, a truly radical and always – to some of us – heartening trumpet blast. Our own declaration was a more modest affair. Life, liberty and the pursuit of happiness were the set goals. But liberty hardly means the levelling of classes to those rich white conservative men who fancifully called the forcible separation of colonies from British Crown a revolution when it was simply an inevitable devolution. England

215

was too small and too far away to govern so many people, so much territory.

Pursuit of happiness was an exceptional thought and, like the Holy Ghost for serious Christians, something to brood upon. In any case, the American day has pretty much run out. The Ks speak for no one except energetic political hustlers within the Washington Beltway. But as the US grows shakier at home and abroad, accidents can still happen. That is why, in the light of the current uproar over President Clinton's boycotting of entire countries, it might be a good idea to start, as tactfully as possible, the removal of the United Nations from the United States and then of the United States from the United Nations (unless, of course, a billion dollars of dues owing are paid).

This sign of world solidarity would clear the air, to riot in understatement, and serve notice that no house in such economic and domestic disarray as that of the very last global power can exercise hegemony over anything other than itself. Such was the intention of our truly conservative founders two centuries ago when they adjured us to follow our own course toward some more perfect – if ungrammatical – union, making true in the process Ajax's hope: 'Ah, boy, may'st thou prove happier than thy sire.' And not, dementedly, slaughter sheep.

The Sunday Telegraph
11 August 1996

8

Race Against Time

Immigration, emigration. Race. Let them in. Keep them out. Should we do the jobs that they do that we don't want to do? Last month an American poll showed that for the first time immigration is the number one anxiety of our stout, sugar-fed people as they restlessly switch channels and ponder the fate of dinosaurs and the nation state.

Recently I toured seven German cities, and spoke at various meetings. The German press was full of anxious reports on the neo-Nazi racists in its midst. It was even more upset by the *non* neo-Nazi racists. The unemployed in particular were attacking Turks and East Europeans and other foreigners. What did it all mean?

There is no longer enough work to go around. That is, proper work as opposed to part-time labour with no future, the sort of work that ill-paid foreigners now do. Every day we read how another great industry has let go yet another 30,000 or 40,000 workers. Automation and reduced demand have made them redundant. What will these people do? Is the state to support them? If so, how? This basic question is generally avoided, particularly by professional politicians, so I shall, for the moment, sidestep it too.

Racism. The fear of otherness is an unattractive but constant human trait, and one that we social meliorists like to say education and peaceful co-mingling will do away with in, as always, time. There is some truth in this. There is also some truth in the saying that all men are brothers, as Abel must have reminded Cain, who replied as he lifted his club, 'Yes, and all brothers are men.'

In Germany I used a line that I often use in the United States when I think that the audience is unaware of the world outside its own national and ethnic bubble. I noted that at the start of the next millennium the white race will make up about 13 per cent of the world's population. This statistic makes white Americans look even whiter, while the dusky faces in the audience begin to beam. The German reaction was hysteria. Race, declared a tense young man, is a myth. I said, no, race is a fact, but the prejudices that people have about races are often mythical.

Also, even if everyone was all the same grey-pink shade, the myths of difference would still be invoked, and myths are very potent. For me, God is a myth, but I am quite aware that millions of people have died non-mythical deaths in his name. In Britain, cavaliers and roundheads went into battle, each side shouting 'Kill for Jesus'.

Always accommodating, I said that if I could not use the word 'race' – an everyday sort of word in my country with no built-in resonance – would 'tribalism' do? No, that was unacceptable. People who spoke of races and tribes in Germany were almost always neo-Nazis. What word *could* I use?

'Multiculturalism' was the consensus in Stuttgart. But, I said, an American white and an American black will often be prejudiced against one another, and each shares exactly the same culture, or its absence. We left the subject in the air. But I remember thinking that if one does not have the words to discuss a matter objectively, emotions will ensure that it then becomes dangerously subjective.

Due to poverty in other sections of the world and a declining standard of living for most people in our part of it, emotions are getting pretty raw. The time is over-ripe for dialogue as opposed to the monologues of demagogues. I see this, curiously, more in Europe today than in the United States. We have had a race war

218

between black and white for over a century now. It is like a low-grade fever that, from time to time, flares up and puts the patient at risk. On the other hand, we are used to it. We take or give our quinine, which is known as welfare, a bribe that we pay to the black underclass in order to exclude them from white society. Meanwhile, we never cease to boast that we are a nation of immigrants.

Racial stereotypes are irresistible, particularly in wartime. I know. I was an American soldier in the great race war against Japan. I served in the Pacific. Our indoctrination was crude and hilarious. In early 1941 the government assured us that, should war come, we would easily win it through air power. Apparently, because of the weird configuration of the Japanese eye, they could not see well enough to be able to manage modern aircraft. Not long after, they sank our fleet at Pearl Harbor.

Before I left to go to the Pacific – I was first-mate of an army freight supply ship – we were given an indoctrination course on how to tell our exquisite allies, the Chinese, from our brutish enemy, the Japanese. On a stage there was a life-sized cut-out of a naked Chinese youth and another one of a Japanese. The Chinese was tall, slim and well proportioned. The Japanese was bandy-legged, buck-toothed, sub-human.

These details were shown to us by an information officer with a pointer. 'But the principal difference,' he announced, 'is the pubic hair. The Japanese is thick and wiry while the Chinese is straight and silky.' I fear that I alone raised my hand to ask what sly strategies we were to use to determine friend from foe.

Our war with Japan was deeply ideological. They had the idea that the Pacific Ocean should be theirs, while we had the idea that it should be ours. This is known as a *conflict* of ideologies. As it turned out, our war of conquest was more successful than theirs. In fact, our hegemony in the Pacific and over Japan was the last great military victory that the white race will probably ever know. Now *they* have the technology and the wealth. And *we* decline.

In the fifteenth century it was as if there was a sudden big bang. The white race in Western Europe – itself a sort of Wild West to the

Asian land-mass – burst its cage. Like a plague, we infected the western hemisphere, Africa, Asia. We were also, literally, a plague, carrying with us so many new diseases that indigenous populations often died out. Though our numbers were relatively few, we colonized. The great goal for our race was China: specifically the north-central Shansi province, the world's largest coalfield.

By the start of the century the European powers and the United States were already established on the China coast. But we now had a rival in Japan. They too wanted the Middle Kingdom. So the struggle between our two races over the division of China has been pretty much the history of the century now ending. Yet, through all this, China has endured and is now set to prevail while Japan is finally *a* – as opposed to *the* – master race.

The loss of identity – not to mention wealth, power and empire – makes for melancholy, or worse. As Dean Acheson famously put it, Britain has lost an Empire but not yet found a role. Fifty years later the United States is in much the same situation. So, too, is Western Europe. In the fourteenth century our race was more than decimated in Europe by the plague. In the fifteenth century population revived – too much so. What were we to do with so many people? We broke loose and conquered most of the world.

The wealth of the western hemisphere paid for the Renaissance in Europe. The wealth of India fuelled the industrial revolution in England. We colonized almost every part of the world, imposing, in the process, our peculiar version of monotheism, one that is crude, savage and hostile to life. For most of the world, particularly those with older and subtler civilizations, we were an unmitigated curse. But we never suspected that we were anything but good, as we went about stealing and converting others to our primitive ways.

What is human history but the migration of tribes? The so-called Aryans swept down into Europe and Persia and India in about 1500 BC. They settled and were absorbed. Then came Huns, Mongols, Arabs. They seldom stayed for long, nor did they, by and large, colonize. By the time our race got busy, we had somehow moved ahead in the applied sciences, particularly those relating to warfare. Incas, Mayans, Hindus, Chinese were no match for us.

Now as the twentieth century draws to a close, we seem to have run out of petrol. We still have the power to atomize the globe but then, with a bit of hard work, so can the Pakistanis. We are no longer unique, even in our destructive powers. We have entered a period of uneasy stasis. What are we do do next, if indeed we still are 'we' at all, rather than just an element in a rainbow mix as is the case in many parts of the United States and, here and there, in Britain.

At the moment 'we' are defensive, even paranoid. Are we to lose what's left of our identity? Are we to lose our traditional countries to immigrants of different races? There is much moaning in the West.

Since we have our countries, the desire to keep them reasonably homogeneous is reflexive and hardly extraordinary. Yet minor immigration has been the rule ever since native whites discovered that poorly paid other-tinted people would do the work that the whites find untouchable. But now major population shifts threaten. Everywhere the tribes are on the move. From south and east they converge on Europe; from south and west on North America.

Meanwhile, internal pressures are building up in all the nation states. In fact, a case can be made that the nation state, as redesigned by Bismarck and Lincoln, is obsolete. Certainly no one likes an expensive bureaucratic centralism, indifferent to the needs of the ethnic components that make it up. You cannot, in the name of the Holy Roman Emperor or even the higher capitalism, shove together and try to standardize a number of tribes that do not want to be together. We witness daily the explosions in what were once the Soviet Union and Yugoslavia. Might it not be wise simply to go *with* the centrifugal forces now at work and not try to oppose them anywhere?

The European aim should be a mosaic of autonomous ethnic groups – each as much on its own as possible, whether it be Basques or Scots or Armenians. This distresses old-fashioned statesmen. They want as many people as possible under their control, not a mere fraction of a multi-tribal whole. We shall lose, they say, our power in the world if we are fragmented. This was the Bismarckian, the Lincolnian line. Well, they have little to fear in the long run because the newly independent neighbours will come back together again in new, less confining arrangements.

In February 1987 Gorbachev invited to the Kremlin some 700 non-communist worthies in the arts, sciences and business, to discuss a non-nuclear world. It was the first unveiling of what, he told us, would be a revolution in the Soviet Union. I was called upon to improvise a speech. A Japanese Minister of Trade had just announced that in the next century Japan would still be number one, economically, in the world. 'No one can surpass us,' he said. Then, in an expansive mood, he said, 'The United States will be our farm and Western Europe will be our boutique.'

Something must be done in order for us to survive economically in what looks to be, irresistibly, an Asian world. I would propose that, as our numbers are so few relative to those of China and India, say, we come together in a northern confederacy of Europe, Russia, Canada, the United States. The fact that the small nation states of Western Europe are having difficulty federalizing their relatively small common market means that federalism, at this stage, is a mistake, while a loose confederation for the general economic good is a more achievable business.

It is also just as easy – or vexing – to include Russia and the heartland states of the old Soviet Union as it is to agree, let us say, about the price of milk at Brussels. In other words, much strain in the short run but, in the long run, the creation of a large prosperous entity based upon geographical latitude and the pale, lonely 13 per cent of the world's population.

It does not matter whether a large goal will ever be achieved. Rather, it is the fact that such a goal exists in order to give shape and symmetry to policies; and meaning, perhaps, to societies that otherwise are adrift. Motivate your football louts, continental skinheads, overwrought white American racists.

I realize that the nation state has accustomed us to the idea of conquest by force. It is hard not to think along those lines. In Germany some critics actually thought that my proposal was a white declaration of war on Asia. It is no such suicidal thing. It is a means of economic survival through union. Without links to us, Russia will break up; Europe will decline; lonely little England will drift off along with Ireland and Greenland and Iceland and Newfoundland and all the other Arctic islands; while the United States will take its place somewhere between hypertense Brazil and lachrymose Argentina.

Alexander Hamilton was by far the cleverest of America's founding fathers; he was also the most realistic. Instead of going on about the brotherhood of man, he said, in effect, let us take into account man's essential greed and will to dominate, and let us allow for these traits in our constitution so that self-interest, reasonably harnessed, can become the engine of the state and thus contribute to the common good. So why not extend this insight to our present dilemma, and make new world arrangements?

I regard race as nonsense, but most of the world feels passionately otherwise. In the unlikely event that the human race survives another millennium, there will be no white or black races but combinations of the two, and of every other race as well. But for now, let us use this negative force for a positive end, and create a great northern peaceful economic alliance dedicated – if I may end on a chauvinist American note – to life, liberty and the pursuit of happiness.

The Sunday Telegraph
10 October 1993

9
Chaos

On November 4, 1994, three days before the election that produced a congressional majority for the duller half of the American
single-party system, I addressed the National Press Club in
Washington. I do this at least once a year not because writer-
journalists are present, wise and fearless as they are, but because
cable television carries one's speech without editing or editorializ-
ing. This useful service, known as C-Span, specializes in covering
such eccentricities as myself and the British House of Commons.

I reflected upon the confusion that each of us is feeling as this
unlamented century and failed millennium draw, simultaneously,
to a close, and there is no hint of order in the world – and is *that*
such a bad thing? As for my own country, I said that there is now
a whiff of Weimar in the air. Three days later, to no one's surprise,
only a third of the electorate bothered to vote. The two-thirds that
abstained now realize that there is no longer a government which
even pretends to represent them. The great – often international
and so unaccountable – cartels that finance our peculiar political
system are the only entities represented at Washington. Therefore,
in lieu of representative government, we have call-in radio programmes, where the unrepresented can feel that, for a minute or

two, their voices are heard, if not heeded. In any case, a system like ours cannot last much longer and, quite plainly, *something is about to happen*. I should note that one Rush Limbaugh, a powerful radio demagogue, greeted November's Republican landslide as a final victory over what he called the age of Lenin and Gore Vidal. It was not clear whether he meant Moscow's Lenin or Liverpool's Lennon. Then, to my amazement the *Wall Street Journal*, where I lack admirers, took seriously my warning about Weimar, and '*What is going to happen?*' is a question now being asked among that 2 or 3 per cent of the population who are interested in politics or indeed in anything other than personal survival in a deteriorating society.

Certainly, I have no idea what is going to happen, but as the ineffable Ross Perot likes to say, it won't be pretty.

I have now lived through more than two-thirds of the twentieth century, as well as through at least one-third of the life of the American Republic. I can't say that I am any wiser now than I was when I first began to look about me at the way things are, or rather at the way that things are made to look to be, but I am beginning to detect an odd sort of progression in world affairs. And I have noticed lately that I am not alone.

Recently, the literary critic, Harold Bloom, in the somewhat quixotic course of establishing a Western literary canon, divided human history into phases that cyclically repeat. First, there is a theocratic age, next an aristocratic age, followed by a democratic age, which degenerates into chaos and out of which some new idea of divinity will emerge to unite us all in a brand-new theocratic age, and the cycle begins again. Bloom rather dreads the coming theocratic age but as he – and I – will never see it, we can settle comfortably into the current chaos where the meaning of meaning is an endlessly cosy subject, and Heisenberg's principle is undisputed law of the land, at least from where each of us is situated.

I shall not discuss Bloom's literary canon, which, like literature itself, is rapidly responding if not to chaos to entropy. But I do have some thoughts on the cyclic nature of the way human society evolves as originally posited by Plato in the eighth book of the

Republic and further developed by Giovanni Battista Vico in his
Scienza Nuova.

Professor Bloom skips Plato and goes straight to Vico, an early
eighteenth-century Neapolitan scholar who became interested in
the origins of Roman law. The deeper Vico got into the subject, the
further back in time he was obliged to go, specifically to Greece.
Then he got interested in how it was that the human race was able
to create an image of itself for itself. At the beginning there appears
to have been an animistic belief in the magic of places and in the
personification of the elements as gods. To Vico, these legends,
rooted in prehistory, were *innate* wisdom. Plainly, he was something of a Jungian before that cloudy Swiss fact. But then the age
of the gods was challenged by the rise of individual men. Suddenly,
kings and heroes are on the scene. They in turn give birth to
oligarchies, to an aristocratic society where patricians battle for the
first place in the state. In time, the always exciting game of who will
be king of the castle creates a tyranny that will inspire the people
at large to rebel against the tyrants and establish republics that,
thanks to man's nature, tend to imperial acquisitiveness and so, in
due course, these empire-republics meet *their* natural terminus in,
let us say, the jungles of Vietnam.

What happens next? Vico calls the next stage Chaos, to be
followed by a new Theocratic Age. This process is, of course, pure
Hinduism, which was never to stop leaking into Greek thought
from Pythagoras to the neo-Platonists and even now into the alert
mind of my friend Allen Ginsberg and of numerous California
surfers and ceramists. Birth, death, chaos, then rebirth, and so – on
and on and on.

But though Vico's mind was brilliant and intuitive, the history
that he had to deal with necessarily left out science – as we know it
and he did not – and we must now ponder how chaos may yet
organize itself with the use of computers and faxes and the means
to control all the people all the time, including taping the private
conversations of the British royal family from, let us say, a
command post at Cheltenham. Chaos – our current condition –
may prove to be altogether too interesting to make order of. Will

the next god be a computer? In which case, a *tyrant* god for those of us who dwell in computer-challenged darkness.

A characteristic of our present chaos is the dramatic migration of tribes. They are on the move from east to west, from south to north. Liberal tradition requires that borders must always be open for those in search of safety or even the pursuit of happiness. In the case of the United States, the acquisition of new citizens from all the tribes of earth has always been thought to be a very good thing. But now with so many billions of people on the move, even the great-hearted are becoming edgy.

So, what is going to happen? Well, Norway is large enough and empty enough to take in 40 or 50 million homeless Bengalis. If the Norwegians say that, all in all, they would rather *not* take them in, is this to be considered racism? I think not. It is simply self-preservation, the first law of species. So even those of us usually to be found on the liberal end of the political spectrum are quite aware that the tribes must stay put and be helped to improve wherever it is that they were placed by nature or by our dissolving empires, to which all sorts of odd chickens are presently coming home to roost.

Now, as world climate changes and populations increase, the tribes are on the move, and the racial composition of Europe, say, has changed. As an American, I think that this is not such a bad thing, but there does come a moment when there are simply too many people on the move and not enough space or resources to accommodate them in the old established societies.

As we start the third millennium of what we in our Western section of the globe are amused to call the Christian era, we should be aware, of course, that most of the world's tribes are, happily for them, not Christian at all. Also, most of us who are classified as Christians and live in nations where this form of monotheism was once all powerful now live in a secular world. So chaos does have its pleasures. But then as Christian presuppositions do not mean anything to others (recently Buddhists sternly reminded the pope of this in Sri Lanka), so, too, finally, Plato and his perennially interesting worldview don't make much sense when applied to societies such as ours. I like his conceit of the political progression of societies and a case can be made for it, as Vico did. But Plato, as political thinker, must be taken with Attic salt, which John Jay Chapman brilliantly supplies in an essay recently discovered in his archives; he died in 1933. Although he was America's greatest essayist after Emerson he is almost as little known in his native land as elsewhere. This is a pity, but then these are pitiful times, are they not?

Watch as Chapman plays around with the notion of chaos – and of order, too. First, he is not well pleased with what passes for democracy in the great republic. No anglophile, he does have a nice word or two for the British, in an essay that begins: 'All good writing is the result of an acquaintance with the best books.' Chapman, like all of us who dwell in what Vice-President Agnew once called 'the greatest nation in the country', often feels obliged to invent the wheel each time he addresses his readers. He goes on: 'But the mere reading of books will not suffice. Behind the books must lie the habit of unpremeditated, headlong conversation. We find that the great writers have been great talkers in every age.' He cites Shakespeare, as reported by Ben Jonson, Lord Byron, and our own Mark Twain. He then generalizes about other tribes, something now forbidden in the free world. He writes:

The English have never stopped talking since Chaucer's time. And the other Europeans are ready-tongued, vocal, imaginative people, whose very folklore and early dialects, have been preserved by the ceaseless stream of talk on castled terraces and on village greens since Gothic times.

But our democracy terrifies the individual, and our industrialism seals his lips. The punishment is very effective. It is simply this: 'If you say such things as that, I won't play with you.' Thus the average American goes about in quite a different humour from the average European, who is protected and fortified by his caste and clique, by his group and traditions, by manners and customs which are old and change slowly. The uniformity of the popular ideals and ambitions in

America is at the bottom of most of our troubles. Industrialism has all but killed the English language among us, because every man is afraid to make a joke – unless it be a stock joke. We are all as careful as diplomats not to show our claws. We wear white cotton gloves like waiters – for fear of leaving a thumb mark on the subject. Emerson's advice about this problem is covered by his apothegm, 'If you are afraid to do any thing, do it!'

Chapman on Plato:

Plato somewhere compares philosophy to a raft on which a shipwrecked sailor may perhaps reach home. Never was a simile more apt. Every man has his raft, which is generally large enough only for one. It is made up of things snatched from his cabin – a life preserver or two of psalm, proverb or fable; some planks held together by the oddest rope-ends of experience; and the whole shaky craft requires constant attention. How absurd, then, is it to think that any formal philosophy is possible – when the rag of old curtain that serves one man for a waistcoat is the next man's prayer-mat! To try to make a raft for one's neighbour, or try to get on to someone else's raft, these seem to be the besetting sins of philosophy and religion.

The raft itself is an illusion. We do not either make or possess our raft. We are not able to seize it or explain it, cannot summon it at will. It comes and goes like a phantom.

As for Plato:

He was primarily an entertainer, a great impresario and setter of scenes, and stager of romances great and small where fact and fiction, religion and fancy, custom and myth are blended by imaginative treatment into – no one knows exactly what the mixture should be called.

The aim of his most elaborate work, the *Republic*, is

identical with the aim of the Book of Job, of Bunyan's *Pilgrim's Progress*, of Milton's *Paradise Lost*, and indeed of half the great poems, plays and novels of the world, namely to justify the moral instinct.

But Chapman is a literary critic as well as a moralist. He wrote:

> As a work of art, the *Republic* is atrocious, but as a garretful of antiquity it is thrilling. It is so cracked and rambling that Plato himself hardly knows what is in it. While clearing out a bureau drawer one day, he finds a clever little harangue denouncing sumptuary laws as both useless and foolish . . . 'There's a glint of genius in that,' says he and throws the manuscript into a big Sarcophagus labelled *Republic*.

Which is where, Chapman notes, it plainly does *not* belong, since Plato's entire work is based on the *necessity* of sumptuary laws.

> We see then what sort of a creature this Plato was – with his poetic gift, his inextinguishable moral enthusiasm, his enormous curiosity, his miscellaneous information, his pride of intellect and, as his greatest merit, his perception that spiritual truth must be conveyed indirectly and by allusions. In spite of certain clumsy dogmatisms to be found here and there in him, Plato knows that the assault upon truth cannot be carried by a frontal attack. It is the skirmishing of Plato which makes his thought carry; and all the labours of his expounders to reduce his ideas to a plain statement have failed. If the expounders could reduce Plato's meaning to a statement, Plato would be dead. He has had wit enough and vision enough to elude them all. His work is a province of romantic fiction, and his legitimate influence has been upon the romantic fiction and poetry of the world. Plato used Philosophy as a puppet on his stage and made her convey thoughts which she is powerless to tell upon her own platform. He saw that philosophy could live in the sea of moving fiction,

but died on the dry land of formal statement. He was sustained in his art by the surrounding atmosphere of that Hellenic scepticism which adored elusiveness and hated affirmations. His age handed him his vehicle – to wit, *imaginary conversation*. Is there anything in the world that evaporates more quickly and naturally than conversation? But *imaginary* conversation! Certainly Plato has protected himself from cross-examination as well as ever man did. The cleverest pundits have been trying to edge him into the witness stand during sixty generations, but no one has ever cornered him. The street is his corner.

Of Plato, as a voice from somewhere at the far edge of a democratic age, Chapman notes, with quiet pleasure, that:

It has thus become impossible for anyone to read Plato's dialogues or any other creation of the Greek brain with real sympathy; for those creations speak from a wonderful, cruel, remote, witty age, and represent the amusements of a wonderful, cruel, remote, witty people, who lived for amusement, and for this reason perished. Let us enjoy the playthings of this clever man but let us, so far as in us lies, forbear to cloy them with our explanations.

Vico saw fit to systematize, if not to cloy, Plato in order to give us a useful overview of the evolution of human society, as glimpsed in the dark shadow of the cross of his day. It should be noted that Vico made far more of Plato's ideal theory than Plato did. But then, alas, Vico, like us, is serious and schematic.

Plato and Vico, Montesquieu and Jefferson, Margaret Thatcher and Ronald Reagan – the urge to devise model states is a constant and if chaos does not absolutely disintegrate us, we might yet endure as a race – if it is not a form of racism to suggest that human beings differ in *any* significant way from the mineral and the vegetable, two realms that we constantly victimize and are rude to.

Apropos of human political arrangements, I have been listening, lately, to a pair of voices from the century before ours; two voices often in harmony, more often in gentle dispute, I refer to Gustave Flaubert and George Sand. Put simply – too simply, I confess – George Sand was a nonromantic socialist while Flaubert was a romantic reactionary. Neither had much illusion about the perfectibility of man or too many notions as to the constitution of an ideal state. They wrote each other during the Franco-Prussian war, the collapse of the Second Empire, the rise of the Commune at Paris, and each wondered, 'What next?'

Flaubert is glum: 'Whatever happens, it will be a long time before we move forward again. Perhaps there's to be a recurrence of racial wars? Within a century we'll see millions of men kill each other at one go. All the East against all Europe, the old world against the new? Why not?'

Flaubert then teases George Sand:

The general reverence for universal suffrage revolts me more than the infallibility of the Pope. Do you think that if France, instead of being governed, in effect, by the mob, were to be ruled by the 'Mandarins', we'd be where we are now? If only instead of wanting to enlighten the lower classes we had bothered to educate the upper classes!

Sand strikes back:

In my view, the vile experiment that Paris is undergoing in no way disproves the laws of eternal progress that govern both men and things, and if I have acquired any intellectual principles, good or bad, this business neither undermines nor alters them. A long time ago I accepted the necessity for patience in the same way as one accepts the weather, the long winter, old age, and failure in all its forms.

Flaubert comes to the point: 'I hate democracy (at least as it is understood in France), because it is based on "the morality of the Gospels", which is immorality itself, whatever anyone may say: that is, the exaltation of Mercy at the expense of Justice, the negation of Right – the very opposite of social order.'

Sand remains serene: 'I've never been able to separate the ideal of justice that you speak of from love: for if a natural society is to survive, its first law must be mutual service, as with the ants and the bees. In animals we call this collaboration of all to achieve the same end, instinct. The name doesn't matter. But in man, instinct is love, and whoever omits love omits truth *and* justice.

'Tell me whether the tulip tree suffered from the frost this winter, and whether the peonies are doing well.'

That tulip tree may symbolize a benign way out of the current chaos. In the interest of shutting holes in the atmosphere, the human race may yet cooperate to survive, though I doubt it. For a new centre to hold we must understand why it is that things fall apart the way they do. I have spent my life trying to understand what it was that so many others appear to need that I don't – specifically, a sense of deity, preferably singular, anthropomorphic, and, to explain the general mess of life that he has made on earth, an inscrutable jealous off-the-wall sort of god. I do not doubt that something new in this line is on its way but, meanwhile, there is something to be said for creative chaos. Certainly order, imposed from the top down, never holds for very long.

Like everyone else, as the millennium is now ending, I keep thinking of how it began in Europe. Does a day pass that one does not give at least a fleeting thought to the Emperor Otto III and to Pope Sylvester II? I should highly doubt it. After all, they are an attractive couple; a boy emperor and his old teacher, the intellectual pope. Together, at the start of our millennium, they decided to bring back the Christian empire that two centuries earlier Charlemagne had tried to recreate or – more precisely – to create among the warring tribes of Western Europe. If Charlemagne was the Jean Monnet of the 800s, Otto III was the Jacques Delors of the 900s. As you will recall, Otto was only fourteen when he became king of Germany. From boyhood, he took very seriously the idea of a united Christendom, a Holy Roman Empire. Like so many overactive, overeducated boys of that period he was a natural general, winning battles left and right in a Germany that rather resembled the China of Confucius's era – a time known as that of the warring duchies.

By sixteen, King Otto was crowned emperor of the West. An intellectual snob, he despised what he called 'Saxon rusticity' and he favoured what he termed Greek or Byzantine 'subtlety'. He even dreamed of sailing to Byzantium to bring together all Christendom under his rule, which was, in turn, under that of God. In all of this he was guided by his old tutor, a French scholar named Gerbert.

As a sign of solidarity – not to mention morbidity – Otto even opened up the tomb of Charlemagne and paid his great predecessor a visit. The dead emperor was seated on a throne. According to an eye witness, only a bit of his nose had fallen off, but his fingernails had grown through his gloves and so, reverently, Otto pared them and otherwise tidied him up. Can one imagine Delors – or even Helmut Kohl – doing as much for the corpse of Monnet?

Now we approach the fateful year 999. Otto is nineteen. He is obsessed with Italy, with Rome, with empire. In that year he sees to it that Gerbert is elected pope, taking the name Sylvester. Now emperor and pope move south to the decaying small town of Rome where Otto builds himself a palace on the Aventine – a bad luck hill, as Cicero could have testified.

Together, Otto and Sylvester lavished their love and their ambition upon the Romans, who hated both of them with a passion. In the year that our common millennium properly began, 1001, the Romans drove emperor and pope out of the city. Otto died at twenty-two in Palermo, of smallpox. A year later, Sylvester was dead, having first, it is said, invented the organ. Thus, the dream of a European union ended in disaster for the two dreamers.

I will not go so far as to say that the thousand years since Otto's death have been a total waste of time. Certainly, other dreamers have had similar centripetal dreams. But those centrifugal forces that hold us in permanent thrall invariably undo the various confederacies, leagues, empires, thousand-year-old reichs that the centripetalists would impose upon us from the top down.

Some years ago I had a lively exchange at an Oxford political club. I had remarked that the nation state, as we know it, was the nineteenth-century invention of Bismarck when he united the German tribes in order to beat the Franks, and of Lincoln in North America when he deprived of all significant power our loosely federated states in favour of a mystical highly centralized union. A not so kindly don instructed me that, as *everyone* knows, the nation state was the result of the Thirty Years War and the Treaty of Westphalia. I said that I was aware that that was indeed the received opinion, which he had been hired to dispense, but it was plain to me that the forceful bringing together of disparate peoples against their will and imposing on them universal education – to make them like-minded and subservient – as well as military conscription, signified the end of one sort of democratic era, to advert to Vico's triad, and the beginning of our modern unwieldy and, for their unhappy residents, most onerous nation states.

What is happening today in the old Soviet Union and Yugoslavia – as well as the thousand-and-one rebellions of subject tribes against master tribes – seems to me a very good thing if we are able to draw the right lesson from all this turbulence. Thanks to CNN and other television networks, we follow, day by day, at least one or two of the thousand or so wars for 'freedom' that are simultaneously being fought as worn-out centralized political structures collapse. Instead of wringing our hands and dreaming dreams of a peaceful world order centred upon Brussels or Strasburg, why not accept the fact that if people want to separate they should be allowed to? The sky will not fall in. In due course, the Muslim states of the southern tier of the old Soviet Union may want to come together in some sort of loose trade and cultural and, alas, religious federation. Why oppose them? Western Europe has already gone about as far as it needs to go toward unification. A common currency will mean a common tax collector, which will mean a common police force, which will mean tyranny in the long run and a lot of time wasted in the short run. Despite the

Norwegians' insistence on giving peace prizes to the wrong people, they are not entirely stupid when it comes to their common good.

The dream of Otto and Sylvester, if ever made even partial reality, will hasten a new theocratic age, which will promptly become imperial thanks to modern technology. The world could then, most easily, become a prison for us all and with no world elsewhere to escape to.

Great centrifugal forces are at work all around the earth and why resist them? For the centripetally minded – theocratic or imperial or both – the mosaic of different tribes that will occupy Europe from homely Bantry to glittering Vladivostok are bound to come together in the interest of mundane trade. Is not that quite enough? At least in the absence of a new god.

Certainly, there is greater safety for the individual in a multitude of states where the citizen is computerized, as it were, upon a tape, than there can possibly be in any vast centralized state. Although the United States is only a middling-size country, it is often at the so-called cutting edge when it comes to the very latest technologies of control. Recently a government spokesman noted that by the year 2008 there will be a central computer that will contain everyone's financial dealings, including bank balances, use of credit cards, and so on. At the touch of a button, the Treasury will know who has what money and the Treasury will then be able to deduct what it thinks it may need in the way of tax. 'The power to tax; the power to destroy', as Emerson is said to have said.

Meanwhile, total control over all of the people all of the time is the traditional aim of almost every government. In earlier times, this was only a tyrant's dream. Now it is technically possible. And has any technology ever *not* been put to use? We are told that democracy is a safeguard against misuse of power. I wouldn't know. I have never lived in a democracy. There are several near-democracies in Europe, small countries like Denmark, Holland, Switzerland, small relatively homogeneous – or, like Switzerland, ingeniously balanced heterogeneous – populations that are able to put important issues immediately to the people through referenda.

Large states cannot or will not do this. Certainly no serious attempt to create a democracy has ever been made in the United States – and now it is far too late in the day for us. At least Great Britain has never gone around proclaiming itself a model democracy as we have done. Even so, I am only able to present these ideal thoughts because both the United Kingdom and the United States still cling to ameliorative liberal traditions that keep us from being entirely totalitarian, even if we are not entirely – or even adequately – free as citizens or subjects.

John Adams proudly proclaimed that Americans would have a government not of men but of laws. We have; but *what* laws!

There are young men and women in prison for life for having been caught a third time with marijuana. Thanks to the criminalizing of so many areas of human activity from drugs to sex we have more than one million people in prison and over two million on parole or probation. Far more men are raped each year in the American prison system than are women on the outside. But no one cares. A state with too many laws becomes, in effect, law-less, mind-less, and heart-less.

For those interested in how to control an entire population, we have invented a magnetic bracelet, which is worn, tastefully, on wrist or ankle, thus making it possible for a central guardian to keep track of the bracelet's movements. At first, the European union will use this jewellery to keep track of aliens; then possible criminals; then. . . . We have surpassed Orwell's innocent imaginings.

As you may gather, I hate the nation state as it has been evolving in my time and now looks to be metastasizing in all of Europe and, perhaps, parts of Asia. I am literally a grandchild of the American Civil War, and I belonged to the losing side. Had the issue of that war been the abolition of slavery, I could not have faulted our defeat – morally at least. But Mr Lincoln – the first of the modern tyrants – chose to fight the war not on the issue of slavery but on the holiness and indivisibility of a union that he alone had any understanding of. With his centralizing of all power at Washington this 'reborn' [*sic*] union was ready for a world empire that has done us as little good as it has done the world we have made so many messes in.

I live part of each year in Italy, which is not, properly speaking, a state at all as many Italians are beginning to note, some wistfully, some angrily. Devolution is very much in the air on the Italian peninsula. Why should the capital of Savoy be at Rome and not where it has always been at Turin? It is my impression that most of the old Italian city states – and some larger entities – would like autonomy within a loose trade federation centred on Brussels – or anywhere except Rome. The region from which the Vidals came to America – the Veneto, Friuli, southern Tirol – has recently asked to be excused from the Italian republic. This universal centrifugal force is now the central fact of world politics. Why does any government stand in its way? The answer is stupidly simple. Rulers like to have lots of subjects. They like a large tax base. They enjoy showing off to one another. When Bismarck introduced universal education for all children whether the parents wanted it or not, each empire was then able to use the educational system to promote patriotism and obedience to the status quo, which meant fighting, usually as conscripts, in any war that looked financially appealing to the rulers.

Now I notice that elements of the British Labour Party are discussing devolution for Scotland and Wales – I dare not mention Ireland in any context. Since no one anywhere much cares for Westminster or Whitehall why not let Edinburgh, say, make its own arrangements with the Common Market, bypassing the Southeast.

Europeans think, rather smugly, that they are not given to such primitive Christianity as Americans, but this is wishful thinking. In bad times who knows what terrible gods will emerge from under the flat rocks of this old continent that has given the world so much mindless savagery in the twentieth century alone.

For as long as possible, let pluralism and diversity be our aim. There is already more than enough union, through international cartels, which pay no nation loyalty, much less tax, and through television, which is better off in the hands of numerous minor states that it can ever be as the 'public' television of any great united state.

Should a theocratic age be upon us – and certainly fundamentalist Christians, Jews, and Muslims have never been busier – then the larger the political entity, the greater the danger for that administrative unit the citizen. Currently, in the United States, militant Jesus-Christers are organizing in order to take political control not only at the local level but at that of the Congress itself. This is disturbing.

In the last century a Speaker of the American House of Representatives was so reactionary that it was said of him that if God had consulted him about creation, he would have voted for chaos. Considering the alternatives, for now at least, so would I.

Oxford Amnesty Lecture, 1995

STOP PRESS

Through a Vote, Darkly

In 1964 I watched the election returns in a ballroom at London's Savoy Hotel. The room had been taken by Pamela Berry, whose husband owned *The Daily Telegraph*. As one would expect, considering our hostess's powerful political views, the guests were largely Conservative, though the odd transatlantic visitor could stare at the vast screen which, historically, the first British 'television' election was filling with faces and numbers. Whenever Labour won a seat, there were boos and hisses. When a Tory prevailed, applause. Then the moment of awful truth: Labour had won and the next Prime Minister would be Harold Wilson. Lives and sacred honour, not to mention fortunes, were now at risk as universal darkness buried all.

Gladwyn Jebb, former ambassador to the United Nations, said to me, 'Parish pump politics. Let's go watch the real news.' He led me into a side room where, on a small screen, the fall of Khrushchev was being gloated over. Jebb: 'Now *this* is the real thing.'

A third of a century later I was again in London at the start of the election just concluded. BBC Television had hired me to chat about it. Most of the surviving Tories from the Savoy – or their children and grandchildren – were voting for something called

240

New Labour, headed by Tony Blair, while the Conservatives were led by John Major, a Prime Minister who made much of the fact that he was a lower-middle-class Everyman pitted against a posh elitist who had gone to public school. The startling difference between 1964 and 1997 was that where Labour once represented the working classes and poor (today's 'disadvantaged'), it is now a home for prosperous suburbanites on the go as well as disaffected Scots and Welsh. In the end, the Tories did not win a single seat in Scotland or Wales, something that has not happened in a century.

The only real issue was: Should the British, if they ever meet the required standards, join a common European currency? But no politician was about to stick his neck out on that one. Another big issue that the local press was fretting over: Are British elections becoming Americanized? Presidentialized? Devoid of relevant content? The answer is, more or less, yes. The tabloids have created a terrible Clintonian atmosphere. 'Sleaze' is the principal word one sees in every headline. Since Rupert Murdoch, a devotee of honest government, has abandoned the Tories for New Labour, and as this Australian-turned-American is allowed to own Britain's most popular daily paper (*The Sun*) as well as the weekend *News of the World*, Tory politicians are being wildly smeared as sexual degenerates and crooks.

With a BBC crew I made the rounds of the three parties. Each presented its programme to the nation. Liberal Democrat Paddy Ashdown received the press in a small crowded ecclesiastical room. 'To make it look like a great crowd', a journalist whispered in my ear. Pamphlets were distributed. Ashdown is blond, athletic-looking; also quick-witted by American standards, but then any public schoolboy in England speaks more articulately than any American politician except for the great Oval One.

Ashdown played the honesty card, something of a novelty. He wants better education for everyone. He admits that this will cost money. The two other parties swear they will never raise taxes, which, of course, they will . . .

I go to the Royal Albert Hall. Major points out Tony Blair's contradictions and evasions. I suspect a few ancient heads in the

241

audience were at the Savoy that night so many years ago when Harold Wilson won and socialism would level all. (Once in Downing Street, Wilson quickly said that, actually, he had never read Marx.) As the hall filled with the gorgeousness of Elgar, I intoned for the camera: 'Land of hope and glory, of Drake and Nelson, of Clive and Crippen.'

The fascinating kickoff was Mr Blair's. We were in an early nineteenth-century building with a dome, dedicated to engineers. Press milled about in the rotunda downstairs where stood a tall dark man, Peter Mandelson, reputedly Blair's Rasputin. He gave solemn audience to the journalists of the lobby! Words murmured to one, hand held over his mouth. TV cameras, including ours, avoided. He has the insolent manner of one born to the top rung but three. The mood of the Labourites was paranoid, particularly the handsome blonde girls in black suits with curled lips and flashing eyes. Blair's lead was so great in the polls that only a blunder on his part could stop his irresistible rise. So one could not be made. Although the BBC and I had been cleared by the press party office, I suddenly looked like a possible blunder.

We take our seats. Blair enters, followed by what will be much of his Cabinet. He has been told not to smile. The smile has been criticized by the press. Too loopy. Too youthful. He is 43, J.F.K.'s age in 1960. He is slender with a beaky, mini-Bonaparte sort of nose. The dark hair does not entirely convince. He holds up the party manifesto with his own face, smiling on the cover. I am close enough to him to realize that he does much of his breathing through his mouth. Lips pressed tight together cause his nostrils to flare as he tries to get enough air in. The speech, his programme, was written, we have been told – as if it were from the hand of St John of Patmos – in his own garden in his own longhand. As it turns out, he has no programme. But things will be better, he tells us. Afterwards, to every question he says simply, 'Trust me.' He departs.

The press, seeing that I'm all that's left in the room, surround me. The blondes try to shoo them away. Question: 'Are we becoming more Americanized?' Answer: 'Well, you do resemble us in that you now have a single party with two right wings.'

Question: 'Which wing is more to the right?'

Answer (in my gravest and most reverential voice): 'One does not bring a measuring rod to Lilliput.'

Then we were all thrown out. Labour complained to the BBC that I had pre-empted their affair to 'slag Blair'.

In the next six weeks, Blair makes no errors. He now has a huge majority in the House of Commons. Although he has no plans, I am sure that whatever it was that Mr Murdoch wanted him to do, he will do. I talked to a Scots MP who knows Blair well. 'He's another Thatcher. Authoritarian. Hands-on control freak.' I go to my splendid ancient friend and former head of the Labour Party, Michael Foot: 'Blair is excellent. Really excellent.' I ask, 'Whatever happened to socialism?' At this Mrs Foot looked grim. 'Yes,' she asked her husband. 'What did?' He smiles. 'Socialism? Oh, social-ism! Yes! Yes! . . . Well, there's time. . .' I move on. 'The young, even in America,' I said, 'are reading Gramsci.' Foot was delighted. 'Good. Good. While you and I are reading Montaigne.'

But I was still uneasy. 'That Peter Mandelson is such an unpleas-ant piece of work.'

'He's Herbert Morrison's grandson. Didn't you know?'

'Are you trying to reassure me that there have been shits in Labour before?'

'*You* said that, Gore, not *I*'.

Question I never got answered by anyone: You are an offshore island. But off whose shore? Europe's or ours?

The Nation
26 May 1997

Appendix

One of the advantages of a written constitution is that every government department (save the rogue Central Intelligence Agency, currently in defiance of the constitution) must submit to Congress – its paymaster – expenditures for the year. Here is what the US Defense Department spent in 1995 on the not-so-virginal British Isles, with our various military installations duly noted.

MAP NO. 72
UNITED KINGDOM

CAPITAL
ARMY INSTALLATION
NAVY INSTALLATION
AF INSTALLATION

SHETLAND ISLANDS

ORKNEY ISLANDS

THURSO

SCOTLAND

OUTER HEBRIDES

INVERNESS
ABERDEEN
EDZELL
NAVAL SECURITY GROUP ACTIVITY
DUNDEE
HOLY LOCH
NAVAL SUPPORT ACTIVITY
GLASGOW
EDINBURGH
NEWCASTLE

LONDONDERRY
BELFAST

NORTHERN IRELAND

ENGLAND

LEEDS

LIVERPOOL
MANCHESTER

RAF ALCONBURY

RAF MILDENHALL
RAF LAKENHEATH

BIRMINGHAM

RAF WOODBRIDGE

RAF BENTWATERS

WALES

CARDIFF

RAF FAIRFORD
BRISTOL

LONDON
NAVAL ACTIVITIES U.K.
DOVER

PLYMOUTH

RAF UPPER HEYFORD

Prepared by: Washington Headquarters Service
Directorate for Information
Operations and Report

UNITED KINGDOM

FISCAL YEAR 1995   (DOLLARS IN THOUSANDS)

Personnel/Expenditure*	Total	Army	Navy & Marine Corps	Air Force	Other Defense Activities
1. Personnel – Total	31,351	791	4,697	24,847	1,016
Active Duty Military	12,131	343	1,805	9,983	0
Civilian	2,322	316	445	672	889
Military Dependents	15,964	66	2,222	13,676	0
U.S. Civilian Dependents	934	66	225	516	127
II. Expenditures – Total	$1,041,420	$71,031	$411,497	$456,229	$102,663
A. Payroll Outlays – Total	575,056	23,722	89,320	422,061	39,953
Active Duty Military Pay	438,447	9,019	52,189	367,239	0
Civilian Pay	93,098	10,695	20,142	22,317	39,953
Reserve & National Guard Pay	968	0	968	0	0
Retired Military Pay	42,543	4,017	6,021	32,505	0
B. Contracts Over $25,000 – Total	464,051	47,106	320,530	33,705	52,710
Supply and Equipment Contracts	236,458	39,707	172,945	19,174	4,632
RDT&E Contracts	37,895	7,075	24,754	1,392	4,674
Service Contracts	189,693	260	122,890	13,139	53,404
Construction Contracts	5	64	59	0	0
Civil Function Contracts	0	0	0	0	0
C. Grants	2,313	203	1,647	463	0

Prime Contracts Over $25,000 (Prior Three Years)	Total	Army	Navy & Marine Corps	Air Force	Other Defense Activities
Fiscal Year 1994	$419,062	$71,352	$200,032	$44,135	$103,543
Fiscal Year 1993	620,895	156,142	202,157	38,765	223,831
Fiscal Year 1992	575,968	93,115	262,654	116,443	104,755

Top Five Contractors Receiving the Largest Dollar Volume of Prime Contract Awards in this Country	Total Amount	Major Area of Work	
		FSC or Service Code Description	Amount
1. Rolls-Royce plc	$199,998	Installation of Eq/Engines, Turbines & Com	$95,839
2. Bombardier Inc	35,316	Aircraft Fixed Wing	35,316
3. Martin-Baker Aircraft Co. Ltd	25,524	Ma1 Aircraft Accessories and Components	15,839
4. Ministry of Defence	19,326	ROTE/Aircraft-Demo/Valid	8,016
5. Lockheed Martin Corporation	16,084	Maint & Repair of Eq/ADP Equip & Supplies	14,913
Total of Above	$296,248	(63.8% of total awards over $25,000)	

Prepared by: Washington Headquarters Services
Directorate for Information
Operations and Reports

* For cost of operation information, refer to applicable DoD Budget Exhibits.